THE POWER OF COLLABORATIVE LEADERSHIP

TESTED PRACTICES FOR TODAY'S WORLD

Ichak K. Adizes, Ph.D.

Revised new edition of *The Ideal Executive:*
Why You Cannot Be One and What to Do About It

Adizes Institute Publications

Published by Adizes Institute Publications
Carpinteria, CA 93013

2023 Edition

ISBN: 978-1-952587-05-4

Library of Congress Control Number: 2023931343

THE POWER OF COLLABORATIVE LEADERSHIP

Dedicated to my teacher
Professor Kirby Warren
Columbia University Graduate School of
Business Administration, NYC

Contents

Acknowledgments   ix

Foreword   xi

Introduction   xiii

PART I Organizational Health

1.   PAEI, the DNA of Organizations   3

2.   The Incompatibility of the Roles   31

PART II Styles

3.   PAEI for Personality Codification   49

4.   (P)-Type Managers and Leaders   55

5.   (A)-Type Managers and Leaders   67

6.   (E)-Type Managers and Leaders   77

7.   (I)-Type Managers and Leaders   89

8. The Deadwood (----) 97

9. The Ideal Executive 103

PART III Building the Complementary Team

10. The PAEI Team 123

11. Team Membership Characteristics 127

12. Implementation 141

13. Managing Conflict 157

PART IV Building Mutual Trust and Respect

14. Collaborative Decision-Making 177

15. Complementary Diversified Structure 229

16. People 257

17. Common Mission, Vision, and Values 275

Summary 279

Appendix 281

About the Author 299

Books by the Author 301

Videos by the Author 303

Websites 303

The Adizes® Symbergetic™ Methodology
for Managing Change 303

The Adizes Institute 304

Acknowledgments

I want to express my appreciation and gratitude to Yechezkel Madanes, who has organized my notes and lectures and worked hard and well in producing this book with me. I want to thank the numerous people who wrote me over the years to say how my theories parallel different religions, political science developments, and other fields of social sciences, all of which I mention in this book. Shawn Richardson and John Landry edited the book and made it significantly more readable. I also want to thank Larry Schiller, my literary advisor and publishing guru, who encouraged me to write this book. To all, a big *thank you*.

Foreword

I'm a raving fan of Ichak Adizes. We first met more than twenty years ago when we were frequent teachers and resources for Young Presidents Organization (YPO) chapters around the world. Whenever Ichak spoke, my wife, Margie, and I would be in the front row furiously taking notes. To me, he continues to be one of the real giants in the field of leadership.

The Power of Collaborative Leadership: Tested Practices for Today's World includes a summary of all of Dr. Adizes's greatest thinking through the years. This includes an extensive review of his PAEI Model — the four management roles needed for organizational health (Producing, Administering, Entrepreneuring, and Integrating) — and how you can apply the concepts to your own organization.

The book also features Dr. Adizes's revolutionary paradigm shift in leadership theory: the philosophy of complementary, collaborative leadership, which has been successfully tested by Dr. Adizes and his associates in organizations of every size throughout the world for more than five decades. The basis for this concept is simple. In today's organizations, there is no ideal executive as an individual. A healthy organization needs a collaborative leader and a complementary team of individuals with diverse interests and styles to build and nourish it in a culture of mutual trust and respect.

As you read *The Power of Collaborative Leadership*, I know you will become as big a fan of Ichak Adizes as I am. His leadership concepts can be universally applied in any organization that wishes to make a difference in today's changing world.

Ken Blanchard
Chief Spiritual Officer of The Ken Blanchard Companies®
Coauthor of *The New One Minute Manager*® and *Leading at a Higher Level*

Introduction

In the United States, ten thousand baby boomers reach retirement age every day, and the millennials that replace them in the workplace are becoming the largest employee demographic in the world.[1]

In a world driven by technology, these "digital natives" — familiar with the Internet, mobile devices, and social media — have become the teachers of their elders instead of, as in all previous generations, their pupils. They resist authority, unlike those raised in scarcity and in fear of losing a job.

Add to this resistance the feverish pace of change, the blurring of industry boundaries, and the creation of a complex, multicultural business environment,[2] and we need a new paradigm of leadership. The millennials who are assuming leadership positions reject the old paradigm of a single leader with a hierarchical, autocratic, and nonparticipative authority structure.

1. Ashira Prossack, "How Millennials Are Changing the Way We View Leadership," *Forbes*, May 18, 2018, https://www.forbes.com/sites/ashiraprossack1/2018/05/18/how-millennials-are-changing-the-way-we-view-leadership.
2. In a recent meeting with my client Applied Materials, I noticed that despite being a California-based corporation with $17 billion in revenues, there was not a single American leader in the room. There were leaders from India, Pakistan, Israel, Iran, China, and Serbia.

Up to this point, organizations relied on a series of solutions within the old paradigm — but these solutions were not sustainable. First we had the "business administration model," then the "process of management." Next came "executive action," and now everybody is encouraged to be a "leader." Ranging from Michael Porter's vision of an all-powerful, "super-decider" quasi-god CEO[3] to Patrick Lencioni's depiction of a leader[4] to the top-viewed TED talks on leadership — the field continues to seek answers.

These successive attempts to improve the old structure worked only because the changes were cosmetic and marginal. They were not the paradigm shift that the new reality required. The changes did not truly alter how we lead in a world that is transforming at a rapidly disruptive rate.

The main questions were unanswered: How can leaders deal with these new realities? How do we catch up to rapid change created by technology? How do we structure an organization that can quickly, flexibly, and dynamically adapt to change but without losing control? How do we manage change without destructive conflict — conflict that wastes energy and prevents the organization from competing successfully in the marketplace? What are the characteristics of such an organization? And what is the role of leaders in making this happen?

To begin answering these questions, let me start with an analogy. You probably remember that when you were a child, your parents told you, "Don't take a hot shower and then go outside in the cold weather! You'll catch a cold!" Well, I always wondered why this would happen because I knew that in Finland and Russia, people like to go to the sauna, sweat,

3. Steve Denning, "What Killed Michael Porter's Monitor Group? The One Force That Really Matters," *Forbes*, November 20, 2012, https://www.forbes.com/sites/stevedenning/2012/11/20/what-killed-michael-porters-monitor-group-the-one-force-that-really-matters/?sh=89d1d28747b5.
4. Patrick Lencioni, *The Ideal Team Player* (New York, NY: John Wiley and Sons, 2016).

then go outside and roll in the snow. They claim it invigorates them! In Siberia even some aged people cut a hole in the ice on a lake or river, then dive into the freezing water! If I did that, I would probably get pneumonia and die.

Why the difference? It's not the cold that makes us sick. It is the rapid *change* from hot to cold.

It's all about the strength, or lack of strength, of our organism. How well can our organism handle change? If our organism is robust, change makes us stronger. But if it is weak, change can kill us.

This phenomenon applies to organizations as well. In today's frenetically paced world, organizations prepared to deal with change are invigorated by it. Those that are not fall ill and risk failure.

This book is about what it means to have a "strong organism," and the leadership that makes an organization healthy so that it can navigate and thrive through rapid continuous change.

APPLICABILITY

This book presents a new paradigm: the concept of complementary, collaborative leadership. It has been tested by me and the certified associates of the Adizes Institute in over seventy countries for more than fifty years, from start-ups to the largest companies on Earth, and with eight prime ministers testing how it applies to country level systems (not easily). Our success documents the validity of what the methodology offers.[5]

The tested methodology presented in this book is value-free and applies to all cultures, technologies, and industries, whether profit-oriented or not-for-profit. It provides tools that can be universally applied to diagnose leadership styles, predict behavior, and recommend

5. See www.adizes.com.

how to develop, train, and staff organizations — how to structure organizations correctly and communicate and reward staff. These tools allow organizations to manage change with the least amount of wasted energy.

This book builds on the vast collection of books covering the Adizes Methodology. To give a necessary foundation and understanding of collaborative leadership, previous publications will be discussed and summarized here.[6]

Ichak K. Adizes, Ph.D.
Santa Barbara, California

6. To further your knowledge of the Adizes Methodology, see the "Books by the Author" section at the end of this book.

PART I

Organizational Health

CHAPTER 1

PAEI, the DNA of Organizations

WHY ORGANIZATIONAL HEALTH?

An organization is an organic system, whether it is a family,[1] a business, a nonprofit organization, or a country. It is composed of subsystems that change at different speeds. Marketing changes faster than sales, which changes faster than production, which in turn changes faster than accounting or IT systems. The slowest to change is the human capital within an organization. On a country level, the technological subsystem has advanced the most in changing, trailed by the economic subsystem that is nevertheless changing faster than the legal system, which is changing faster than the political system. The slowest to change is the social values subsystem.

---

1. For the application of Adizes theory to the leadership of families and couples, see: Ichak Adizes with Yechezkel and Ruth Madanes, *The Power of Opposites* (Santa Barbara, CA: Adizes Institute Publications, 2015).

This disparity in the speed of change in the subsystems creates gaps in the system, and those gaps manifest into what we call problems.

Disintegration is a sign of a malady, of dysfunctionality manifested by what we call "problems."

All problems are a manifestation of
disintegration caused by change.

The faster the change, the more problems a company will have, and if not treated (since change is ongoing), the disintegration will continue and compound till the problem becomes a crisis. At that point, the organization is very "sick."

According to Milton Friedman and his school of thought, the purpose of a business organization is to increase the owners' equity. Many business corporations seek profits, and in their pursuit of profits the organization has to continuously change, which can cause it to fall apart internally. It becomes dysfunctional and sick. To avoid internal problems it might not hold off from change, but then it gets disassociated form the market. In the long run, in both cases, the level of profitability cannot be maintained. The same goes for people who chase materialist goals: they might make a lot of money, but in the process, they fall apart physically or mentally or socially, losing their marriage. I propose an alternative purpose: to make and keep the organization healthy. If an organization is healthy, it will be profitable in the short *and* long run.

A healthy organization — whether it is a marriage, a government, a multinational corporation, or a candy store — is effective externally by satisfying market needs and efficient internally by aligning all subsystems to work in unison, both in the short and long run.

Being healthy means being effective (integrated with the external environment) and efficient (integrated in its internal environment) in the short and long run. In other words, the organization satisfies the needs of its present and future clients efficiently and profitably.

A healthy organization can measure its success according to its mission. If the organization is a for-profit company, it can measure success by profits. If it is a political party, success might be measured by whether its candidates are elected or reelected. If it is a research institution, the honors and prizes won by its scientists might be its measure of success.

The role of leadership is to develop and nourish a healthy organization that will produce the indicators of success appropriate for that organization — to build, nurture, and protect organizational health as the organization strives to reach the goals it was established to achieve. The function is value-free, without sociopolitical or cultural biases. Conceptually, the leadership process is one and the same, the only difference may be in how it is applied, taking into account the size and nature of the unit being led, the location of the organization on its lifecycle, and the culture of the country where the organization operates.

THE FOUR ROLES NEEDED FOR ORGANIZATIONAL HEALTH

Being healthy is the ability to perform the function for which you exist — to be effective and to do it efficiently, in both the short and long run. It is a system that can produce the immediate desired results and at the same time keep changing to satisfy long-term needs.

How to build such an organization? The function of leadership is to see to it that the roles are performed and the organization stays integrated while continually changing, adapting or (even better) proacting to change.

Four roles are essential for making an organization effective and efficient in both the short and long run. These roles contribute to the success of an organization in the same way that vitamins contribute to the health of a human being. If any one role falls short, the organization falls into a "disease." (Those diseases are covered in my book about corporate lifecycles.[2] In this book we will cover only how they affect leadership.)

Over the last five decades, I have studied the relationship between each role and specific types of organizational behavior. Furthermore, I have analyzed which role combinations result in which leadership style and noticed how a deficiency in any one role can lead to a predictable leadership failure. This insight has led naturally to a diagnostic and therapeutic methodology that we have tested successfully at hundreds of organizations worldwide.[3]

The four roles are: (P)roducing, (A)dministrating, (E)ntrepreneuring, and (I)ntegrating, known as PAEI.

Role	Makes the system	In time span
(P)roducing	Effective	Short run
(A)dministering	Efficient	Short run
(E)ntrepreneuring	Effective	Long run
(I)ntegrating	Efficient	Long run

The (P)roducing role — to produce results, to perform that for which the organization exists — satisfies client's needs when performed properly. This can be measured by how many previous buyers come back to obtain company products or services in a competitive environment. For a political party, it will be how many of the voters remain loyal to the party. For a country, as a system, it will be how many are immigrating versus emigrating.

(A)dministering, the second role, ensures that the organizational processes are systematized: that the company does the right things in the right sequence with the right intensity. (A)dministering ensures efficiency in the short run.

2. Ichak Adizes, *Managing Corporate Lifecycles: Why and How Organizations Grow, Age, and Die and What to Do About It* (Santa Barbara, CA: Adizes Institute Publications, 2004).
3. See www.adizes.com.

Next, the organization needs to adapt to its environment. It needs to be proactive in an environment of constant change to ensure the company's effectiveness over the long run. This is the role of (E)ntrepreneuring, which combines creativity with the willingness to take risks. If the organization performs this role well, it will have the services and/or products that its future clients will want and seek.

Finally there is (I)ntegrating, where leaders build a climate and a system of values that motivate individuals in the organization to work together so that no one is indispensable. This ensures that the organization will be efficient and survive in the long run. It enables the organization (that is, an organic entity) to function well interdependently.

If the (P)roducing and (A)dministering roles are performed well — the organization achieves the expected results and the company runs smoothly — then the company will be effective and efficient in the short run (i.e., it will be profitable but in the short run only). If only the (E)ntrepreneuring and (I)ntegrating roles are performed, it will be effective and efficient in the long run, but the company will suffer in the short run.

> *A healthy organization is one that is effective*
> *and efficient in the short and long run.*

For a company to be profitable in the short *and* long run, it must perform all four roles well. In a not-for-profit business (a government agency, for example), capably performing the four roles will lead to achievements in service, political survival, or whatever the goals of the agency may be.

Even parents must perform these roles, because a family is an organic organization, a system that requires all four roles to function properly, too. In a traditional family, one of the spouses performs the (E) and (P) roles of building a career and bringing home the bacon. The other assumes the (A) and (I) roles, transforming a house into a home and the adults and children into a family.

What might happen *if* the roles aren't carefully *divided and shared* in a two-career family? If both spouses perform externally the (P) and (E) roles, but are deficient or have no time to perform the (A) and (I) roles, they may need a maid to do the housework (A) and a family therapist to help them relate to each other (I).

In any organization, people's differences in these four roles — if handled correctly — cross-pollinate and create synergy and growth.

Let us now discuss the four roles in detail.

The (P) Role: A Raison D'être

The first role that leadership must perform in any organization is (P)roducing the desired results for which the company or unit at any level exists.

Every organization has its raison d'être; it is not put together just to be put together. To survive is not an acceptable goal. Cancer wants to survive, too. A functioning organization must have a larger mission than survival.

What is the purpose of a given organization's existence in the short or long run?

Let's use an analogy: Five friends get together on a Friday night and have some beers. As they are drinking, someone suggests they go on a hike to the nearby lake the next morning. The rest of the group enthusiastically agrees.

The next day, the five friends follow a mountain path that leads to the lake. It's a very narrow path so they must walk single file. They have been hiking on the path for hours. They're singing, whistling, joking, and laughing. At a certain point on their journey, they encounter a big rock blocking their passage that none of them alone can lift.

This group can be described as an organization; it has common goals that change over time. The first goal was to get together on Friday night. The second was to have some beers. The latest is to hike to the lake. Each of these goals had a task that needed to be performed — find a place to get together, provide the beer, and now the new one is to lift the rock. Let's assume they cannot lift the rock. They may then decide to camp somewhere instead and have a nice time camping and playing ball. Notice how the task is changing.

Organizational leadership is born when a task that needs to be performed evolves: a task — a common purpose to be achieved — that cannot be performed by one person alone. That task, once defined, will drive the behavior — the interactions and the interdependencies — of the group in the short run: to provide the beer, to lift that rock, or to camp and relax — each of these requires doing, acting, and producing expected results.

Every organization must satisfy today's need — that is the (P)roducing role. But what is needed today may not be what is needed tomorrow because the purpose might change. For that the (E)ntrepreneuring role is required — to choose what those needs of tomorrow might be.

Lifting the rock is the (P) role. Deciding to hike to the lake is the (E) role. The (P) role focuses on *what* to do now. The (E) role focuses on what for, on the *why*: Why are we doing what we are doing? What is the purpose that we are trying to satisfy? Swimming in the lake is the future need we want to satisfy. Lifting that rock, which is blocking our path to reach the lake, is the short-term need we need to satisfy.

The rock, and the immediate need to be satisfied, may change across the same organization. Two different branches of the same bank might have different client needs. One may require parking, while the other doesn't. A leader must ask: what is my particular "rock" that needs to be "lifted"? Military commanders, when retiring from service, often go into business but miss this point in their new endeavors. The "rocks" are not the same as those they faced in their military careers, and the leadership style required is, by definition, not the same.

What is Effectiveness?

If an organization fulfils the (P)roducing role, it is effective in the short run but what does it mean to be effective?

Let's look at an example. You have a car; you turn it on and notice that the engine is running. Is the car working? Not really. Why? Because it's not yet satisfying a need. The fact that the engine is running doesn't mean that the car is effective. "Effective" means it satisfies a need. This brings us back to the question: What is the need? Do I need a truck, a sports car, a sedan, or a limo? Is transportation my need, or is my need to show off? Or both?

So, what is the purpose of a business organization in the short run? Why does the business organization exist? What result is it supposed to give?

The typical answer, particularly from students of economics and those who distrust big business, is "Profit!"

But we all know of organizations that are very profitable in the short run yet go bankrupt in the long run — not *in spite of* but *because of* being profitable. In other words, constantly thinking about profit instead of about what the client needs is as futile as saying, "The purpose of my existence is to be happy." If every morning you wake up and ask yourself, "Am I happy?" you will soon become quite miserable. You need to focus on *what makes you* happy.

Profit is the goal. It is the lake you are hiking to. It is not the rock you are supposed to lift if you want to get to the lake.

I often find that companies ignore the critical importance of "the rock" and focus only on "the lake." To get there they might look for a sidetrack or just climb over the rock and ignore its existence. It is called, in some cases, "corruption" or just unethical behavior.

Playing tennis provides another analogy. If you want to win, you don't look at the scoreboard all the time; you watch the ball. If you hit the ball effectively, efficiently, and repetitively, you will win. In other words: I know you want to win the game, but for now you need to focus on hitting the ball well and repetitively.

And what is "the rock"? Concentrate on who needs this organization. Who will cry if you die? Who needs you? What for? Unless you produce something that attracts clients, you are not going to be effective; you're not going to get revenues.

Amazon excels in applying this philosophy. I was on a stage with Bezos when he had started Amazon and was looking for investors. He said he was not going to have dividends, not even profits, for a while. His focus was and I still think is customer satisfaction. Few understood him then. With his success all understand him now.

Profit is a *result* of good leadership, not the purpose of it.

The purpose is to be healthy, to excel in performing all four roles, and then profit will occur in the short and long run. Profit in a competitive market economy is not a dirty word as many Millennials think. It is a measurement of how well an organization adds value. Let me explain.

When people buy a product or a service *in a competitive market*, they are telling you — literally in dollars and cents — how much it is worth to them to satisfy a particular need. But (P)roducing that desired service or product means a company must spend money.

When the company's costs to *produce* a product or service that satisfies a client's need are lower than the price said client is willing to pay to have their need satisfied (and the client chooses to have their need satisfied with your company, despite other options), the result is profit. The company is (P)roducing that need-satisfying service or product at a lower cost than its perceived value to the client. What is wrong with that?

How about the leader of an accounting department where the clients are internal and have no choice but to use the internal-accounting resources? The same principle applies here but with a twist. The leader of the accounting department should ask himself or herself: Who needs our accounting services? It is not only the tax authorities. Internally, every leader in the company needs accounting reports to know where they stand in their endeavors. So the accounting department leader (and every leader) should know who needs their services, externally or internally — who their clients are.

And this accounting department that has a monopoly of providing accounting services for the internal clients should ask itself, "If our internal clients had a choice to go somewhere else for the services they need, would they? Could they get the services they need cheaper than the overhead charges that the accounting department levies on the organization?"

This route of reasoning applies to marriage, too. Ask yourself, what are your spouse's needs? If they had a choice to go somewhere else, would they? If your spouse is continually coming home late, there must be a reason. If the kids, who are also clients of the entity called "family," leave and rarely come back, there must be a reason.

Clients are all those entities whose needs the organization was established to satisfy. And how do you measure satisfaction? Are they coming back to get their needs satisfied? Would they come back if they had a choice? Clients are different from *stakeholders*, who are the people you must consider or hold at bay and treat properly and satisfy their needs — so that you can fulfill the purpose of your existence, to satisfy your present and future clients' needs.

Clients vs. Customers vs. Stakeholders

Thirty years ago, I did some consulting for the Los Angeles County Department of Children and Family Services. This is the division of the city that takes care of abused and underprivileged children. The division deploys social workers who specialize in the needs of these children. At the start of working with them, I asked them to define the (P) role: "What are you here for? Why does this department exist? Who is the client? Whose needs are you satisfying?"

To my surprise, I got responses such as "We need to pay attention to the court system, because they decide whether to give the child to the parents or to assign them to custody," and "We need to pay attention to the press, because they often give us a hard time," and "We need to pay attention to the state government because they approve our funding." Somewhere on their list, at the bottom, there was the category "Children." They almost forgot the children. So, I went down to the street, found a little kid with his mom, and asked them if they would please come inside for a moment to join us. I said: "Guys, this is the client. This is whose needs we satisfy. All the others — government, press, courts, etc. — are stakeholders. Stakeholders we have to satisfy only enough to retain their continued support, so that we can serve the client, which is the child."

Truth be told, the abused child does not make any decisions, so how can they be the client? Here came the illumination: the social workers represent the absentee natural parent who is supposed to be responsible for making decisions that satisfy the child's needs. For that purpose, I had to coin a new word: a "parenter." When a child has absentee parents — either because they are abusive, incarcerated, mentally incapable of parenting, or physically absent — the social worker performs that role of the *parenter.* The social worker representing the child becomes the client. And in that case, it is their professional integrity that needs to be met and satisfied. Not the integrity of the court system, nor of the media. It is of the social worker who represents the child.

After this session, the department designed a logo of an adult hand holding the hand of a child to continuously remind everyone of their role and of the client and what the client needs.

It is important to distinguish between clients, customers, and stakeholders. Customers are the end users, the ones enjoying the product or service. A client is the one who makes the decision to buy the product or service, the one whose need ultimately must be satisfied or he or she won't buy, won't pay for it, or cause it to be paid. Stakeholder, as the name implies, are those entities whose cooperation is needed for the client's needs to be satisfied.

Client needs must be satisfied — the more the better, or there will be no revenues. Stakeholders' needs, on the other hand, must be satisfied only to the level that they will continue to cooperate.

Clients, customers, and stakeholders have different needs and, thus, need to be dealt with differently. When my kids were young, I used to take them for brunch every Sunday. I loved a certain restaurant that unfortunately does not exist anymore called LOVE. But guess where we went? McDonald's, obviously. Who decided? The kids. I was the one paying. McDonald's Corporation knows very well who the decision makers are — who the clients are. Look at the playground in front of the restaurant. Look at the children's menu. The children are the clients. I was a customer who consumed the food or maybe just a stakeholder who carried the wallet to pay.

McDonald's has the kids as clients for which it must design and provide the right tasty food, and me as a stakeholder for whom it must price the product attractively and provide parking.

This is a major distinction because there is no way leadership can maximize all needs. Client satisfaction goals are *deterministic* (more or less, depending on the goal), while for stakeholders we need *constraint* goals (avoid violating certain values). Increasing sales is a deterministic goal, with a constraint goal of no more than five percent bad debt.

So what, then, is the purpose for which your organization exists? What must your organization *produce*?

The answer is: client satisfaction. That is the (P) function of every organization. Please note that I did not say *customer* satisfaction. Customers belong only to the sales department; they are *external*. But every organization has clients, which are either external or internal. If your accounting department does not satisfy the information needs of its internal clients (i.e., the operations or marketing departments), this will lead to a problem, won't it? "Clients" are those entities whose needs the organization or unit was established to satisfy; the decision makers who decide to part with their money to satisfy a need they have.

Marketing people use research to find out client needs — how they need it, when, and at what price, etc. The same applies to any leader of production, accounting, or safety. First, find out who your internal clients are; then, find out what they need; and finally, go and do what needs to be done.

Your organization is effective in the short run if it provides for the present needs for which it exists — and this is verified by the fact that your clients are coming back even if they could get the same or similar services elsewhere.

To perform the (P) role, a person must be knowledgeable of the needs that are supposed to be satisfied and have what psychologists call "the achievement motivation" to get the job done, accomplished, and finished.

The (A) Role: Running the Railroad

Is (P)roducing results sufficient for being healthy at least in the short run? What happens when the leader is an excellent Producer of results and a knowledgeable achiever? This type of person is good, productive, diligent, and reliable, and so we reward them with a promotion to head the department.

But now, this person is no longer merely a Producer; they must work with five or six or more people. They must coordinate, delegate, control, and oversee. Instead of (P)roducing their own results, they must make the *system produce* results. And that is a different task altogether. That's why we need another role: (A)dministering.

The (A) role is also indispensable for good leadership. It is the role of Administrators to pay attention to details, to systematize how the (P) role is carried out, so that a wheel does not have to be reinvented each time something needs to be wheeled around. Administrators also ensure that the organization follows those systems and routines. (A)dminvistering ensures that the company does what it was intended to do — *efficiently*. It moves the organization up the learning curve so it can capitalize on its memory and experience. It analyzes successes and programs them so that they can be repeated.

If you *produce* results, your organization will be effective. If you also *administer*, your organization will be efficient. If you perform both the (P) and (A) roles, your organization will be effective and efficient in the short run, and it will be profitable in the short run, if that is how you measure success.

Input	Throughput	Output
(P) role	Satisfy client needs	Effectiveness in the short run
(A) role	Systematize	Efficiency in the short run

If an individual is (P)roducing but lacks the (A) role, they will be disorganized. They will work hard, probably harder than necessary, but not intelligently. They will waste a lot of time carrying the rock on their back rather than using a wheel cart.

The same applies to organizations. An organization may satisfy client needs but lack an organized *administration*. It has no system, or its systems are faulty. Its supply chain is disorganized; its salary administration is a patchwork of individual agreements; its recruitment processes and policies are haphazard. This type of company will be effective but inefficient. It might manage to get sales but with low profits, if any.

An American analogy for management is "running the railroad." How do we run a railroad? First, we need the railroad engineer to *produce* results, i.e., transportation. The engineer takes the train from station A to station B.

To run a *profitable* railroad organization at least in the short run, we need supplies, revenue collection, and universally communicated time-tables to get the right train to the right town at the designated time. Budgets must be adhered to, costs must be controlled, systems developed, and the implementation of those systems supervised.

All this is the role of the Administrator, which should be a person whose style is compatible with the needs of this role. He or she must be detail-oriented, thoughtful, and organized — while an achievement, task-focused person is needed for the (P) role.

The (E) Role: Seeing Through the Fog

Beyond (A)dministering and (P)roducing, the railroad company must also plan what to do next — deciding what direction the organization should take — as it acts to address change. There are demographic changes, market-needs changes, and rising competition from trucks and airlines. How should the railroads meet those changes? Making that decision is the role of (E)ntrepreneuring.

Whereas the (A) role involves systematizing and implementing plans that have already been determined, the (E) role must generate a plan for what the organization should start doing differently now. Planning is not what you are going to do tomorrow. It is what you should be doing *today* to prepare for the needs of tomorrow, in light of what you expect tomorrow will yield.

A metaphor I find useful for the ingredient of creativity for the (E) role is "the ability to see through the fog." The future is foggy. You really do not and cannot see it perfectly well. You must make assumptions based on the limited information available.

A creative person looks into the fog and sees pieces of information appearing and disappearing, and he identifies a pattern. Creative people visualize the image that a large jigsaw puzzle creates well before the full picture has been constructed. They fill in the puzzle's empty spaces with their imagination, picturing the finished puzzle. They see a big ear, then a big trunk, then one big leg, and conclude: "Aha! It is an elephant."

Noncreative people wait until the fog lifts, the sun is shining, and it's totally clear. Then they go and touch the elephant and even smell the elephant. And *still*, they are not quite convinced: "OK, *maybe* it's an elephant!" These people have not added any information or created anything, while creative people, using their imaginations, have filled in the blanks in the fog.

Returning to the railroad analogy, it is the role of (E) to determine which older stations to close and which new stations to open, whether to add or subtract the number of cars on each line, and how often the train should stop at each station. It is the (E) role, in other words, that guides the organization as it deals with changing realities.

Besides business Entrepreneurs, who monetize the opportunities of the commercial market, there are social Entrepreneurs, who initiate cultural and political change; and educational and artistic Entrepreneurs, who satisfy aesthetic needs and generate new ones. All are of value to society, and in a society of material abundance, economic entrepreneurship will eventually decline in importance and even come under political attack. Social entrepreneurship is on the rise.[4]

Since change is inevitable and constant, the (E)ntrepreneuring role is essential for good leadership. When performed well, it makes the organization effective in the long run. It prepares the organization to satisfy future needs. If there is no one to perform the (E)ntrepreneuring role

---

4. In 1970, I established at UCLA the first master's program in the world to train art administrators — the "social animateurs," as Andre Malraux called them.

in an organization, that organization will eventually lag behind its more creative and proactive competitors.

In this role, the focus is on the future: What are the future needs of our present clients, as well as the needs of our future clients? To predict the future, one needs to be creative. No one can predict the future for sure, but one must prepare for that future in the present, and that entails taking the risk that all those preparations might not be valid. To perform the (E) role, a leader must be creative and willing to take risks.

The (I) Role: Getting Integration

With the five friends hiking to a lake, their friendship and sense of belonging expressed a need to do something together: first by drinking beer, then by hiking, then by working together either to lift the rock or come up with another plan.

The process of identifying a new way to satisfy that ultimate purpose (going on a hike rather than drinking beer) was (E)ntrepreneuring, the (E) role. The organizing of the hike (where to meet, what time to meet, who would bring the picnic basket) belonged to the (A) role, or (A)dministering. The actual act of hiking to the lake or removing the rock from the path so they could get the purpose realized was (P)roducing, the (P) role.

But what is the common denominator in all these activities? Why are these people drinking beer together, going on a hike together, and lifting a rock together in the first place?

Physiological studies show that humans need to interrelate. Imprisonment is confinement from the public and, thus, a punishment. What is the worst level of punishment in a prison? Solitary confinement. Notice the psychological effects on people since the COVID-19 pandemic began: paranoia, depression. We all need to relate to and have contact with other people.

Therefore, no matter what the current or future need is that an organization satisfies, the (I) role is permanent and ongoing. The (I) role is the most important, and every leader should ensure that it is not diminished in pursuit of the other roles.

Some leaders divide and rule. Using only the (P) and (E) roles in their strategies might make sense for external integration, but one should analyze how they implement those decisions, those strategies, and that affects the (I) role, the internal integration.

Michael Platt, a neuroscientist at the University of Pennsylvania and at Wharton, said: "Human beings are wired to connect, and we have the most complex and interesting social behavior of all animals." We are social; we need each other. We even keep dogs or cats sometimes for no other reason than to feel needed, to interrelate. In the United States, dogs are trained to visit patients in hospitals; some studies have shown that a dog's attention and affection can speed up the healing process. (There is even a company in southern California with miniature horses that visit hospital patients and veterans.)[5]

Everything in this world exists to serve something else. That is the (P) role. If it serves only itself, then it is a cancer and serves death. The pen I write with is useless if it does not leave a mark on paper. Breathing has no meaning unless the oxygen feeds my body. Nothing is functional by itself; everything is functional in relation to something else for which the (I)ntegrating role is needed.

If performed well, the (I) role causes long-term efficiency because when people work well in unison they do not waste energy. As the team works well, it does not depend on any single individual for survival. What integrates is the social system of values. It depends on no single individual and no energy is lost. Developing and nurturing affiliations is what makes an organization efficient in the long run.

---

5. See https://www.minitherapyhorses.com

People who perform the (I) role well (those with the capability of integrating others) have the potential to go beyond being good managers and to become leaders.

While the (I) role is critical, it should not be performed in vacuum or be the only role performed. An organization that is performing the (I) role for an (I) purpose is just a social, feel-good, "get together to laugh and be merry" organization. It is not a performing organization. If it has economic purposes for its existence but is performing only the (I) role, it will happily go bankrupt.

What would happen if your organization was managed by an executive who performed the (P), (A), and (E) roles in an outstanding way? If they were a knowledgeable, achievement-oriented, task-oriented, effective, no-nonsense Producer, as well as an outstanding Administrator running a tight ship (systematic and well-organized, everything done right and on time)? In other words, what if your organization was effective and efficient? In addition, what if this executive was an outstanding Entrepreneur, constantly adapting and improving the organization so that it really moved and adjusted to the changing environment? Now, what would happen to that organization when this leader died?

The organization would also die. Why? Because although the (P), (A), and (E) roles are necessary, they are not sufficient if the organization is to be effective and efficient *in the long run*.

Organizations should be managed to survive for the long run. Look at the Catholic church, for example. It has existed for two thousand years, and it will likely go for another two thousand. Why? Because it has established a set of values that each individual in the organization identifies with, independent of who the Pope is.

To achieve that, the (I) role needs to be realized.

(I)ntegrating means to change the consciousness of the organization from mechanistic to organic. It means developing a set of accepted values that are adhered to by the organization.[6] If the role of (I)ntegrating is performed well, people will learn to work as a team instead of as individuals.

(I)ntegrating builds a climate, a system of ethics and behavior, that encourages everyone to work together so that no one is indispensable.

The (I) role can be performed by an individual or by a system of institutionalized values. In a democracy, the (I) role is realized by the constitution that people honor and defend. In a dictatorship, it is done by an individual, often with demagogy and/or oppression.

(I)ntegrating can be either mechanistic or organic.

Look at a chair: it is integrated, but only mechanistically. If one of the legs breaks, the other legs do not pitch in to hold up the structure. There is no internal interdependency, no organic relationship among the parts of the chair. Only external intervention can help.

Something similar happens in mechanistically oriented organizations. Let's say there is a problem with sales. The company is going broke. The production department says, "That's not my problem. That's a sales problem." However, there may be something production could do differently that would improve sales. This is "the silo syndrome."

That is also what happens in international relations. Each country takes care of its interests, less so the broader ones. When I was in college studying political science, in a class on international relations, the professor told us right off the bat that international relations are not handled following the ethics that govern interpersonal relations. What drives countries is self-interest. And the result is polluted air, polluted

---

6. On the role of (I)ntegrating, see an early writing by P. R. Lawrence and J. W. Lorsch, "New Management Job: The Integrator," *Army Organizational Effectiveness Journal*, no. 2 (1984).

oceans, polluted water. No one takes care of the open seas. The air pollution of China ends in California, and California smoke, caused by big fires, ends in Sweden.

If we will ever solve the problem of a deteriorating environment it will be when we develop an organic consciousness, where we are concerned about what is happening in China as if it is happening to us here.

If the four legs of the chair were internally interdependent (i.e., organic), when one leg broke the other three would realign themselves into a tripod to maintain the chair's functionality.

Look at your hand. If one finger breaks, your whole body feels it. There is empathy. And not only that: when one finger breaks, the other four fingers on that hand will try to compensate for that loss. That is organic consciousness, with interdependency and cooperation; it's symbiotic instead of individualistic, independent, and frequently adversarial.

"Yes, but in the case of a hand, the fingers all share the same head," a cynic might argue. Not always. What if the finger that broke belongs to your four-year-old son? It's not *your* finger. So why are *you* in pain and unable to focus? Because it belongs to someone you love, and his pain is your pain.

So (I)ntegrating does not have to be physical. It can be emotional and/ or spiritual. It is driven by a sense of belonging and affiliation.

When your kids are fighting, you don't always solve their problems for them, do you? Why not? Because you are trying to promote their sense of interdependency and affiliation. You might say, "Hey, you're family; you're supposed to be helping each other. I'm not going to be here forever. You must learn to solve your own problems."

Let's say that you and your family are packing up the car for an outing, and you find your son sitting in the car, waiting for the rest of the family. "Why are you sitting?" you might ask him.

"My stuff is already in the car," he responds.

"Get moving and help the family!" you'd probably respond. "You are not alone here. Your job is done when the *whole family's* job is done." Right?

A family is more than a group of people; a hand is more than just five fingers. There is a sense of interdependence fostered by common values and vision.

(I)ntegrating involves creating and nurturing a culture of constructive collaboration and cooperation. Within this culture, then, the group can continue to function if something happens to the leader or any other individual member

Take a sports team. If you pull players from various all-star teams — who have never played or trained together — and play them against a team that is above average but has been playing together for a long time, who might win the *first* game? It's possible that the above-average team will win because the all-star team has not yet developed its team consciousness; its members cannot yet predict: "If she does that, I can back her up by doing this." That sense of cooperation while working toward a common goal is what we mean by teamwork.

Companies that rely on any single individual for continuous success in their operations inevitably face a crisis if that individual leaves or dies. Organizations that have been managed by a (PAE-) — the dash in the (I) code signifying that the (I) role is missing or deficient — will find success as long as their leader is alive and functioning but will be in trouble if that leader leaves before a cohesive team (an esprit de corps around an effective course of action) has been developed.

Since an organization's life span should be longer than the life of any individual, effective long-range continuity depends on building a team of people who understand, trust, and respect each other — and who complement each other's abilities and share a common vision, mission, and values. The (I)ntegrating role, when performed well, creates that effect.

To remember the four PAEI roles and how they work together, think of a car. For a car to function well, it needs to have a good engine (the (P) role), so it will move and be capable of fulfilling the function of transportation. It also needs to have a steering wheel (the (E) role), so it can change directions as it moves toward its destination. It needs to have brakes (the (A) role), so the car is controllable. And it needs to have oil, or the electronic system (the (I) role), to keep all the different parts working together.

When my kids were toddlers, I bought them a xylophone. One Sunday morning I was reading the newspaper in the living room. My kids were in their room playing. All at once I heard shouting: "Daddy, Daddy. . . ." They were fighting. I went to their room and found that they were fighting over the xylophone. Both wanted it.

Here is the test question: How would you solve this problem employing the (P) role?

Often, I get the answer: Let them share it, one child gets it for ten minutes, the other gets it for ten minutes, and so on. But that is not a (P) solution. It is an (A) solution. For a solution that uses the (P) role, you must first identify: Who is the client? What is the client's need?

You need to ask yourself what the *kids* need to satisfy their fighting over the xylophone.

If you asked them, I bet they would not know. They would say something but do not assume that *is* the need.

Likewise, grown-ups do not always clearly know what their need is." Do you know *exactly* what you want when you go to buy a car? Probably not. You test drive cars and rule in what you want and rule out what you don't want until something clicks. So a good leader, in performing the (P) role and trying to satisfy a need, must explore the client's needs and address these by trial and error. Are the kids really fighting because they want to play music, specifically on a xylophone, on Sunday morning. If so, buy another xylophone.

They probably just want to make noise. In that case, go bring some pots and pans from the kitchen, one plays the pots and the other the xylophone. If that works, you are done. If not, maybe it is sibling rivalry, and they are vying for dominance. In that case, let them keep fighting (unless blood flows), or teach them brotherhood: supporting each other rather than dominating each other. (For the (I) role, see below.

The (A) solution, for instance, would be to flip a coin and the winner plays the xylophone for ten minutes and then the other one for ten minutes, back and forth, until they get tired of the toy.

In the (A) solution, whose need was satisfied? Not the kids if their need is for dominance or to play music or just to make noise. The (A) solution solved the need of the parent to have some peace and quiet.

In many companies a person comes to a manager with a problem. The manager does not solve the need of the client, only their own need for order and peace. This is why bureaucracies have a terrible reputation for service.

What would be the (E) solution? Find another need that is bigger and stronger than the need the kids are currently fighting over and redirect their attention to it: "Kids, who wants to go to the movies?" or "Who wants to play ball?"

And that is what you have to do if you own a restaurant — always have a new dish of the day. If you are a pharmaceutical company, it is your latest medicine. Many medicines are not new at all. Just a small change of a molecule here and there. But they are marketed as *new*, improved, more powerful, more effective drugs because that is what the market wants.

Audiences want something new, something different. That is the need.

How about the (I) role solution?

Do not say: "Make them play together."

That is a mechanistic solution because the solution is provided from the outside: *You!* For organic (I)ntegrating, they need to find the solution themselves. They need to own their solution.

So?

I told them brothers should not fight. "I am not going to solve your problem. When I am not around anymore, who is going to solve your problems? A judge? Will you go to court? (That is external, mechanistic integration.) *No!* Both of you to the bathroom. Give me the xylophone, close the door and do not come out till you decide how to solve your problem.

How long do you think it took them to agree? They looked at each other and in no time came to an agreement.

Now if I did not take the xylophone from them and sent them to the bathroom, how long would it have taken them to resolve their problem? They would probably have continued fighting in the bathroom. Why? Because I would be putting them in a situation where they need to employ two roles simultaneously: the (P) and the (I), and that is not easy. The roles are in conflict, a subject we address in later chapters.

Let us look at an application of the PAEI model on the macro level.

Years ago, Mexico's then-President Vicente Fox invited me for consultations. I diagnosed a pattern common to developing economies. The executive-branch structure had plenty of ministries for (P)roducing, such as dealing with the economy, industry, housing, telecommunication; and (I)ntegrating, such as health, education, social development. But the (A)dministering function was unrepresented — it lacked essentials such as federal prosecutors and federal police. The judicial system was weak and there was no ministry for (E).

Mexico and other developing countries did not develop their own indigenous (A) and (E) for a reason. In working with indigenous Mexicans, the rank and file, I found that their aspirations tended to the short term, looking at the future in weeks rather than years. Their (E) role was limited to some small offerings on the street or a small store. This demonstrated a lack of a big (E) role. They lacked in the (A) role as well. The (A) develops during industrialization, and developing countries were industrialized by foreigners. This results in indigenous people lacking in (A) and using the (I) instead. As an executive in a developing country once told me: "We do not have institutions here. We have connections."

Without the (A) function, law and order, countries rely on (I) relationships to drive and regulate interdependencies — which yields corruption. Deals are made among people who trust each other and do not necessarily follow country-wide rules.

To fight corruption, it is not enough to persecute the wrongdoers. And it is very difficult to achieve results with persecution when the courts are corrupt. What is needed is a ministry for de-bureaucratization (tasked with wiping the slate clean of obsolete laws from the colonial era or legislation that benefits the multinationals) and redesign of the administrative structures to reflect the changing needs of the nation: Change the education system to nurture (A). Bring (A) to replace (I) — i.e., students must deliver homework on time and according to specifications, or work is rejected. Be on time, leave on time, etc. Also needed is the establishment of a major government agency that encourages (E)ntrepreneuring and provides not only financial but also professional advice to small businesses — one that builds business incubators. In developing countries the (E) is weak, too, because in an agricultural society plans form one season to the next. It is the industrial society that needs a long term view.

Agricultural and tribal societies excel in the (P) and (I) roles. The (A) and (E) roles develop through industrialization performed by imported leadership sent by the colonialists or, later, the expatriates of multi-nationals, not by the indigenous people. And the imported leadership often does not share the same interests as the indigenous people

I found this same phenomena in Ghana and India, where I also consulted.

In my consulting to leaders of developing nations, I have emphasized the need to change the education system to develop the (A) and (E) roles, within the culture, if the country wishes to emerge from its underdeveloped status.

CHAPTER 2

The Incompatibility of the Roles

We have established that there are four PAEI roles, all necessary to make an organization healthy.

The roles, however, undermine each other's performance. Any of them can be performed well over time, as long as only one or two are performed together. But all cannot be performed well at any single point in time. Let us see how it happens.

Managerial Roles are in Conflict

P ⚡ E	P ⚡ A	P ⚡ I
Conflict	Conflict	Conflict
Present / Future	**Function / Form**	**Results / Relationships**
E ⚡ A	E ⚡ I	A ⚡ I
Conflict	Conflict	Conflict
Innovation / Tradition	**Provocation / Harmony**	**Mechanistic / Organic**

Incompatibility of (P) and (E) Roles

How many times have you said, "I'm working so hard. I have no time to think!" In other words, moving the rock (i.e., satisfying present demands) is so overwhelming that you have no time to think about future opportunities. But while you've been sweating and pushing that rock out of your path, performing the (P) role, someone else has been performing the (E) role and planning to build a big highway close by. As one works hard, day and night, focusing on short-term results (the rock), it is difficult if not impossible to also stay aware of and capitalize on the changes that are coming our way (the highway).

It can be hard to have both perspectives, short-term and long-term, at the same time. Our minds are like a camera. We can either focus on the close-up view, rendering the long-range view out of focus, or vice-versa.

I have met many exceptionally successful entrepreneurs who were lucky enough to be fired from their former jobs, where they were busy performing the (P) role. If they had stayed put, they would never had started their own company. Once they were freed from the (P) role, they could afford to start to (E)ntrepreneuring.

Conversely, the (E) role, by its very nature, threatens the (P) role: (E)ntrepreneuring means change, and (P) sees change as a threat because it can interrupt *productivity*. People in production are forever complaining to the engineering department, "If you guys don't stop changing things, we'll never get anything done!" At some point, you must freeze the planning, the (E) role, so you can proceed with the doing, the (P) role.

Incompatibility of (P) and (A) Roles

When you play doubles in tennis, and a ball comes at high speed directly to the center of the court, do you wait until you're sure where it's going to land before deciding who is responsible for hitting it back? Obviously not. Do you make a line in the middle with some white-wash, so you and your partner know *exactly* who is responsible for what area? I don't think so. You divide the court among yourselves, *more or less*. And when the ball hits the middle of the court, in the "gray area" of responsibility, then you both move for the ball. This is effective because one of you will hit the ball, but it is not very efficient. Both of you moved.

The most efficient scenario might seem to be that no one moves until the ball has landed, and it is clear whose responsibility it is. Only one moves to hit the ball. This may be an efficient solution, but most likely it will be too late for anyone to return the ball. Thus, it is an efficient but ineffective solution

Effectiveness (the outcome of the (P) role) and efficiency (the outcome of the (A) role) are incompatible processes.

When you want to be very effective, you have difficulty being efficient. That's why start-up companies, which are constantly putting out fires and dealing with unanticipated problems, are somewhat disorganized and inefficient. They accept the fact that organization and order, the (A) role, will have to wait.

The opposite is also true. If you are very efficient, you could end up less effective. That is the case with bureaucracies, in which every de-tail is planned, and no variable is left uncontrolled. Ironically, the more control you have, the less control you *feel* you have — because the more control you have, the more deviations you can identify that need to be controlled. Let us look at the tennis analogy again and adapt it to make the case.

In a game of couples tennis, one opponent might send the ball in be-tween the two of you, to the area where there is uncertainty about whose responsibility that is. To decrease the chance of not hitting the ball back, the (A) type (one who wants most control and thus mini-mum uncertainty), would put a third person on the court, in between the two of you. But now there are two areas of ambiguity between the three. So, in the next round, again to reduce uncertainty, the bureau-crat would add two more people (in business this is called throwing people at the problem). Now we have four areas of uncertainty. four more people are added to the court to reduce uncertainty and increase controllability. Before we know it, there will be fifty people on the court, but no one is watching the ball (which is what the client needs). Instead, each is watching that the other guy does not step on their toes. They are watching their turf and the only ball they hit back is the one that hits them right in their forehead.

That is bureaucracy for you.

As the granularity of control increases, the system becomes increas-ingly inflexible, and thus nonresponsive to the changing needs of its clients. The more and more efficiency one might want, the greater the inefficiency. And bureaucracies in searching utmost efficiency usually end up being inefficient.

Here is another tennis analogy: Assume a player stands in one place, practicing and practicing hitting the ball until his hand and body move-ments are perfect, and then tells his opponent, "Send the ball *here*," to the spot he practiced in, where he can be the most efficient. The result is that he hits only those balls that come directly to his racquet.

Instead of going after the ball (following his clients' changing needs), he expects the clients to follow his system for efficiency. Instead of the racket following the ball, the ball is to find the racket. He is just going through the motions, hoping that when he swings, the ball will be there to be returned.

This is what I call being precisely wrong rather than being approxi-mately right. And this is how bureaucracies work. Everything is planned and controlled to the minute detail. No variable is left unattended. The fact that the ball — the client's changing needs — is over *there* now instead of over *here* does not do much to change their behavior. They just go through the motions as planned for maximum efficiency and control. They are efficient to the extreme, making them inflexible and, thus, eventually extremely ineffective.

To be approximately right, but be effective, you must go to where the ball is, even if it means your body is not moving in the most efficient way.

This dichotomy of form versus function, effectiveness versus efficiency, could be observed as the Berlin Wall came down and the communist system started to thaw. This system experienced tremendous difficulty in its transition to a market economy. In order to be market-driven and -oriented (in other words more effective), people had to learn to be less efficient, with less regulation, less government planning and supervision. But when I lectured at the Academy of Economics in Russia and tried to explain that to be more effective their system must be less efficiency oriented, it was like selling pork to orthodox Jews. The whole communist system was based on the (A) role, on production efficiency — five-year plans in detail. Switching to perform the (P) and the (E) roles and focus on market needs was a much bigger challenge, a huge cultural change, than just learning how to measure profit by accounting principles.

The incompatibility of the (P) and (A) roles is, in essence, a struggle between form and function.

Think of a teapot: perhaps you bought it because the shape was attractive, but the tea spills all over the table. In this case, you gave form priority over function.

When something is created in which form and function (i.e., effectiveness and efficiency) are in perfect balance, that creation is put in a museum. It is a piece of art.

Incompatibility of (A) and (I) Roles

Both the (A)dministering and (I)ntegrating roles are concerned with form. Each is concerned with an accepted set of rules that both drives and puts boundaries on behavior.

The (I) role represents organic form, whereas the (A) role represents mechanistic form. By mechanistic, I mean that the (A) role is externally driven: (A) establishes parameters, and you must accept these parameters as they are given to you, whether you agree with them or not. If you break the rules, or deviate from them, you understand that there will be a penalty.

The (I) role also sets parameters, but the (I) role's parameters are internally driven by your affinity to the group values you have internalized and accepted as your own. Thus, an (I) role can be even more constraining than an (A) role. When you are both rule maker and rule enforcer, cheating is impossible. You cannot deviate — even in the darkness where no one can see you — because you are watching *you*, and you cannot escape yourself.

Here is an example: A man says to a married woman, "Why don't we make love?"

She says, "No, I cannot."

He says, "Why not? Your husband will never know."

She says, "Yes, but *I* will know."

That's the (I) style. "Why not?" Because "I will know." Whether or not anyone else knows is irrelevant because *I* will know that I did something I shouldn't have done. It's internal, in contrast to the (A) style, which is external: "If I break these rules, I may be caught and punished but maybe not."

The (A) role undermines the (I) role as a regulator of interdependencies because the organization will rely on its legalistic, manualized rules to control those interdependencies and relationships, and draw less on its members' cultural values. And it is easier to legislate a rule than to develop a value. To make a new law might take a few months. To develop a new code of ethics that people internalize and adhere to might take a lifetime. Thus, the (A) function will always tend to increase as a regulatory mechanism, which will make the (I) function less necessary and poorly reinforced. The more (A) you have, the less (I) you will have.

In the beginning years of a new religion, for example, the founding believers won't have a lot of the (A) role. What they will have is a commitment to their God and a shared value system, which will enable them to decide among themselves about what is right and wrong. They'll have lots of (I).

As time goes on, the religion will become codified into a set of rituals and practices. New practitioners of the religion might forget the initial (I) values and just follow the (A) manual — whether it is the Old or New Testament or the Koran or another text — and become more and more rules-driven. Eventually, the tail will begin to wag the dog: The (A) rules will start to dominate. Instead of (I)ntegrating — a system of values serving as the "glue" that unites the community through consistency of beliefs — the organization now emphasizes rituals and rules, the (A) role, and the religion becomes rigid. It becomes an *organized religion*, and its believers conform to the rules of conduct rather than the spirit of the content.

In the Middle Ages, the inquisitors in Spain put my ancestors who converted to Christianity — but did not practice Christianity correctly (they practiced Judaism in hiding) — on a burning stake. Is that what God (absolute love) wanted? The (A) role destroys the (I) role.

There is one God. So why is there fighting among religions? We all have the same goals in serving God, no? The schism and the religious wars are over *how* we serve — the (A) role. That is where the fighting and anger and persecutions are. Jews cover their heads when entering a house of prayer. Christians take their hats off. Muslims take their shoes off. Jews acknowledge Saturday as a sacred day of worship. Christians Sundays. Muslims Fridays. Hey, you want to start a new religion? Thursdays are still available.

I am Jewish, but I have no problem with going to a church if it is across the street and the synagogue is too far away. God is everywhere. What is the difference? Follow the (I) role. Let go of the (A) role.

Here is another example of the (A) role undermining the (I) role: Which country has the most lawyers per capita? The United States. (A) is very high and growing; our court system is overloaded. The (A) role is penetrating deeper and deeper into our social fabric. It dictates how we should raise our children, how to address our spouses, where and how we can or cannot smoke, eat, talk.

Look at the bumper stickers as they zoom by on American cars. "LOVE" is probably the most repeated word: "I love New York," "I love my dog," "Jesus loves you," etc. Why do we have this preoccupation with love? Because love is the ultimate (I)ntegrating factor, and it is in high demand because it is threatened by change. Change brings alienation, which seems to be the overwhelming result of modern life. Furthermore, the bigger the city, the lesser the (I)ntegrating role impacts, and the lonelier the people will be, accordingly.

So the need for the (I) role continues to grow because of change, but this need is often satisfied with the (A) role. At your local bookstore, the largest and fastest-growing section is very likely the "self-help" aisle, where you can find "the rules" for doing everything from finding a life partner to planning a party, to resolving an argument, to making friends. There are rules for everything. (A)-role solutions for (I)-role needs. Endless books and courses on intimacy, love, relationships, communication, self-growth, and self-actualization. Read the books and note they are giving you (A)-role instructions, a manual, on how to perform the (I) role. They are (A)dministering (I)ntegrating.

The more you rely on (A) rules to solve whatever interrelationship issues you have, the less you will rely on your internal guide, your internal voice (your values). The (A) role is easier to follow. It is mechanical. You just go to the self-help aisle, find the prescribed list of steps for your issue, and follow them.

Now let's look at the reverse: Is it possible for the (I) role to undermine the (A) role?

Actually, "undermine" is inaccurate in this context. Rather, the (I) role slows the growth of the (A) role — the more (I) you have, the less (A) you need. You do, however, need at least a threshold level of the (A) role, or the (I) role will deteriorate. Without some rules, you have chaos.

In a tribal community, the tribe relies on its internally developed values to make decisions and resolve conflicts. They do not need external intervention, like police or the courts, to solve problems. They have a very strong value system that tells them what's right and what's wrong; they don't need anybody else to intervene.

I belong to a meditation mission: Heartfulness. I have visited its center in Kanha Village, next to Hyderabad, India. It is a very large settlement with not one policeman and no regulations. On the birthday celebration of the guru, as many as twenty thousand people might come to celebrate. Food is distributed. Sleeping arrangements made. When I was there, I did not see one manager directing or intervening what to do. They were in the background. Minimal intervention. People just lined up and did what was right and cooperated. They were driven by values, by caring for each other.

Here is how you can tell if a hotel or a restaurant is any good: By the *absence* of management. The manager is there but in the background. Only watching, not directing. Keep in mind, however, that the (A) role should not be zero. (in this book, a void in the PAEI code will be referred to as a zero, a dash, or a blank, and represented by a dash in the code, such as (P-EI).)" With all due respect to (I)ntegrating, without at least a threshold level of the (A) role, the (I) role will deteriorate. Without some rules, you have chaos even at the Heartfulness center, and the (I) values will be impacted.

If you accept a code of external rules *and* make it your own, if you have your (I) role as the exclusive role for integration and it serves as your (A) to integrate externally — if you, for instance, believe in communism and are willing to die for it, it might make you extremely inflexible. Some Russians committed suicide when Stalin's atrocities were disclosed. The revelation destroyed many people's internal belief system.

People with only (I) driving their behavior are fanatic. Depending on what they believe in, they can be Mother Theresa or Hitler. Same with the Taliban. They believe in their religious rules and practice them meticulously in running the country. It's tough to win a war against people with a belief system for which they are willing to die.

Those people who have the (I) take the role of (A) if they get disillusioned and lose the (I) are all (P-E-), cynical. No values. That is what I believe happened to Russia. As the Soviet Union was dismantled and the communist ideology bit the dust, people were left with no God, no belief system, and only money to guide them. They cared only for results now and in the future. They became materialistic, and more capitalistic than the capitalist countries.

Incompatibility of (P) and (I) Roles

Have you ever attended a course or workshop that promised to teach you how to be a better Integrator: how to relate better to people, be a good communicator and a more sensitive human being? Then you returned to work and a crisis came about, and it was time-sensitive, and you had to have a meeting on the spot to deal with it, in which you had to *produce* results. There was no time to convince, explain, or motivate — only time to *do*. What happened to your new team-building skills and techniques for patient listening?

When there is time pressure to *produce* results, it is normal to become rather dictatorial and assign a lower priority to (I)ntegrating and the needs of some stakeholders. The (P) role squeezes out the (I) role.

No matter how many times you may have gone to a meeting promising yourself that *this* time you'll be patient and understanding and people-oriented, situations inevitably arise in which decisions must be made *now!* And what are you thinking, as you sit fidgeting in a meeting and checking your watch for the fifteenth time? *"To hell with people's expectations of speaking their piece! We have a business to run here!"* Right? The (P) role erases the functionality of the (I) role

By the same token, the (I) role undermines the (P) role by applying boundaries, very much in the way of the (A) role.

Here is an example, again from religion: Imagine that the very religious Jews, the ones dressed in black, don't have much to eat and no work. When you ask them, "What are you going to do?" What will they say? "God will help." "God will provide." Period. They have total confidence and faith. This is true of very religious Muslims and Christians, as well.

Now, if you are not religious, you are not going to sit around waiting for God to provide, are you? You're going to go out and find work or food or both. You're going to *produce* results.

So, people with a large amount of faith, or (I) role, will stay within the parameters of their value system, and this can interfere with their ability to *perform*. Even if it is a matter of life and death, they will not violate their religion.

For an interlude, here is a scenario that I believe makes the point:

A man was a very righteous man. Prayed religiously and never sinned. One day there was a serious life-threatening flood. He climbed to the roof. A boat came to save him. He refused. "God will save me," he said. "I am a righteous man."

Then a helicopter came to save him. Still, he refused with the same excuse.

Eventually he drowned.

When he came to the other world, he asked God why he did not save him. He never sinned. He was a righteous man.

"What do you mean I did not try to save you?" asked God. "I sent you a boat; you refused it. I sent you a helicopter; you refused it."

Relying on the (I) role to *produce* results is not going to help. God helps the sailor who rows the boat. Performing the (I) role will help to *produce* results but it does not replace the (P) role.

In recent years, a new form of performing the (I) role has begun suffocating the (P) role. It's called *political correctness*. We must get along and make no waves. It's a different kind of pressure. It may even be more pressurizing than the political oppression of the (A) role.

Incompatibility of (E) and (I) Roles

Why are the (E)ntrepreneuring and the (I)ntegrating roles in conflict? Because the (E) role seeks to change, create, and make a difference, whereas the (I) role seeks to harmonize, agree, and collaborate." While the (I) role tries to put things together or keep them together, the (E) role will try to change things and take them apart.

Here's a rather complicated example of how the (I) role undermines the (E) role: Japan. Until just a few years ago, the Japanese had not, historically, been individualistic innovators. The Japanese education system has always been weak in the (E) role. They teach their children to recognize each other's value and avoid disagreeing in public or standing out as an individual. To perform the (E) role, however, you have to move out of the box, to challenge the status quo, to seek change, and that threatens consensus.

When I work in any other country in the world, and the group I am working with agrees on a subject, we clap our hands and shout, *"Yes!"* When I work in Japan, I reverse my rules: When somebody in the room says, "I have a different opinion," *that's* when we clap hands and shout, *"Yes!"* Because the Japanese rarely disagree with each other. They are watching to discover the consensus. They are driven by (I).

Japan was once the envy of the world. An economic marvel. They worked hard, executing the (P) role, and (I)ntegrating to work together. And with immaculate order and attention to quality and detail, they also developed the (A) role. But they were weak in (E). They imported the (E) function by copying technologies and importing (E) executives like the founder of SoftBank, the CEO of Nissan, and the CEO of Sony.

When the rate of change worldwide began to accelerate, and decision-making needed to be faster — but with too much (I)ntegrating and too little indigenous (E)ntrepreneuring — Japan could not adapt and accelerate their decision-making. At the same time, interdependencies increased (governments with corporations; banks with governments, etc.), and their (A) function increased.

With high (I), the (A) role increasing, and the (E) culture low, *performing* economically, the (P), had to decline and Japan lost its standing in the international community as a miracle economy.

To change course, Japan needs to change its educational system so that it supports and nurtures and increases the (E) role; in other words, it needs to start teaching people how to *learn* rather than just to *know*. It must begin to value "deviant" thinking — out-of-the-box thinking — and reward individualism instead of rewarding the (A) role; and it must do so without losing its own cultural competitive advantage of the (I) role.

If these changes can't be realized, then the Japanese need to open their gates and stimulate the immigration of nationalities with a lot of

(E) in their cultures — the Greeks, the Jews, or the Indians — a practice that Japan, a particularly closed society, rejects.

Incompatibility of (E) and (A) Roles

Finally, how are (E)ntrepreneuring and (A)dministering incompatible? This one is easy to see. (E) people are the liberals, whereas the (A)s are the conservatives. (A) people want to maximize efficiency through control, and they try to achieve this by minimizing deviations; whereas (E) people *live* to create deviations, to introduce change, which (despite the mess that it sometimes causes) is necessary for long-term effectiveness. Thus, the (E) role threatens the (A) role because too much change hinders systematization, routine, and order.

And the opposite is also true: the (A) role endangers the (E) role. As you freeze new ideas for the sake of efficiency, your ability to be proactive and effective in the long run will become limited. Policies, rules, and institutionalized behavior inhibit change.

Let's take the example of communist Soviet Union. The (A) culture was so dominant that anybody who was an (E)ntrepreneur was called a *spekulant*, or speculator, which definitely had a negative connotation: it meant somebody who would undermine the centrally planned economy of the country.

And why was it so easy for Hitler to convince the German nation to reject the Jews? (Also, Spain expelled my ancestors in the fifteenth century. I am a Sephardi.) It was an (E)/(A) roles cultural conflict (obviously there are other reasons, this is just one of them): Jewish people being very strong in the (E) role (needing to survive, moving from one country to another), and Spain and Germany (in each era, respectively) being very dominant in the (A) role. And (A) rejects (E) whenever it can. The Italians who were collaborators with Nazi Germany were less prone to execute its Jewish population. My insight? The Italians were more (E)s and very much less (A)s. The biggest achievement attributed to Mussolini was that he made the Italian trains run on time.

———————————

Because the PAEI roles undermine each others' performance and because energy is fixed, some roles are stronger than others in driving personality style and behavior. That creates mismanagers, managers, leaders and misleaders.

PART II

Styles

CHAPTER 3

PAEI for Personality Codification

The PAEI codification is a kind of shorthand for communicating a "style." If the PAEI combination is known, the style is predictable. The different combinations and the degree of ability to perform the different roles allows us to classify a person's style and to evaluate them as a *manager* or a *mismanager*, a *leader* or a *misleader*.

To function well as a manager a person must be able to perform all four roles at least at the threshold level needed by the organizational role assigned. Thus, when one or more of the PAEI roles is not being performed at the level required by the task or the situation — signified by a dash in the code, with extreme cases containing three dashes — a corresponding extreme of mismanagement style emerges: A (P---) is a mismanager whom I call a Lone Ranger; an (-A--) is a Bureaucrat; an (--E-) is an Arsonist, and an (---I) is a SuperFollower. The more dashes a person has in their code, the higher the degree of mismanagement.

Managers don't have blanks in their code, and they may excel at one or more of the PAEI roles. A manager may excel at (P)roducing while being merely competent at the other roles. I would "code" that manager's style, then, as (Paei) — the upper-case (P) designating excellence in that role and the lower-case (a), I, and (i) designating competence in those roles.

Another manager may excel at organizing (pAei), while a third may be good at sensing future trends (paEi). A fourth might be great at "reading people" (paeI).

There are people who might excel in two letters of the code, for instance, (PaEi). Usually these are the founders of companies or the leaders of revolutions. A (pAeI) would be a very human, participative, open Administrator. A (PAei) would likely be known as a "taskmaster" who tells their subordinates what to do and how to do it, not giving people the right to think independently or even asking if they agree with the orders. A (paEI) represents a statesman-style leader who unites a nation to achieve a vision that is supported by people who make that vision realizable.

Remember, energy is fixed. The bigger one letter in the code is, the smaller one or more of the other letters in the code must be. If someone excels in (PAE), predictably he or she will be approaching zero in the (I) role. If someone is an outstanding (PEI), he or she will be deficient in the (A) role. Energy is fixed and is allocated accordingly.

Any permutation of the combined performance of these four PAEI roles (if each role varied from one to one hundred) yields a style — there will be innumerable permutations, as many as there are people on Earth. We are all the same, subject to variations.

A "leader," contrary to a manager, must excel at two or more roles — one of which must be (I)ntegrating — while also meeting the threshold needs of the other roles.

There are many leadership styles, depending on the code combination,[1] like the Little League Coach (PaeI), the Statesman (paEI), the friendly Administrator (pAeI), etc. Whether a leadership style is functional will depend on the demands of the tasks involved, which also can be PAEI codified.

A misleader is a person who excels in two roles, one of which is (I)ntegrating, but has a blank or two in the rest of the roles.

Examples of misleaders are:

- (P--I) — A misleader who mobilizes people and *integrates* them around the (P) role but who lacks orderly systems (A) and vision (E).

- (-A-I) — A misleader who *integrates* around the (A) role but does not focus nor serve well the current or future needs of the clients.

- (--EI) — A misleader that I call "the Demagogue," who *integrates* people around a vision but doesn't deliver on its promises; he or she lacks the (P) and the (A) roles.

Personality vs Style vs. Behavior

There is a difference between personality, style, behavior, character, and function. Your personality is the core PAEI orientation you are born with.

---

1. For an in-depth exploration of management and leadership styles, see Ichak Adizes, *Management/Mismanagement Styles: the Good, the Bad and the Ugly* (Santa Barbara, CA: Adizes Institute Publications, 2004).

It is genetically determined. Medical research suggests that each role is driven by a specific gland[2] or the relative dominance of parts of the brain[3].

Your style is the behavior you exhibit over time (i.e., your ongoing, consistent way of acting). Style is impacted by your genetics and environment, by the role you perform in a company or a system.

Behavior is what you are doing *right now*, in this very moment. Since a mentally healthy person can perform all four roles — albeit some better than others — in various situations, this person might exhibit a variety of different behaviors, each dictated by the situation at hand. For instance an (E) person needs to manage her direct reports in the department in an (A) *style*. When she goes home and kisses the children, she is behaving in the (I) *style*.

The healthier mentally is an executive is, the better and more effectively he or she can respond to the problems and challenges that the workplace inevitably brings, even if what is required is very different from the natural inclination of their personality. What makes a good leader is the ability to adapt to new situations, and to call upon the elements of the PAEI roles that are needed in that moment. Thus, behavior is driven more by the situation than by genetics while personality is driven more by genetics than the situation.

Personality, style, and behavior, in this definition are free of value judgements, of ethics. When a behavior or style is driven also by values, I consider it *character*.

---

2. Elliot Abravanel and Elizabeth King Morrison, *Dr. Abravanel's Body Type Program for Health, Fitness, and Nutrition* (New York: Bantam Books, Inc., 1985).
3. Stephen M. Kosslyn and G. Wayne Miller, *Top Brain, Bottom Brain: Harnessing the Power of the Four Cognitive Modes* (New York: Simon and Schuster, 2015). https://www.amazon.com/Top-Brain-Bottom-Harnessing-Cognitive/dp/1451645112#detailBullets_feature_div

Function is what an organization requires you to do in your job and it can also be coded with PAEI. When I describe a function I reverse the sequence of the PAEI code.

For example: The marketing department requires a person to perform the (Ep) roles, to analyze what future needs the company should satisfy. I am changing the sequence of the roles in the code to communicate that the E role is dedicated to the P role. It is Eing the p, like innovating how to better P, how to better sell or produce. In the sequence pE, the person is Ping the E, such as working hard doing marketing research. If the person's style is (paEi), then they match the function of the job and are suited to it. But as we said before, a person's behavior can change according to the situation

An interesting point about *behavior* of the moment: if a person with a large (E) personality interacts in decision-making with another (E) personality, whoever is stronger in the (E) role will perform the (E) role while the other one automatically will behave as an (A) or (P) — whatever the first person is weak in. The situation calls for a complementary interaction. If both refuse to behave contrary to their personality and insist on (E)ing, there is going to be a clash.

Psychological tests will tell you about a person's personality, but not necessarily how this person will behave in different situations, and that is no less important to know.

This distinction is important. If we want to hire a new person, we need to know their personality to analyze if their profile fits what is needed. In order to analyze a person's satisfaction at work, we should watch their style and compare it to their personality. If we see a difference, it means the person is in the wrong job. In order to know how to relate to a person at any point in time, we should watch their behavior in the moment, ignoring their style or personality. While a person might have an (E) personality, *most of the time* their style is of a (P) because they have been put in a sales job that calls for (P). If *right now* they are in an (A) mode, they need accuracy and order and we should treat them as if they are (A) style if we want to relate to them constructively.

For staffing decisions look at personality, for human resources development look at their working style, and for how to communicate at the moment watch their behavior of the moment.

In the following pages we describe leadership or managerial styles or behavior. This description of mismanagers, where only one role is being performed and none of the other three, is an exaggeration of what happens in most cases. It is abnormal mismanagement.

It is valuable to know the extremes because the difference between normal and abnormal is one of degree. You could say a normal person is a diluted abnormal. Knowing how abnormal people behave allows us to better manage the normals.

Psychologists study the abnormal to understand the normal. It is easier to see what is going on. We are doing the same here. I am describing extreme mismanagement styles because normal mismanagement is just a behavior of lower intensity or less variables. A diluted abnormal.

CHAPTER 4

(P)-Type Managers and Leaders

Leaders who have (P) as a dominant role in their style can be, among many others:

- (Paei) — the Producer
- (P---) — the Lone Ranger
- (PaeI) — the Producing Leader, or Little League Coach

The Producer (PAEI)

A manager who excels in *providing* for the needs of the clients and thus *produces* the expected results — while also meeting the threshold needs of (A)dministering, (E)ntrepreneuring, and (I)ntegrating — is a manager whose code is (Paei), and whom I like to call a Producer, or a (P) style.

To *produce* as a manager, you must possess several qualities. The first quality is knowing what your clients' needs are and why they are coming to you. What is your particular niche in the marketplace? Second, but just as important, you must know something about the technology required to provide what your clients seek.

Input	Throughput	Output
(P) role	Satisfy client needs	Effectiveness in the short run

It's not true to say, "You can manage anything if you are a professional manager." That is dangerously oversimplified unless we add three more words — *after some time*. And what do you do during that time? You try to learn the peculiarities of the organization that you are managing because, as in the example of the two branches of the same bank that I gave in chapter one, there are no two "rocks" alike in the world. You must know the particularities of what you are trying to manage, so that you can *produce* results and *provide* for the expected needs.

But even that's not enough. Some people, despite being very knowledgeable, do not *produce* results. They can give you a beautiful report, they know the client needs, the technology, and their judgment is correct. However, they lack what psychologists call "achievement motivation," the urge to get in there and do it! Don't just talk about it — do it! This is the desire to see the finalization of a task, like a salesman who won't stop selling until he has a signature on the dotted line. They won't let go until the need of the client is satisfied or the task is done and completed.

A manager who is a Producer of results, must be a knowledgeable achiever.

The Lone Ranger (P---)

What happens when an organization has a manager who is a knowledgeable achiever, a doer, performs the (P) role outstandingly well, but cannot perform the (A), (E), or (I) roles? A (P---). Let's say his function was that of a railroad engineer. You showed him the track, told him what stations to go to, gave him the train, and off he went, full speed ahead — through walls if necessary. He was such a good doer, such a good achiever, so diligent, that he got promoted to a managerial role.

Suddenly, problems start to arise. He can't be an Administrator (doesn't organize, coordinate, delegate, follow up, supervise, or control), nor can he be an Entrepreneur (doesn't come up with new ideas, isn't creative, dislikes taking risks). And he's not an Integrator (insensitive or oblivious to interpersonal relations, doesn't consider group dynamics or individual's feelings; does not relate well to people or build a team and develop the capabilities of others around him).

In the United States, he is called The Lone Ranger. In Mexico and in Scandinavia, he's called the Lonely Wolf. Every country has a different name that reflects this managerial style, but the behavior of the style is identical. He is a hard worker. That is it.

His style: first to arrive to work, last to leave. It is like inventory control system. He is neither a LIFO (last in, first out) nor a FIFO (first in, first out). He is a FISH: first in, still here. Works non-stop. Pays attention to what needs to be done now. Hates intellectualizing, talking, and dreaming. Wants results now. Action now. This person is task-oriented and detests big talkers or wishy-washy, people-focused styles. What you see is what you get. A simple, to-the-point person. No masks, no makeups, no make believes, just a straight shooter. Do not expect innovation from him or her, or much interpersonal sensitivity, or that they will follow the rules religiously.

Once he identifies a task, the Lone Ranger is a good soldier. He will get the job done. That's his advantage: he's loyal, dedicated, and a compulsive doer. But because he overdoes it in one aspect or role of management, to the exclusion of the other roles, he can become a liability as a manager or even more as a leader.

The Lone Ranger focuses on the *what* (not the *how*, not the *who*, and not even the *why)*. "What do we need to do now? Come on, guys, let's get to it. Let's not waste any more time." He doesn't really care whether he is doing the right thing as long as he is doing *something*.

In fact, the Lone Ranger measures his success and his value to the organization by how hard he works. When you ask him, "How are you doing?" his typical answer might be, "I've been working till midnight lately." And "lately," in his case, might be his entire working life!

How is his desk: clean? It's piled to the ceiling with papers, and although he's always working hard, he's somehow always behind, always complaining that the day is too short. "The new week has already started, and I haven't even finished last week's work!"

Yet how would he feel if he came to work and found his desk clean and nothing to do? He would panic. Why? Because he's worried when he's not busy. He constantly needs to be doing something.

The Lone Ranger is just like an alcoholic. He is a workaholic.

One of the characteristics of an alcoholic is that he's never far away from a bottle. Similarly, the Lone Ranger is never far away from work. It's 11 o'clock at night. What is he carrying home with him? A briefcase full of work in case he can't sleep, at least he can do some work.

To a workaholic, going on vacation is a punishment. It's like saying to an alcoholic, "You must go to a dry island for two weeks." That's *scary*. So, what will he pack for his vacation? A trunk full of work, like an alcoholic who hides a bottle in his suitcase.

If you say to an alcoholic, "I have a bottle of the best booze there is. What should I do with it?" Predictably he's going to say, "Give it to *me*." Similarly, if you go to a Lone Ranger and say, "I have a problem; what should I do with it?" he's going to say, "Put it on my desk." In fact, the more difficult the problem is, the more likely he is to say this.

The tons of overdue paperwork and projects on the Lone Ranger's desk aren't work. They are all bottles. Bottles, bottles, bottles. Only when he's sure he cannot do a task by himself (i.e., only when he is so drunk that he cannot drink more), only *then* will he delegate (i.e., give you the bottle). Of course, by then the problem is already a crisis. Thus, the style of a person who performs exclusively the (P) role is one of management by crisis.

Lone Ranger types are like bulldogs; they get their teeth around the other dog's neck and lock their jaws and don't let go. They stick to a task till it is done even if it turns out to be the wrong task.

If they want to make something happen, they do not touch, they hit. A Lone Ranger will come down on others in a dictatorial style, telling them what he wants them to do and when he wants them to do it.

By the same token, if you want to convince a (P)-style manager to change direction, hinting will not work. You'd better hit him with everything you have. The (P) style will hear you only when you are deafeningly loud.

The Lone Ranger takes things literally: "yes" means yes, and "no" means no. Lone Rangers do not understand nuances. For them, everything is simple. Everything is literal. Give them a "yes" or a "no"; just don't give them a "maybe."

Lone Rangers hate to deal with uncertainty, with alternatives, with ambiguity. They see everything as either black or white and are exceedingly uncomfortable with gray. They can't take the pain of sitting in a meeting, thinking things through. They cannot accept that it might take three days to solve a major problem. They want things simple, and they want them *now*. Going full speed ahead makes the Lone Ranger feel good — even though he might be speeding directly into an abyss.

The Lone Ranger has a very limited, short-term perspective; he sees only the nearest horizon. Thus, he is typically an improviser. "All right let's get going! Does it work? Done! *Finito*! Go! Next!" He won't take the time to pay attention to the larger questions: What is ultimately needed? What are the details that are necessary to make it work? His view of time is that it should be used to solve the immediate problems of the organization. He has no concern for "ten years down the pike" and is always promising to plan later: "After I finish clearing my desk." But of course, that never happens.

The Lone Ranger prefers doing the job himself over directing others. Let's take a Lone Ranger architect as an example. She is such a good architect that eventually she heads her own firm and hires other architects and draftsmen to work for her. But when she comes to work, where do you think she drifts? Does she drift to the accounting department? No! She drifts to the design department. She watches her employees work for a little while; then she says, "Okay, let me show you how to do it." And she sits down at the drafting table and starts designing.

Why does the Lone Ranger prefer to do everything himself or herself? One reason is that he wants to make sure things are done properly. "If you want to be sure something is done right, you'd better do it yourself" is one of his typical expressions. Also, he hates being idle. The Lone Ranger measures himself by how hard he works, so if he were to delegate, what would be left for him to do? He needs to be indispensable, to have problems waiting in line for him. He is always rushed, and he likes it that way.

His subordinates hang around, waiting, coming in late, doing very little. Then all at once there's an emergency — everybody's running here and there, firefighting. The Lone Ranger thrives in this type of environment. That's why another nickname for the Lone Ranger style is the Firefighter.

Managing, to the Lone Ranger, means managing the task, getting the job done. To him, people are merely tools for serving that goal. As a result, the Lone Ranger is politically naive. He doesn't realize that people's judgments might be colored by their own needs and desires. He can make political blunders that lead you to seriously question his intelligence.

The ultimate do-it-yourselfer, the Lone Ranger hates meetings with a passion. If she is required to come to a meeting, she will do so reluctantly.

The same principle applies to the Lone Ranger's own staff meetings. She will avoid them as long as she possibly can. "There's too much work to do; I have no time for meetings." If you force her to hold meetings, she'll probably initiate a conversation, one-to-one, very likely standing in the hallway on her way to somewhere else, and she'll call that a meeting. Because she's addicted to email and voice mail, she truly believes that leaving messages or short instructions are sufficient for fostering teamwork and are certainly a fine alternative to those time-consuming meetings.

The Lone Ranger's subordinates are the same everywhere, though their nicknames vary from one country to another. In the United States, they are called gofers. In Mexico, they are called *inginiero ibeme*, which means, "Engineer, go bring me something." In Israel, they are called *errand boys*. In the US television series, *The Lone Ranger*, the subordinate was called Tonto.

Since the Lone Ranger cannot do everything herself, she uses her subordinates as "expediters" who assist her with errands and short-term assignments but have no permanent, long-term responsibilities. These people spend most of their time waiting to be summoned to deal with the next crisis, for which they generally have no experience or training.

These gofers and errand boys are not always low-level managers. In many companies, top vice presidents are gofers for a Lone Ranger. I once worked in a developing nation with a prime minister whose style was predominately (P). He had cabinet ministers waiting in the corridors, never knowing when they might be summoned in.

When do these gofers come to work? Late. When do they leave? Early. What do they do in the meantime? They wait.

Does the Lone Ranger delegate to her subordinates? No. When you ask her, "Why don't you delegate?" she responds, "They can't do it. They're not ready. They're not prepared."

"How long have they worked for you?"

"Twenty-five years."

"So why don't you train them?"

"I have no time to train them."

"Why don't you have time to train them?"

"Because I have no one to delegate to."

Because everything must go through her, the Lone Ranger inevitably becomes her own bottleneck. Since she has limited time, so not everything gets done and things get lost on her desk. This is ironic. The harder she works, eventually, the less she gets done.

The (P---)-style leader sees no value in the systematic, ex cathedra, classroom training of subordinates. She prefers the apprenticeship approach: subordinates learn how to perform a task by watching her do it herself. "In this business there aren't any secrets. Just get the job done," she insists. "If someone is willing to work hard, they should have no problem getting the job done."

The organization that a Lone Ranger manages cannot grow, since the Lone Ranger is not growing. She is inflexible and simple-minded. She can easily burn out and become obsolete. When she leaves a company, she leaves untrained people behind.

For comparison let us look at another manager's style. No dashes in the code, but this does not mean they excel in everything. They still have some weaknesses. They are just a normal person with strength and weaknesses.

The Little League Coach (Paei)

The (PaeI) Little League Coach is a leader who excels both at (P)roducing results and (I)ntegrating subordinates. He integrates people around the *production*. This leader is a wonderful facilitator, an expert at using compromise to *produce* short-term results. With enough competence in the (A)dministering and (E)ntrepreneuring roles, he can function well as a people-oriented, first-line supervisor. He does not concern himself with the external environment of the company — its market, its suppliers, its bankers, its community — and he does not stand on formality. He encourages and supports the people as they do their job.

Unlike the Lone Ranger (P---), the Little League Coach seeks agreement and is people-oriented. Because of his leadership abilities in (I), he rarely establishes a top-down command, as the Lone Ranger does. But unlike the SuperFollower (---I), he *produces* results. This leader resembles a youth leader or a small-town politician. He seeks to generate excitement and then channels that energy into (P)roducing results.

You can make your own description of any other combination of roles. How about (PAei), or (PaEi), or just a (Paei), or even (P-E-)?

Now, let's try our hand at analyzing a known person, as she has been described in the media

Claire Hughes Johnson, Stripe's Chief Operating Officer

Until recently, Claire Hughes Johnson was responsible for a significant part of Stripe's success. She's part of the new generation of women COOs helping young companies grow rapidly over the past decade. Driving the execution of strategies outlined by CEO Patrick Collison, Johnson allowed him to focus on the vision while leading the short-term, tactical, and operational side of Stripe.

Some of Johnson's key phrases and my PAEI interpretation of them:

"I'm very collaborative, which means I like to discuss decisions and options and whiteboard big stuff in a group. I will rarely get stuck in one position or opinion." (I)

"I expect you are making decisions a lot without me and if you come to me, I'll usually put it back on you with, 'What do you want to do?' or 'What should you do?' and just help you decide." (PI)

"I take action items really seriously, and I expect you to know what yours are, when they are due, and get them done." (P)

"I want us to be ruthless in priorities." (P)

"I dislike being bogged down in data and torturing the numbers [low A]. Let's review consistent information on what really matters and use data to get insight, not to lull ourselves into thinking we know what's going on or to try to find answers that might involve going with our gut." (P)

"I love meeting with people, but sometimes don't spend enough time on the strategic stuff because I am working on other things."[1] (P)

Based on this writeup (I do not know her personally), her style is (PaeI).

1. Elad Gil, *High Growth Handbook: Scaling Startups from 10 to 10,000 People* (San Francisco, CA: Stripe Press, 2018).

CHAPTER 5

(A)-Type Managers and Leaders

The (A)Dministrator (Paei)

This person has the capability and natural inclination to pay attention to detail, especially details of implementation. He or she is methodical and likes their environment to be well thought-out and organized. They think in a linear fashion.

When you have a business idea, especially an innovative one or one for which you have doubts about *how* to do it, you go to this leader to help you cool your enthusiasm. She will think things through for you. She will ask you questions you hadn't thought of. She will see pitfalls you didn't consider. Give her a business plan and she will tear it apart, and you will be grateful! It costs less and hurts less in the long run if problems are anticipated. Either you find ways to solve them before they become crises, or you reject the plan as unworkable.

A good Administrator, or (A) type, can foresee the problems inherent in an idea. In psychological terms, the (A) role is best served by a person with a need to control, while the (P) role requires a person with the need to achieve.

If you trust them, and your idea passes their scrutiny, you will know you can do it. And *should* do it. And if it does not pass the (A) type's strict scrutiny and you decide to do it anyway, at least you will know ahead of time what risks you are taking.

A good Administrator always knows what is going on. They cannot sleep if they don't know what is going on. They keep track of the details. They are well organized and concerned with follow-up and implementation. They have an excellent memory (or are fortified by systems, which means they do not have to rely only on memory), and they work to see that the system operates as it was designed to operate.

The Administrator is good at worrying. They worry about precision, about the integrity of information. They worry that the organization will lose its files, its database, or its intellectual property.

A good Administrator is indispensable to a growing organization. A young organization usually grows too fast and in too many directions and can easily trip and fall on its face (i.e., go bankrupt) without even realizing that it's been in trouble for quite a while.

Good Administrators have your back. They keep the gateway to the castle closed so that the enemy — chaos — cannot enter.

What they do *not* do, however, is *produce* that for which the organization exists.

If you look up the word "administration" in a thesaurus, you will find that its synonym is "to serve." (A)dministrators serve (or at least "should" serve — they often forget that) those who *produce* (i.e., they meet the needs of their clients). One *administers for* someone, *for* something. In public-service organizations, government *administers* for the society, and the people who work in such organizations, are called public administrators, or public servants.

A lawyer who has a (pAei) style is the one you want to write up your contract, but do not ask him to be your trial lawyer. He might lose in court. He can write an agreement that is faultless, but if you must sue, you're much better off finding a creative (paEi) lawyer who can interpret night as day and turn a liability into an asset.

The same is true for accountants. One to advise on taxes is the (paEi) type. The one to *file* taxes is the (pAei) type. If the (E) style *files* the taxes, you might find yourself in trouble for creative accounting. If the (A) style *plans* taxes, you will probably pay more than necessary.

A (PA?-) PROFILE: COCA-COLA'S DOUGLAS IVESTER

Douglas Ivester was Coca-Cola's CFO and the right hand of legendary CEO Roberto Goizueta. Upon Goizueta's death, Ivester was appointed Coca-Cola's CEO.

Ivester was, in the best sense of the term, a number-cruncher supreme, an expert with financial instruments, balance-sheet mechanics, and the like [(A) style]. But Ivester was emotionally inept; he was not a people person [low in (I) role]. He didn't like to schmooze — another word for listening in informal settings where honest feelings often are expressed — and he couldn't empathize with the personal concerns of others. In 1999, when Belgians by the hundreds took sick after drinking Coke, Ivester dawdled in Atlanta for a week before flying across the Atlantic to show he cared about his product's impact on customers. The loss of a potentially lucrative merger with Orangina in France can also be attributed to Ivester's emotional clumsiness. He wouldn't, by all reports, deal with or dissipate anti-Americanism among Orangina's executives.

Then there was the avoidable loss of Coke's highest-ranked African American executive, Carl Ware, who had been relied upon to handle a

*messy discrimination suit in race-charged Atlanta. As most of Atlanta —
and Coke employees — watched in horror, Ivester essentially demoted Ware
during a reorganization [No (I) style].*

*Accounts of Ivester's follies may have surprised shareholders and the general
public, but most Coke executives, especially people who had worked closely
with him, knew full well that he lacked the human touch, that his political
skills were underdeveloped, and that he was a one-man band who seldom
involved others in big decisions [(P) style]. Indeed, Ivester was widely seen
within Coke as someone lost in the details [(A)] while failing to grasp the
big picture [no (E)]. Granted, the company considered him an excellent CFO.
But if the board had bothered to ask, it would have quickly discovered that
few Coke employees considered him a leader.*[1]

THE BUREAUCRAT (-A--)

What happens if a manager is exclusively (A)-oriented? At zero or
borderline in all the other roles? In other words, an (-A--) style?

What is the (-A--) interested in? While the Lone Ranger (P---) is exclusively interested in *what*, the (-A--) is interested only in *how*. That's
why I call him a Bureaucrat: "Never mind what we do. It's *how* we do
it that counts."

Bureaucrats tend to rise in their organizations by following the rules,
often to the point of excess. Bureaucrats may be the easiest to spot of
the four mismanagement types. Certainly, he is one of the easiest to
satirize.

Literature has a great example of a Bureaucrat. Captain Queeg, in Herman Wouk's novel *The Caine Mutiny*, has risen through the ranks of
the navy, not because he was especially competent at leading a crew or
running a ship, but because he followed the rules. He says so himself:

1. Warren Bennis and James O'Toole, "Don't Hire the Wrong CEO," *Harvard
Business Review* (May–June 2000, https://hbr.org/2000/05/dont-hire-the-wrong-ceo).

"Now, I'm a book man, as anyone who knows me will tell you. . . . When in doubt, remember we do things on this ship by the book. You go by the book, and you'll get no argument from me. You deviate from the book, and you better have a half dozen damn good reasons — and you'll still get a hell of an argument from me." [2]

What are the characteristics that typify an (-A--) type, or Bureaucrat?

The Bureaucrat spends an excessive amount of time worrying about (A)dministering the details. He or she prefers to do things right rather than do the right thing. In other words, he would rather be precisely wrong than approximately right.

Here's a joke that will illustrate this point: I was flying over Brazil some years ago. Sitting next to me was a leading accountant from a prominent accounting firm, a big (-A--). We were looking through the window, and we saw the Amazon River. He said, "Dr. Adizes, did you know that this river is a billion years and seven months old?"

"How did you get a billion years and seven months old?" I asked, amazed.

"Well, seven months ago someone told me it was a billion years old."

Bureaucrats pay attention to the form, to the number (straight through to the very last digit), at the expense of the total picture. The Bureaucrat may be focused on the wrong market, the wrong product, the wrong direction! But his reports always look very good because the numbers are calculated to the third decimal.

Here is another joke about the (A)-style person.

Two people are flying in a balloon and get lost in the clouds. They descend a bit and see a person on the ground, so they shout to him: "Where are we?"

---

2. Herman Wouk, *The Caine Mutiny* (New York: Bantam Doubleday Dell, 1951), 131.

He replies: "In a balloon."

One looks at the other and says: "That guy down there must be an accountant. He gave us excellent, perfect information, but it was totally useless."

If you ask a Bureaucrat to give you a report analyzing whether your company should try to penetrate the New York market, he'll say, "Sure," and disappear for a while. He'll accumulate data and analyze it ad infinitum. But by the time he comes back with his recommendation, that market may already have been claimed by your competitor.

In decision-making, the Bureaucrat prefers not to take risks. He does not want to be embarrassed by deciding wrongly. He wants everything safe and organized. He's precisely wrong. He's running a very well-controlled disaster: the company is going broke, but on time.

When does he come to work? On time. When does he leave work? On time. How is his desk? Clean, all in neat piles.

He wants everything to be perfect and under control, and he can spend an inordinate amount of time and money on marginal control that is really not worth it. Such demanding perfectionism can suffocate a company.

While the Lone Ranger focuses on *function*, assuming the form will follow, the Bureaucrat operates under an opposite belief that *form* produces function. Now, sometimes that is true; military leaders assume that if you polish your shoes and shave exactly as required, and hold your head and march exactly as required, that when the time comes to attack and sacrifice your life, you will run and do exactly that — the form will produce the function.

But here is the danger: sometimes the form is so inflexible that it will *not* produce the function. That's why partisans and guerrilla forces invariably defeat organized, established armies. They rely more on the (I) role than the (A) role in asking people to put their lives on the line.

Bureaucrats have an organizational chart readily accessible; if it is not on paper, then it is in their head. They have no trouble finding any of the organization's rules or procedures at a moment's notice. They manage by means of directives, usually in writing. Even when violations are necessary to produce the right results, they won't tolerate a subordinate that breaks the rules.

The (-A--) type's free time is spent looking for new transgressions against the system. When they find one, they design a new form, a new report, or a new policy to prevent the transgression from being repeated. This is why standard operating procedures, rules, and policies multiply and suffocate a company over the years.

Bureaucrats are prone to what is called "manualitis": everything is documented, processes are monotonously described step by step, and the written word begins to dominate the organization's behavior. People who are managed by an (-A--) spend an enormous amount of time reading and writing memos, and filing and responding to memos. This cuts down efficiency tremendously. Thus, trying to be too efficient ends with being inefficient and wasteful.

A Bureaucrat knows the cost of everything but the value of nothing for the following reason: cost is certain; value is maybe. She will tell you, "We cannot do this, it's too expensive." But the truth is that very often the cost of *not* doing may be higher than the cost of doing. "If you think education is expensive, consider the alternative." But an (-A--) will prefer not to take the risk or spend the money. She will waste precious time gathering more information and more details and more justifications and more studies and more analyses — all to minimize risk. But time costs money, and meanwhile the opportunity slips away.

Bureaucrats can subvert the goals of the organization through their insistence on observing the letter of the law, even when departures from it are essential. Their primary and often exclusive commitment is to the implementation of the plan, regardless of its wisdom or even its ethics.

At his 1961 trial in Jerusalem for implementing the genocide of European Jewry, Adolf Eichmann's defense was a morbid and extreme example of this type of behavior. Eichmann described his role in the Third Reich as having been "an administrator of trains." The fact that at one end of the railway line were the victims and their homes, and at the other end were the extermination camps, did not concern him.

A Bureaucrat will frequently have difficulty revisiting a decision during the implementation phase. "We decided," he'll say. "We spent a lot of time on this decision. We spent a lot of money on it. We are not going to open this chapter up again!" Unfortunately, the world often changes even faster than you can implement a plan or attempt to adapt to the changes. A typical Bureaucrat resists such change.

While Lone Rangers evaluate themselves by how hard they work and the results they achieve, Bureaucrats evaluate themselves by how well they *control* the system and their success in eliminating deviations and minimizing uncertainty. Because of this, they tend to be a crowning example of Parkinson's law.[3] They get increasing numbers of subordinates to implement the same task, trying to control every detail, without achieving any apparent increase in productivity.

Bureaucrats are linear thinkers — A, B, C, D, E, F, G. They do not understand that sometimes "G" relates to "H" and "H" relates to "A" and "A" relates to "J" and "J" relates to "B." They get upset when they perceive a discussion as getting out of order. Discussions need to be open to lots of different options, but an (-A--) can't see that.

I call the Bureaucrat's subordinates yes-yes men or office clerks. But although they have a clerk mentality, they are not necessarily clerks. They could be vice presidents. Regardless, they must arrive on time, leave on time, and do everything by the book.

---

3. "Work expands so as to fill the time available for its completion." C. Northcote Parkinson, *Parkinson's Law: Or the Pursuit of Progress* (London: John Murray, 1958).

Bureaucrats hire people like themselves: people who will do as they are told and will not take the initiative. People who do not ask questions that challenge the status quo. People who will avoid rocking the boat.

There's even a joke about this behavior. A new person arrives in Hell and is assigned to work in a bureaucratic department. When he gets there, he finds that all the other workers are standing in fecal matter up to their lips. Horrified, he asks, "How do you work here?"

"Just don't make waves," is the reply.

The Bureaucrat's subordinates know that if a problem is revealed, the Bureaucrat is going to have to find out who did it, and why, how, where, and when. In a word, there is going to be a witch hunt.

Does the Bureaucrat hold staff meetings? You bet: every Monday and Friday from 9 to 12. Assistants take the minutes, the last meeting's conclusions are discussed and verified as to their implementation. There is order, and along with it there is boredom with the myriad of details that the Bureaucrat insists on covering.

Does he have an agenda? Absolutely. In detail. Does the agenda deal with important subjects? Not necessarily. The company might be losing market share, even going bankrupt, but the Bureaucrat will drone on about the need to fill out the necessary forms in duplicate and on time.

The Bureaucrat loves training. He wishes he could program everybody and make every process a routine.

Change, to a Bureaucrat, is a threat of major proportions. His ingenuity in finding reasons to discourage new projects makes him an obstructionist. The organization must find ways to achieve its goals despite him (and those in the organization who are committed to getting things done will quickly learn to bypass him in trying to implement change).

What is an (-A--) type's typical answer when a subordinate asks for permission to do something different? "No." Before you even finish the sentence: "No." Here is a typical Bureaucrat on the phone (this is a Russian joke): "No. No. No. Yes. No. No. No."

"What was that one 'yes' about?" you ask.

"He asked me if I heard him clearly. Yes, and still NO!"

Under the Bureaucrat, strategic planning is at best an exercise in forecasting, but quite often it simply analyzes the past and projects it into the future. So, what is next year's budget or goal? What he is sure he can achieve?

By the time an (-A--) is eliminated from an organization, that organization may have become so mired in regulations and rules that it will have difficulty adapting to long overdue changes, either internally or externally or both.

CHAPTER 6

(E)-Type Managers and Leaders

The Creative Contributor (PAEI)

A person who focuses on the (E) role, with an adequate but not strong (P) orientation; and is a leader with plenty of ideas, some good, some bad, that flow nonstop; is one I call the Creative Contributor. Remember the kid in school whose hand would go up even before she heard the end of the question? Likely a (paEi) type. She is the person in a meeting who does the most talking. Whatever solution is proposed, she has another option. In my previous books, I called this style an Entrepreneur. I was wrong. To be an Entrepreneur, creating and developing organizations, one must be strong in the (P) role as well as the (E) role. A focus on (E) alone is not enough. Without a strong (P) role being performed, the (E) type will constantly move from one idea to the next without finishing much. And she will not be capable of building an organization.

Faculty members at business schools often fit this profile. Why? Because they are *only* creative. They may even be prolific in their creativity, as measured by the number of articles they publish. And the focus of their creativity may even be (E)ntrepreneuring, or how to make money. Nevertheless, if they do not have the additional characteristics that I believe are necessary for an Entrepreneur — the willingness to *proact*, to walk *into* the fog, to take risks, to follow a vision to *produce* actual results, in other words to *(P)*, then they cannot *be* an Entrepreneur. They will not succeed at making money even if they wrote the book on how to do it.

The Statesman (PAEI)

The (paEI) is a leader who excels both at the (E) and (I) roles and mobilizes and integrates people around a vision. He is creative and adaptive and listens to people; but unlike a Demagogue (--EI), his style meets the threshold of the (A) and (P) roles and he attempts to deliver on what he promises.

The (E)ntrepreneur (PAEI)

To be entrepreneurial, managers must have two major characteristics: First, they must be creative, able to visualize new directions and adept at devising strategies for adapting the organization to a perpetually changing environment. Second, they must have a feel for the organization's strengths and weaknesses, the imagination and courage to identify strategies that capitalize on these characteristics, and they must be willing to act and follow their own ideas.

It is risky to follow a dream in the fog. There may be dangerous pitfalls. When you finally get to your destination, you may find that where you are is not where you wanted to be. So, Entrepreneurs must not only have a vision, but also be willing (and able) to risk what they have in order to get what they want.

The Entrepreneur knows what he wants and why he wants it. He is creative, but in the service of a goal. He has an idea, a purpose, and if he has at least threshold capability in the (A)dministrator and (I)ntegrator roles, then he likely can translate that idea into a reachable and achievable outcome. His creativity is focused on how to make the vision (E) a reality (P). He is a no-nonsense person, ideas without results annoy him, and results that are not born out of big ideas are a waste of time.

Input	Throughput	Output
(P) role	Satisfy client needs	Effectiveness in the short run
(A) role	Systematize	Efficiency in the short run
(E) role	Proact	Effectiveness in the long run

Jeff Bezos

"We started Amazon in my house. I have tons of stories from the early days, where we made so many mistakes, and we learned a lot. I can put everything I know in a short list:

"First: You need to obsess over customers. We have been doing this from the very beginning. When given the choice of obsessing over competitors or obsessing over customers, we always obsessed over customers; we pay attention to what our competitors do but it's not where we put our energy, it's not where we get our motivation from. We like to start with customers and work backwards. That is the key, and it covers for a lot of other mistakes, a lot of errors. (Big (P) here)

"Second: Invent. When we have a problem, we never accept either/or thinking. We try to figure out a solution that gets both things and that often requires invention. You can invent your way out of any box if you believe that you can (E). And what we talk about is inventing on behalf of customers. It's not a customer's job to invent on up for themselves; you need to listen to customers. It's critical. If you don't listen to customers, you will go astray. But they won't tell you everything, so you need to invent on their behalf. (PE)

"Third: Think long term. This is really critical. Any company that wants to focus on customers and put customers first, any company that wants to invent on behalf of customers, has to be willing to think long term, and it's actually much rarer than you might think. I find that most of the initiatives we undertake take five to seven years before they pay any dividends for the company. They may start paying dividends for customers right away, but often take a long time to pan out for shareholders. The company needs to have the ability to think in five-to-seven-year time frames. It's a huge competitive advantage to be able to think long term, and you get to serve customers much better. (E)

"Fourth: A willingness to be misunderstood. Many of the inventions that we undertake may be disruptive. They may not be understood in the early beginnings, and it's always been very important for us to think long term so that we can tolerate being misunderstood. We've been called 'Amazon dot toast,' 'Amazon dot con,' and many other different things. If we think we're right, then we continue. If we think we're wrong, if we're criticized about something, and we think we're wrong, we change it, we fix it."[1]

The Arsonist (--E-)

What happens if the (E)ntrepreneuring role is performed exclusively, and the other three roles are not? This manager's efforts would consist entirely of innovating, just charging at any target that appears on his organizational horizon.

---

1. Jeff Bezos, "Video from Jeff Bezos about Amazon and Zappos," YouTube video, 8:09, July 22, 2009, https://www.youtube.com/watch?v=-hxX_Q5CnaA.

I call him the Arsonist because he enjoys creating crises — like an arsonist who starts a fire, then sits back to watch the ambulances and fire trucks arrive with sirens blaring. As people jump out of windows, he is delighted, thinking, "I did it all."

The more commotion, the more *appearance* of productivity, the happier he is.

If you have a problem and need help from your manager, a Lone Ranger will tell you to put it on his desk. "I will take care of it," he will say.

A Bureaucrat will interrogate you: "Who did this? When? Why? With whom?"

An Arsonist will give you a solution, but his solution might create more problems for you than the problem you had to start with.

Following is a description of the Arsonist, from my book *Leading the Leaders.*[2]

Arsonists act out of emotion and nervous energy, and very often out of negative energy. They have a huge need to build something new, which often means destroying what's already in place. To "own" their idea, they feel they must start from scratch or change what is there even if it is more than adequate already.

But this can be expensive. If an (E) brings you a new idea, ask yourself if it is better or just different. For an (E), different is better, but this is often far from true.

In my experiences, I have learned to beware of new marketing managers. They tend to automatically criticize whatever their predecessor did and recommend something new, which often is just different but

2. Ichak Adizes, *Leading the Leaders: How to Enrich Your Style of Management and Handle People Whose Style Is Different from Yours* (Santa Barbara, CA: Adizes Institute Publications, 2004).

not better — or if it is better, it is just marginally so and not worth changing.

The Arsonist is only concerned with *why not*. Change. Ideas. *What* we do is not as important. *How* we do it is not important, either.

When does the Arsonist come to work? Who knows? When does he leave work? Who knows? When do his subordinates come to work? Before him, by the time he arrives they'd better be there. When do they leave work? Right after him. I've seen vice presidents working for this type of mismanager: it's seven, eight, nine o'clock at night; there's nothing to do, but they can't leave because if they leave what might happen? The boss might call a meeting: "Drop everything you're doing. Everybody to the meeting room, right now. I have an idea I want to share."

He might call on Christmas Eve and take you away from your family celebration. He has an idea that cannot wait. He will ask you to join him on a trip somewhere, even though it interrupts your holidays, or your anniversary, or a birthday.

Oh, and he will call you any time of the day or night and you'd better drop whatever you are doing and take the call.

In meetings if there is an agenda, he violates it anyway, moving from subject to subject at will. Nevertheless, he expects everyone to be prepared for the meeting. And who will do all the talking in these meetings? He will. Meanwhile, what will everyone else do? Nothing.

Picture a army. Out of the trenches emerges the captain — in a beautiful blue uniform with red sashes, all the decorations, golden epaulets, hats, and feathers. He looks dashing. He pulls out his sword and shouts: *"Advance!"*

The soldiers clap their hands in approval. But nobody gets out of the trenches.

Why? The Arsonist captain doesn't say, "Attack in *this* direction!" He says, "Attack in *this* direction, *that* direction, that *other* direction, and that *fourth* direction." All simultaneously. Working for an Arsonist feels like running in circles and getting nowhere or running full speed in neutral.

And who usually gets out of the trenches and attacks? Only the people who are new to the organization. Those with some experience know there is no use in getting out of the trenches and attacking. Very soon, the (--E-)-type captain will change direction or decide on a new strategy.

So, what can the soldiers do? They stay in the trenches and shout "*Bravo!*" And when they're asked, "Are you going to attack or not?" their typical answer is, "We're working on it."

Here is another analogy: picture an organization as an axle. There is a big wheel at one end and a small wheel at the other end. When the big wheel makes one revolution, the small wheel must turn many times. If the big wheel is an Arsonist, he will frequently change direction while the smaller wheel is are still in motion. Eventually the gears of the smaller wheels are stripped, and the axle breaks down. The big wheel is left to spin alone.

But the (--E-) does not realize that he himself is responsible for the breakdown. Instead, he thinks, "Somebody must be undermining my efforts." He becomes paranoid and looks for someone to blame.

The Arsonist is usually very likable (despite driving people crazy) because he is stimulating, enterprising, and full of energy. Working for him can be exciting, until you figure out that no matter what you do the Arsonist will find fault with it. His priorities will continually change, and before you've completed one project, he will want to know why you haven't made any progress on a new one.

The Arsonist likes to witness the furor that his initiatives cause. Under such managers, projects are always being completed under pressure. The staff is forced to work overtime, and crucial details remain in a state of flux right up to the last minute.

Details are the Arsonist's Achilles' heel and he tends to ignore them; he works with a big brush on a wide canvas, as if he were looking down from 40,000 feet. For an (--E-), a million is somewhere between 700,000 and 1.5 million (and remember for an (-A--), 999,999 and one million are not the same. (So, you can see why (E)-style people and (A)-style people don't communicate well.)

Picture the (--E-) as an eagle, flying thousands of feet over the mountains and seeing the big picture but not the small details. From up there, everything looks simple. With a movement of its wings, the eagle can fly from one cliffside to another. The eagle cannot comprehend that down on the ground, cover the same amount of distance, human beings must go up and down mountains and canyons. He suffers from what I call the "coefficient of error" — the bigger the (E) type, the bigger the error. If an (E) with a coefficient of error of six, says it will take a week to do something, it might take six weeks.

Because they create on the run, Arsonists often contradict themselves. The mouth is talking, the mind is working, but there isn't necessarily a connection. An (--E-) often says, "It's too late to disagree with me. I've already changed my mind." They start with one angle and then change to another and then switch to a third, and eventually you can't follow what they are saying.

Yet not being understood upsets and offends Arsonists, and they can react with unbelievable hostility when their argument is challenged or even when inconsistencies are pointed out.

An Arsonist habitually works on the *"Why don't we?"* principle: "Why don't we do this?" "Why don't we do that?" But what is a mere question for an (--E-) is assumed to be a decision by his subordinates, especially those with the (P) style. People with a (P) style, who think and understand the world in literal terms, believe they have just heard the boss make a decision. They begin to implement it and get penalized for acting without authorization. As a result, they become cautious. The next time the (--E-) thinks out loud, his subordinates don't act, thinking that this, too, is just an idea but this time the Arsonist is upset: this time it was a decision, and the staff *didn't* implement his instructions. Subordinates feel they can never satisfy him, no matter what they do or don't do.

Of the four PAEI extremes, the (--E-) is the worst listener. Why? Because he's full of ideas and with ease generates new ones. Anything you say might trigger a chain of thought in him, he will be so busy listening to himself that he will not hear anything else you are saying.

In conversation, the Arsonist is emotional and expressive. He uses words like "never," "always," "impossible." He exaggerates to push his ideas through. That might make people mistrust him and call him a liar, a manipulator, one who has no real data to support his claims, a shallow leader.

In a company managed by an Arsonist, Monday mornings, coming back from a vacation, or coming back from a long flight are a dangerous time. The Arsonist has had time to think, and guess what? There will be new directions, new priorities, new goals, new objectives.

One (E)-type executive bought a ranch an hour's drive from the office. Hating long drives, he started coming into the office less frequently (this was before the Internet). Productivity quadrupled.

Not much happens in a company run by an Arsonist because he doesn't like to finalize anything. Even in mid-change he might shuffle things again and send everyone in yet another "better" direction. Every idea leads to another idea. By adding an idea, he's diminishing the value of other ideas because there's a limit to how much one person or one company can handle.

Nor does he measure the cost of his plans against their value. The opposite of the Bureaucrat, the (--E-) "knows the value of everything, but the cost of nothing." An (--E-) is always talking about the brilliant innovations he's going to make, but how much will they cost? "Those are just details," he shrugs. That is why an Arsonist can build a big company and lose it overnight.

Arsonists do not play well with other peoples' ideas. If you give an (--E-) an idea, he might say, "No, I don't agree with you." But the next week he will give you back the same idea, rephrased, as if he'd thought of it himself. Arsonists are often seen as narcissistic, self-centered troublemakers. They always act like they know best. Therefore, they are constantly giving advice and can hardly stand to take it; and they need a tremendous amount of approval and applause.

It takes a very strong person to work with an Arsonist, and yet the (--E-) types tend to surround themselves with weak people because they have to win every argument, and weak subordinates will never challenge them.

If the Lone Ranger's subordinates are gofers and the Bureaucrat's are yes-yes men, then the typical subordinates of the Arsonist are *claques*. *Claques*, which is a French word (in Mexico they are called *palleros*), are the hired audience in an opera house who are paid to start clapping when a singer ends an aria. They do so to encourage the rest of the audience to clap as well.

Claques are paid to agree with the Arsonist's ideas, at least in public. The result is that the Arsonist invariably receives tumultuous applause, but it isn't real.

The Arsonist's subordinates learn not to reject his plans outright because he will interpret a rejection of his ideas as a rejection of himself. Thus, the subordinates are forced to accept tasks that they already know are impractical. They come up with creative excuses instead, trying to appear cooperative without actually cooperating.

The Arsonist's typical complaint about his staff is, "Nobody understands me." "No one follows my priorities." He feels he's surrounded by idiots. The following unattributed aphorism was probably first said by an Arsonist: "It is difficult to soar like an eagle when you are surrounded by turkeys."

Sometimes the Arsonist will go through the successive stages of firing someone and then bring in someone new. For a little while, he will think this new person is a genius. He'll put him on a pedestal ("Look at him! Look how good he is!"). The new guy will walk on water, for a while. Six months later, the Arsonist will become convinced that this man does not understand the tasks well either, will find him disappointing, but most probably he will not fire him. (--E-) types dislike firing people personally. Since the (--E-) type seeks applause, and firing might not solicit this reaction, they don't usually fire anyone personally. They prefer to get a hatchet man to do the firing or, more often, they'll make their target's life so miserable — demeaning them, putting them down, criticizing them in public, or humiliating them — that the person will eventually resign.

For the Arsonist, planning does not mean committing the organization to a course of action. Planning means making long lists of ephemeral goals. Whereas the Lone Ranger rarely takes the time to plan at all, and the Bureaucrat derives next year's budget by adding some percentage to last year's results, the Arsonist may not even have a budget. If he does, it is usually unrealistic.

The Arsonist is so preoccupied with opportunities that he sees few if any threats. He can endanger an organization by recklessly trying to exploit too many opportunities at once and spreading himself and his organization too thin.

One might expect to find creativity throughout an organization managed by an Arsonist. Isn't the Arsonist extremely creative? But the opposite is usually true. The Arsonist will set a course, but change direction multiple times, causing confusion within the organization. Since he monopolizes who can make changes, no one else dares to be creative. The end result is that his creativity runs on empty or as one executive described it: "He runs full speed in neutral." Lots of noise but no action. Or as it says in the Hebrew Bible: Lots of clouds and wind but no rain.

Since details bore him, the Arsonist's attitude and preferences are to decentralize, but it's equally important for him to maintain control of the decision-making process. The result is a catch-22 for his subordinates. They are *expected* to decide, as long as their decisions coincide with the decision *he* would have made. But they don't know what he would have decided because he keeps changing his mind. For his subordinates, that decision is a moving target, being expected to know what to do without knowing what the boss would have preferred. It produces organizational paralysis or a culture of finger pointing and accusations.

Like the Bureaucrat (who is so focused on efficiency that he over controls and creates an inefficient bureaucracy) and the Lone Ranger (who wants so much to be effective that he does it all by himself, thus creating an ineffective organization), the Arsonist is so exclusively focused on causing change that he creates paralysis.

When an (--E-) type leaves an organization, it is usually in shambles and its people are exhausted. They're desperate for peace and quiet, for stability. As a result, they usually ask for, and eventually get stuck with, a Bureaucrat (-A--) or a SuperFollower (---I).

CHAPTER 7

(I)-Type Managers and Leaders

THE (I) ROLE IN LEADERSHIP

(I)ntegrating is a very creative process since it must bring together diffused and unstructured information about diversified people with diverse styles and interests. These people must jointly agree to a decision they will support. It is even less programmable than (E)ntrepreneuring because (E)ntrepreneuring does not necessarily deal with people.

In the case of (I)ntegrating entrepreneurs, one has the additional burden of forging their individual creativities into a cohesive unity — to develop group risk-taking out of individual risk-taking — to fuse an *individual* sense of responsibility into a *group* sense of responsibility.

A functional Integrator is one that excels in (I) but meets at least the threshold of the other roles; clarifies issues by finding the common threads of deep — not just superficial — agreement; and assimilates contrasting values, assumptions, and expectations.

A successful Integrator also must make herself dispensable. Her subordinates should be trained to be capable of replacing her. Ideally, in a cohesive group almost any member should be able to lead. To take a military example, if any soldier in a squad can take the squad leader's place and be accepted when the leader is killed, this demonstrates that the leader was a good Integrator. If the squad scatters when the leader is killed, then the (I)ntegrating of the unit was insufficient, although the leader may have been a competent commander in other respects.

The Integrator is sensitive to others (empathetic) and capable of deductive thinking (able to infer what people really want to say from what they *do* say). A good (I) has her ego under control, which enables her to hear and respond to other people's expectations, problems, and needs rather than her own.

The late Juscelino Kubitschek, former president of Brazil, when asked whether he was for or against a certain political program, replied: "I am neither for nor against it: I am above it."[1]

The (I) role is unique in that it not only provides for future organizational continuity, but also enables an organization to function smoothly in the present. This role is essential for success, both in the short *and* long run. (I) is the one role that *must* be present for leadership to occur.

---

1. In some Western democracies, including the U.S., the president is the leader of a political party, as well as head of the executive branch. The executive branch performs the (P) function of government. Leading a political party and being in a (P) role, the president cannot perform the (I) function. The constitution provides the (I) role, formalized within its founding document and its amendments. A monarchy (an entity that is above politics) personalizes the (I) role and represents the country's unity. In some countries, religion provides the (I) role. In others, like Turkey, the military provides the role.

Input	Throughput	Output
(P) role	Satisfy client needs	Effectiveness in the short run
(A) role	Systematize	Efficiency in the short run
(E) role	Proact	Effectiveness in the long run
(I) role	Integrate	Efficiency in the long run

Managers can be strong in two or even three roles — (PAei), (PaEi), (pAEi), (PAEi) — but unless one of them is (I)ntegrating, they will not become leaders. For leadership to occur, the (I) role must enhance whatever other roles a leader excels at performing.

There are two types of (I)ntegrating: passive and active — and three directions: upward, lateral, and downward.

Upward (I)ntegrating is the ability to draw together people who are higher in status, authority, rank, and so on. Lateral (I)ntegrating is the ability to successfully relate with peers into a cohesive group. Downward (I)ntegrating establishes cohesion among subordinates.

A very effective lateral Integrator may function poorly as a downward Integrator, tending to be arrogant with subordinates. In fact, it is unusual for a person to be an excellent Integrator in all directions.

A passive Integrator will integrate herself into a group of people. An active Integrator can integrate a group of people to themselves. Because in leadership, (I)ntegrating must be active, we will concern ourselves here only with active (I)ntegrating.

Why must (I)ntegrating be active? Because you cannot do it only once. (I)ntegrating is a process, not an event. You cannot just bring flowers once to your spouse, and that's it. Think of (I)ntegrating not as a noun, but as an active *verb*.

Once with a client of mine, as we were scheduling our next series of meetings, I suggested a certain upcoming date. He replied, "Oh no, sorry, I cannot do it on that day. I will be on my honeymoon." I was surprised. Just the night before I had joined him and his wife for dinner. How had he managed to get divorced overnight? We were in California, but still it was a bit too fast. He noticed my asking face and said, "Dr. Adizes, in my family, we have a rule. Every year, on the anniversary of our marriage, we have a honeymoon because one honeymoon is not enough for a lifetime of marriage." You must continuously feed *integration* and not take it for granted. The reason why it should be a continuous process is because change is continuous, too. And with change comes, by default, disintegration: things fall apart.

To be a leader it is essential to be an active and downward Integrator because the leader must work through others to achieve organizational goals. Where leadership has succeeded in (I)ntegrating the individual members of an organization into a group, we may expect greater identification with the organization, more job satisfaction, and better performance. The importance of interpersonal relationships for the success of organizations has been repeatedly demonstrated in the literature.[2]

The Superfollower (---I)

How would a manager function if he was deficient in the areas of (P)roducing, (A)dministrating, and (E)ntrepreneuring and was only capable of (I)ntegrating?

What is he mostly concerned about? He's interested in *who*. He doesn't care *what* we agree about, nor *how* we agree about it, nor *why* we agree. The important thing is, "Do we agree?" He's not a leader. He is a SuperFollower. He's the one who asks, "Where would you like to go? Let me lead you there."

He wants everything to run smoothly and accommodates endlessly. He tries to find out what plan will be acceptable to the largest number of

2. Chris Argyris, *Overcoming Organizational Defenses: Facilitating Organizational Learning* (Boston: Allyn and Bacon, 1990 Bernard M. Bass, *The Bass Handbook of Leadership* (New York: Free Press, 2008).

powerful people. He is like a fish monitoring the undercurrent, always seeking the right tide to join.

What is the difference between a politician and a statesman? The statesman worries about the next generation, while the politician worries about the next election. The SuperFollower is not concerned about the future as much as he worries about present support for his political standing. "Do we agree?" is his motto. He might be running a very happy disaster. He negotiates an appearance of agreement rather than resolving the deep-seated issues that cause conflict.

The SuperFollower welcomes any training as long as it improves his ability to understand human nature or contributes to the appearance of unity. He rejects any solution that creates heat, even if it's necessary for the company's success. If the SuperFollower has free time, he spends it socializing, listening to complaints or agreements, and then amplifying and accentuating them by offering his support.

It's difficult to get a SuperFollower to commit to a point of view. In Mexico, they call this type of manager "the soapy fish," because you just can't nail down his argument. He always wiggles out of your hands and slips away. His typical complaint is, "You really didn't understand what I really wanted to say." You can't corner him. That's how he remains in power for a long time. He figures out which side is winning and adapts himself to that side, because his approach is noncommittal. He might say something like, "I have an idea, but I'm not so sure I agree with it," or "I suggest we declare dividends, but I don't feel too strongly about it." He launches trial balloons to see where everyone else stands before he makes any commitment. He wants to see which way the wind is blowing. This makes him a perfect weathervane. If you want to know which changes will most likely be accepted and which will not, watch him.

The SuperFollower tends to avoid making decisions as long as he can. He has no ideas of his own that he would like to implement. He is indifferent to any particular system as long as agreement is achieved or is seen to be achieved. Since he lacks strong convictions, his mind can be changed quickly and easily. He sways along with popular opinion.

At meetings, the SuperFollower is the one who is listening very attentively. Who is saying what? What does the speaker really mean? What is not being said? Where does the power lie? Which way is the decision likely to go?

If the SuperFollower is chairing a meeting and a consensus cannot be achieved, he will probably postpone the decision by establishing a subcommittee to study the problem further. In reality, he is waiting for a political consensus to emerge. Sometimes the consensus he's waiting for will not surface until the situation has become a crisis and the organization's survival is at risk.

The SuperFollower hires people like himself, who are politically intuitive. They have a good nose for how the political power base is moving. They are the first to identify it and to jump on the bandwagon. What do they spend their time on? "What's going on?" "Who said what?" "What does it mean?" "Where is the power base?" I call them informers or oilers. Their main job is to keep the boss up-to-date. It is their duty to feed the boss the latest office "news." No gossip is too insignificant to relate.

The SuperFollower's subordinates know that loyalty to him is paramount if they want to be promoted. In his presence, the (---I) type's subordinates appear peaceful and accepting, remembering that their boss prefers people whom other people like. This often requires them to keep their true feelings hidden from him, which can easily lead to their feeling manipulated and emotionally exploited.

The SuperFollower has no particular goal. Rather, the goal is whatever is most desired at a particular time by a consensus of his coworkers. The SuperFollower doesn't tell you what he thinks; he asks what you think. This is, of course, a very limited commitment toward corporate goals, and as a result short-range interest groups and cliques flourish under the SuperFollower.

When a SuperFollower leaves an organization, the superficial (I)ntegrating he established rapidly deteriorates. At that point a Producer is called in to inject some energy and clarity, and to clean up the confusion that the SuperFollower's political maneuvering has created over the years. This change of styles is stressful because people must change their behavior and learn to follow different organizational cues to be successful.

CHAPTER 8

The Deadwood (----)

So far, we have covered different types of managers, mismanagers, leaders, and misleaders. We have talked about the extreme archetypes, i.e., those people who are missing three out of the four PAEI roles.

In times of accelerated, high-rate change, which creates high levels of uncertainty and risk, some people avoid performing any of the PAEI roles. They become Deadwood, with a PAEI code of (----).

They neither focus on producing results, nor enforce systems, nor come with great new ideas, nor focus on how to deal with people. The goal of a Deadwood is to survive. Deadwoods know that any change can threaten their position. To maximize their chances for survival, they resist nothing because this may expose them. Rather, they agree to everything but act on nothing. They don't rock the boat and, they are agreeable, friendly, and nonthreatening. They are liked but not respected. So, people end up enduring them and don't want to hurt them. In the meantime, it's the organization that suffers.

They apathetically wait to be told what to do. They may work hard, like the Lone Rangers, but no results are produced. They don't get involved with power intrigues like the SuperFollowers, nor do they stir up fireworks like the Arsonists. If they have any good ideas, they keep them to themselves. Unlike the Bureaucrats, Deadwoods care about following the rules insofar as doing so will help them survive until retirement.

Deadwoods very likely started out as one of the other four types of mismanagers, and they still evince their former dominant personality traits. One can still see in them traces of the enthusiastic Arsonists or the meticulous Bureaucrats. But by the time they have become a Deadwood, their number one characteristic is a "low managerial metabolism."

According to their basic orientation, all PAEI styles have a common complaint. Whether it's that there is not enough time, the (P) style; or that things are not being done in the proper way, the (A) style; or that the most urgent priorities are not being pursued, the (E) style; or that the people factor is being left out of the equation, the (I) style — there is always a recognizable direction to their complaints. That's not the case with Deadwoods, who avoid threats to their own existence by never complaining about anything (a complaint could end up requiring them to take responsibility for something they may not be able to handle, so better to shut up and keep going through the motions.)

Another strategy for survival, whenever change is happening, Deadwoods don't resist it. They show approval to any idea suggested in their surroundings and simply go with the flow, agreeing with almost anything and everything (in order not to make waves), while taking no action whatsoever to make things happen.

Competent subordinates may threaten the Deadwood's very existence and end up grabbing their jobs and replacing them. So, to feel safe, they tend to hire other Deadwoods. In this regard, Deadwoods are like cancer: they spread throughout an organization because as they stop changing and learning, those reporting to them stop learning and changing and become Deadwoods themselves.

Causes for Deadwood and How to Treat the Phenomena

Look at the following styles:

- (P---)
- (-A--)
- (--E-)
- (---I)

Do you realize they are three quarters Deadwood, whose code is (----)?

So, all that is needed for a Lone ranger to become a Deadwood is to lose his ability to *perform*. How does that happen?

The Lone Ranger (P---) is not a person with twenty years of experience, but rather, a person with one year of experience that he has repeated twenty times. Over time he becomes obsolete. He might still have the drive to achieve, but he does not know what he is doing.

How does the (-A--) type (the Bureaucrat) become Deadwood? Change the systems. Digitalize the company. They have no (E) thus they do not change easily. They, too, become obsolete.

And how does the Arsonist (--E-) type become Deadwood? She starts too many fires and at a certain point loses control of them. She is ignored and running in circles. As we said before, an organization is like a big axle. When "the big wheel" turns back and forth without warning, and without paying attention to how it impacts the other smaller wheels attached to the axle, the axle breaks down. The "big wheel" keeps turning but on empty. It is full speed ahead in neutral. From a functional point of view, this is a Deadwood although it does not behave like one, at least not right away.

And the (---I)-type becomes a Deadwood when there is a crisis that needs to be handled right away, and she stalls searching for consensus. There is a palace revolution, she is dethroned so that the problem can be solved.

The common denominator is *change*. The more change, the more Deadwood.

Usually, people expect bureaucracies to have Deadwood but their presence only becomes obvious when the bureaucracy is experiencing change. The company most prone to Deadwood is the company that is experiencing the most change, such as a go-go company, which may be on a fast-changing trajectory. It outruns the capabilities of its people.

And in a country experiencing major changes like America, with the high-tech revolution taking place, you find homelessness. Or in previous generations, during industrialization, you find the *favelas* (poor parts of the city in Brazil) or the Soweto township in South Africa.

Deadwood in organizations is like cancer in the human body. You do not know you have it, no pain, all is fine while it spreads. But not all cancer is malignant. Some are Possums. They are just acting dead.

"Possum," not Deadwood

Due to frenetic rates of change and uncertainty, some people end up in the Deadwood condition because — having been impacted by the levels of change and feeling threatened by it — they have simply decided to take a back seat and wait to see what will happen. They simply don't know what's going on, what is right, and what is wrong. Their minds still work, but they don't dare to stick their necks out. So, they retreat into their cocoon and just yield to any demands.

Much like the Australian possum (an animal who pretends to be dead when threatened), Deadwoods behave as if dead, but they may not be dead at all. What to do? The organization needs to create a safe environment in which they can perform. These individuals could still be great and knowledgeable assets to the company.

Before you fire them, make sure that they are not just playing possum. After that, if they are still unable to perform, they may have reached managerial death. No more oomph. No more motivation. Like those employees who just manage to show up, do the bare minimum, offer no ideas, and are the first ones out the door, Deadwoods may have un-officially retired from the job.

CHAPTER 9

The Ideal Executive

All the above styles are not perfect. None fulfill *all* four roles, but for an excellent company all four PAEI roles need to be performed with excellence. This is the ideal leader, the ideal executive. That is the description of the ideal executive the literature describes, or the ethos business schools try to develop.

From classic textbooks on leadership — the old paradigm — to today's best-selling leadership books, to the most-viewed talks on how to lead, there is a consensus: the ideal leader is depicted as a knowledgeable and achievement-oriented Producer; a detail-oriented, systematic, efficiency minded, and organized Administrator; a charismatic, risk-taking, and change-oriented Entrepreneur; and an Integrator who brings people together while being sensitive to their needs. In other words, a PAEI leader.

If you look at the most viewed TED talks on the subject of leadership (from Simon Sinek, Brené Brown, Laura Sicola, Simon Lancaster, Luvvie Ajayi Jones, Patrick Lencioni, and others), which together account for over 100-million views, you'll notice how they tend to equate "leadership" with a collage of relational and emotional abilities — the best traits they can find in different people — and present the collage as if it were a single individual leader.

In *The Leadership Shadow*,[1] Professor Erik de Haan points to this stereotyped image of a leader as having a sort of superhuman nature (my PAEI-role interpretations are in brackets):

To be a high performer in today's world of work, it is necessary for you to be engaged and collaborative [(I)], as well as tough and uncompromising [(P)]. You have to protect the individual as well as look after the whole [(I)]. You must work at the core [(P)] whilst being present at the periphery [(E)]. You are responsible for the detail [(A)] yet are expected to stay out of the detail to be able to imagine the future [(E)]. In a word, you have to be incredibly present to a great many people. You have to be erudite and action-oriented [(P)]; reflective and initiating [(E)]; flexible and warm in relationships [(I)] and decisive in your stance [(P)]. This means you have to embrace quite a few paradoxes and transcend as many contradictions as possible.

The problem is, where do you find such a unicorn?

"Who is wise? He that learns from everyone. Who is powerful? He that governs his passions. Who is rich? He that is content. Who is that? Nobody." — Benjamin Franklin

What else is wrong with the leadership theory in the old paradigm?

It is unidirectional. A Google search found synonyms for "leading" including: manage, head, command, govern, call the shots, go out in front, preside over, conduce, move, prevail, supervise, bring on, run things, prompt, contribute, control, introduce, induce, produce, outdo, be ahead, and dominate.

Is there a common denominator shared by all these words? Yes, they are all a one-way process.

1. Erik de Haan and Anthony Kasozi, *The Leadership Shadow: How to Recognize and Avoid Derailment, Hubris and Overdrive* (London: Kogan Page, 2014);

The implication of these words is that leaders tell those being led what to do. No ifs, ands, or buts. If you were to look at motivation in this context, you could assume that the motivator has already decided what should be done, and you could conclude that motivation is about getting someone else to do it willingly.

> *"Leadership is the art of getting someone else to do something you want done because he wants to do it."* — Dwight D. Eisenhower

There was a cartoon in *The New Yorker* some time ago that illustrated this point nicely. A mother who is a psychologist is trying to convince her son to take out the trash. Wearily, the boy says, "Okay, Okay! I'll take out the trash, but *pleeeease*, Mom, *don't* try to motivate me." Even a child perceives motivation as a kind of manipulation.

A leader is the head of the department, and the subordinate (note the literal meaning: sub-ordinary) is at best the right-hand person. And what does the right hand do? Unless you're left-handed, the right hand does exactly what the head tells it to do.

This does not fly in the modern world we live in — with millennials and people who grew up in abundance and not in scarcity, scared to lose a job.

The present paradigm is elitist. In Hebrew, the word for subordinate is *kafuf*, which literally means "bent at the hips," like someone who bows before you out of respect or fear. Leaders, on the other hand, have superior vision. That is the source of the word "supervision."[2] Military insignias illustrate this principle: A first lieutenant's badge has one branch to denote his rank, a lieutenant's has two branches, a captain's has three. As we ascend in the military hierarchy, we are climbing the tree. A major has a leaf, signifying the top of the tree. And a general, with the highest supervisory authority of all — way above the treetops — has a star.

2. Matthew Stewart, *The Management Myth: Debunking Modern Business Philosophy* (New York: W. W. Norton & Company, 2009).

"Leadership" refers to a certain rank in an organization and implies an individual's role or authority. It delineates the role of those who *make* decisions.

The reality is that there is a difference between making and taking a decision. (Interesting that the French and the Spanish say, "taking a decision" while in English it is "making a decision.") To me, *making* a decision is a process of "cooking" the decision, the process at arriving at a final decision. It is *taken* when it is finalized.

Leaders and managers have the authority to *take* a decision. Granted. But with the complexity of the decisions that the modern world requires, unless it is a mom-and-pop store, the time when they could make and take a decision all by themselves is a long time gone.

It is individualistic. Try the following exercise. Call all of your top leadership into a room. Ask each one of them to write down the company's top five problems. The rules are, first, no names should be mentioned, and second, don't use the word "because" — no explanations for the problem are necessary.

Just ask them to note on a piece of paper (which they do not have to show anyone), the top five most critical and significant problems, undesired results, or processes of the company.

Also, only list problems that are *controllable* by the people in the room. It is not acceptable to define a problem as something "they" are not doing. Focus on what "we" are not doing. In other words, instead of writing, "Competition is increasing," write, "We are not meeting competition head on."

Now ask the group: How many of these problems did the company have last year? (The answer is usually close to 100 percent.)

How about two years ago?

Most of them.

How about three years ago?

Again, most of them!

Now, if this is true, then how many of these same problems are you likely to have three years from now?

Most of them, right? Why is that?

Now invite everyone to look at their list of problems again. How many of them can any individual in the room solve *alone?*

None! Right? If they could, they would have already done so.

Now ask them how many of these problems would disappear if you gave them a magic pill that would permit them, as a team, to agree on a solution?

All of them, right? If they followed your instructions correctly and only wrote down problems that are controllable by the people in the room, then it is true by definition that a solution is possible if only the people in the room would work as a team.

So, what is the problem?

The problem is that we usually have one leader chasing ten problems all at once, rather than ten leaders chasing one problem at a time.

The business world, in other words, is trapped by the misguided principles of individualistic leadership, and it projects these principles onto a single individual who is then expected to excel at planning and organizing and motivating and communicating and building a team.

In reality, such a leader does not exist, because the roles are incompatible at a point in time.

The leadership process is far too complicated for one person to perform.

Traditional leadership theory personalizes the entire process of decision-making and implementation as if practiced by a single entity.

This error leads to a misperception that ultimately hampers our efforts to lead successfully. It may also bring about a witch hunt. Meanwhile, the organization's problems do not get resolved.

The words "leader" or "leadership" should be thought of not as a *person* ("Who is the leader?") but as a *process* (the practice of leadership), which by its very nature can encompass people who may not officially be identified as leaders by rank or title. Anyone who is involved in making a decision and its implementation should be viewed as being involved in leading the company.

5. It is based on industrial experience. Classic leadership textbooks teach that leaders plan, decide, organize, control, and motivate an organization. However, there are organizations in which leadership is *not supposed* to perform some of those functions. Some years ago, I studied the leadership styles of several performing-arts organizations — opera houses, dance companies, theaters, orchestras — and I learned that artists cannot be led in the same way as, let's say, one might lead industrial workers. Both administrative directors and artistic directors are needed to lead these types of organizations. The same is true for universities and hospitals — all professional organizations — and with high-tech companies it is no less applicable. In fact, the professional and the business director must practically co-lead. Decisions cannot be made by either of them alone. "We are the two wings of the Austro-Hungarian eagle," the administrative director of the New York City Opera told me, when describing his relationship with the artistic director. "Without both of us, this opera will not fly."[3]

In high-tech companies, an engineer who knows the technology or may even have significantly contributed to inventing it is indispensable to leading the company. But his financial know-how and business

---

3. Ichak Adizes, *Essays on the Management of Performing Arts* (Santa Barbara, CA: Adizes Institute Publications, forthcoming). This manuscript is available by request from the Adizes Institute.

acumen are usually limited. For successful leadership, he needs someone to make the business decisions with him.

Why do we find ourselves using leadership theory that is mainly based on industrial experience? Because it was developed during the twentieth century almost exclusively on industrial experiences. Fayol was a mining engineer. Urwick was a military officer. Koontz took his insights from the airline industry. Taylor was an industrial engineer. Drucker's early experiences, from which he derived his ideas, were in the automotive and publishing industries. They brought experience from the for-profit and industrial spheres to their books.

In a similar fashion, countries like the United States, Israel, and Argentina have seen in recent years the surge to power of presidents who come from either business or military backgrounds — under the assumption that these backgrounds will translate directly into leadership from one field to another. But managing a company is not the same as heading up a brigade. And managing a business, however large it may be, is not the same as leading a country.

In recent years, management theory has all but disappeared from the curricula of schools. It has been replaced with heavy behavioral-science, which is not based on industrial experience but on applied psychological research. While it adds value it is insufficient to meet the demands required to lead a company successfully in today's frenetically paced world. It does not have enough practical, experience based theoretical frameworks.

6. It is culturally bound. In certain countries that are used to an autocratic tradition, such as Russia, I have noticed that when the manager or leader speaks, everybody listens. And it does not necessarily need to be the CEO or the president of the company speaking; it could be the head of a department. That person dominates the meeting, everybody listens, and no one dares to challenge the speaker because Russia doesn't come, historically, from a democratic tradition.

The disallowing of participation in autocratic Russian culture means that a lot of first-class brains are underutilized. Such is the problem of cultural impact. This contrasts with Israeli culture. Coming from the Talmudic tradition, Israelis seem to go to the other extreme and challenge anything and everything. Kim Scott, in *Radical Candor*,[4] brings the following anecdote from an Israeli company:

"I'll never forget overhearing Noam Bardin, Deltathree's COO, yelling at an engineer, 'That design could be fifteen times more efficient. You know you could have built it better. Now we're going to have to rip what you did out and start over. We've lost a month, and for what? What were you thinking?'

I was a little shocked by this — I don't think I had ever heard such a direct challenge in the workplace. But the engineer seemed to think this challenge was perfectly acceptable."

Culture is also present in the language used to speak about management and leadership. In languages such as Swedish, French, Serbian, and Croatian, the word "manage" does not even have a literal translation. In those languages, words like "direct," "lead," or "administer" are often used instead. When people in those countries want to say "manage" the way we mean it in the United States, they usually use the English word.

In Spanish, the word *manejar*, which literally translates as "to manage," means "to handle" and is used only when referring to horses or cars. *Gestionar* is another Spanish word that has the same connotation. When they want to say "manage" in the American sense of the word, they use "direct" or "administer."

I suggest that there is a confusion in the field — stemming from our difficulty in defining the leadership process and what it is supposed to do — that is manifested in our vocabulary, or lack of one.

4. Kim Scott, *Radical Candor: Be a Kick-Ass Boss Without Losing Your Humanity* (New York: St. Martin's Press, 2017).

Management or leadership is not a group of people in the hierarchy of the organization. It is not a rank. It is a PAEI *process* by which organizational goals are continuously identified and reidentified and eventually achieved efficiently in the short and long run. *Whoever* is involved in this process, regardless of *where* they fall on the organizational chart — whether they are an executive, administrator, consultant, leader, manager, or worker — by definition they are involved in the managerial process, in the leading process.

Usually, we look at the managerial role as one of managing *people.* If no one reports to you, you are not management. (Do you see the elitism and the hierarchy here?) I define management as the process of defining and accomplishing tasks, and all who are involved in this process are part of the managerial team even if they have no direct reports. While no one *reports* to them, they still must interrelate with others to accomplish the common task. They will not be giving out orders or demotions, but they must be "selling" their ideas and perspectives on the task. Thus, it is not the reporting relationships that makes one a manager. It is interrelating for a common cause that makes them part of the process *and* the management team.

7. It may be biased by sociopolitical contexts. The managerial/ leadership process as understood in the West is not universally accepted or practiced. In some countries around the world, the managerial process as taught in western textbooks has been prohibited by law. In the former Yugoslavia, for instance, during the communist era of self-management, managers were constitutionally prohibited from making decisions the way they are made that is, *for* the organization. Rather, the manager's role was to make suggestions and work to convince the workers, who had the ultimate authority for determining salaries, production quotas, investments, etc.

The self-management system — which adapted democratic principles as they had been conceived for nations and then applied them to industrial organizations — was called *industrial democracy.* In industrial democracy, the managers belonged to the executive branch. Their role was to recommend and implement decisions that were made by the workers council, which performed the legislative branch of running the company.[5]

In some countries, management was socially discouraged. During the heyday of the Israeli kibbutzim (which emerged out of a socialist/anarchistic school of thought) management was deliberately rotated every two or three years, so that nobody became what is known in the United States as a professional manager: a person whose profession it is to *decide for* other people what they are to do.[6]

Failed Attempts

The field of leadership has continuously created new words to label new processes in the hope of making the process more effective and efficient. What we know today as "leadership" was originally described as "administration."[7] That is why business schools used to be called Graduate Schools of Business *Administration* (some still are), and the degree awarded from such schools is the MBA, Master of Business Administration. The first journal in the field was the *Administrative Science Quarterly*. But since administrators failed to produce the desired results, the word "administrator" is now used mostly as a synonym for "bureaucrat."

A new word then came into use: "management." Educational institutions became graduate schools of *management* instead of *business administration*. But when the desired outcomes were still not achieved, the word "management" came to denote only the middle level of the hierarchy; thus, the need for a new word emerged. The next word used

5. Ichak Adizes and Elizabeth M. Borgese, *Self-Management: New Dimensions to Democracy* (Santa Barbara, CA: Center for the Study of Democratic Institutions and ABC-CLIO, 1975), 30–31.
6. Ibid., chapter six.
7. Notice the confusion in Wikipedia's "Management" entry: management (or managing) is the *administration* of an organization, whether it is a business, a not-for-profit organization, or a government body.

to describe those at the leadership level was "executive"; and with this we began to hear terms such as "executive training," "executive action," and "chief executive officer." But when even this did not completely fit the bill, the word "leadership" evolved to replace "executive," and this is where we are today in 2022.

Although there are plenty of books that will tell you how leadership is different from administration, which is different from executive action, which in itself is different from management,[8] I suggest that this new fad will not last either. In fact, I would not be surprised if in the next few years another new word is coined to define the process, and the word "leadership" will be redefined to mean some piece of the managerial process or hierarchy — as happened with the words "administration" "management" and "executive."

The root problem is that the paradigm has remained the same; it is the same process in a new dress. The entire managerial process is personified in a single individual, whether we call him Administrator, manager, executive, leader, tsar, or sultan. This is the natural manifestation of a culture of individualism.[9]

In a *New York Times* profile about me, I referred to myself as "the corporate exorcist":[10] one who goes from company to company trying to exorcise leadership from believing they can do that which they cannot.

The paradigm of the "lone leader" — all-wise and all-powerful — has never worked. Furthermore, as the rate of change keeps

8. See John P. Kotter, *Force for Change: How Leadership Differs from Management* (New York: Free Press, 1990).
9. Michael J. Kami and Joel E. Ross, *Corporate Management in Crisis: Why the Mighty Fall* (Hoboken, N.J.: Prentice Hall, 1973). Other authors who oppose the one-rule man include Harold J. Leavitt, *Managerial Psychology* (Chicago: University of Chicago Press, 1989), 297–99; and Peter F. Drucker, *The Effective Executive* (New York: Harper Business, 2017).
10. Elizabeth M. Fowler, "Management: The Team Approach at the Top," *The New York Times* (Business section, Sept. 16, 1977, https://www.nytimes.com/1977/09/16/archives/management-the-team-approach-at-the-top.html).

accelerating, the authority structure is continuously disrupted by a new breed of younger leaders that reject the old notions of hierarchy and nonparticipation. At the same time, the level of uncertainty that needs to be dealt with continues to increase, and as businesses become global instead of local, a paradigm shift is now more necessary than ever.

Traditional Management Squashes Potential

The structure of the modern organization is more conducive to eliminating managerial talents than developing them. Instead of fostering well-roundedness, it inhibits growth.

Consider the modern hierarchical system. It capitalizes on the strengths of individuals. A person who is a strong Administrator will be promoted as an (A) style and will climb the corporate ladder as an (A) style. In the short run, an organization may be getting the maximum out of that manager, but in the long run, his lack of opportunity to develop the (P), (E), and (I) roles will make him inflexible and uncooperative when dealing with people whose styles are different from his. That will ultimately harm the company.

Yet another breeding ground for mismanagement lies in the very rigid boundaries that corporations typically maintain between workers and management.

At the bottom ranks of most organizations, the (P) role is expected almost exclusively. Workers are not expected to be Administrators, Entrepreneurs, or Integrators, nor are they given opportunities or experience in those roles. In particular, management regards as a potential threat any attempts at (I)ntegrating from the lowest levels, which often manifest themselves as unionization efforts or informal, unsanctioned leadership.

Just above *production* are first-line managers, who are expected to have plenty of (A). When a *production* worker is promoted to first-line manager, he needs to reduce his (P) role to a (p) and begin performing (A) tasks with some (e) and (i) roles added in. Lacking crucial experience in the new roles, however, the new manager more often than not continues to exclusively operate as a (P).

This is equally true when a *production* manager is promoted to CEO. In any new job, people tend to repeat the style that has worked for them, and since what made him successful was his *performance* (P), the new CEO will probably continue to *produce*, running the company single-handedly and making all the important decisions himself.

Paradoxically, until an employee rises to the vice-presidential level, the (E) and (I) roles are generally discouraged by the company. But once he reaches that level, he is *instantly* expected to be creative and to facilitate staff interactions. The question is: Where will he find the skills and emotional resources to perform these new functions when he has been harnessed, suffocated, and divested of his creative impulses for twenty years or more? Usually, the answer is: He won't. This may explain why so many companies fill their top management positions from the MBA ranks, who have no experience except (E),acquired from learning to write business plans in school.

Mismanagement Breeds Mismanagement

Corporations founded by (P-E-) types grow rapidly (assuming they are successful). During this phase, they usually lack the cohesion that good (A)dministering provides; in fact, efforts to create controls are sometimes met by antagonism from a (P-E-) founder.

If the organization is to continue to grow, however, the (A)dministering function has to be developed.

When the problem becomes serious enough, a (pAei) is usually called in to establish some order. But her chances of surviving for very long with a (P-E-) are slim at best. The (P-E-) tends to change accountants and *administrative* managers more often than is prudent for organizational stability.

The challenge for the organization at this point is to find a way to distance itself from the (P-E-) founder, to reduce his control over the company. If the organization cannot do that, its (pAei) Administrator will be seriously handicapped in her attempt to substitute structure for chaos.

Sometimes the only way to reduce the (P-E-) founder's power is to replace him. But since he is also the source of much of the company's (E)ntrepreneuring energy and creativity, that strategy can be dangerously self-defeating.

There are several possible scenarios for what happens next. If the company is much larger and it keeps growing at the same explosive pace, over time its founder will lose control simply because the job, or jobs, he's been doing by himself will become too overwhelming. Various roles and responsibilities will start to shift, resulting in confusion and a power vacuum. This leaves the organization vulnerable to a takeover by an outside firm. After a takeover, the founder generally resigns, is forced out, or is shunted aside to some innocuous position. The organization becomes free of the destabilizing influence of an (E) leader, but at what price?

During this phase of its lifecycle,[11] the organization is exposed to other risks as well, some of which may make a takeover look good.

If, for example, an (-A--) leader takes control, bureaucracy begins to grow like kudzu. This is fatal to the organization's (E)ntrepreneuring. Suddenly it is open hunting season on the company's (E) types, who soon find themselves with exactly two choices: either they must give up and adapt (don't make waves; don't stand out), or they will have to go elsewhere.

---

11. Adizes, *Managing Corporate Lifecycles.*

Schools that do Harm

For years organizations have been chasing down the mythical perfect manager. In their quest to find this incredible faultless genius, they raise salaries, increase stock options, and give all kinds of special incentives and rewards to CEOs.

Business schools, as well, have been trying to create the perfect leader. The 20th-century phenomenon of management, as a profession and a "science," has led to a burgeoning of business schools and training courses for both novices and veteran managers. And without question, there is a need for such training. Unfortunately, these schools continue to focus on the wrong goals and wrong strategies.

In fact, most business schools of management do not teach management at all. They teach accounting, finance, the economic theory of the firm, and behavioral science. But knowing how to measure profits, optimize financial resources, or understand group dynamics and personal needs does not provide you with the know-how to manage. Management — the art of defining what you should want and making it happen — is not just the sum of the above management skills. It is something else entirely, and it is not taught.

The schools, by encouraging students to believe they can manage large groups of people without the support of a complementary team, do their students a tremendous disservice, setting them up for a future of perceived humiliating failure.

The schools encourage these unrealistic expectations in ways both direct and indirect. For instance, management textbooks, to illustrate good management practices, often put together a collage of the best traits of the best managers and then present this collage as if it were a single, individual manager. This mythical creature then proceeds to manage (flawlessly, of course) all tasks: planning, organizing, training, developing, motivating, leading, organizing, and disciplining under all conditions in all organizations in the same way.

In effect, then, the textbooks present as a model for their students a manager with no weaknesses — a model who, in reality, could never be emulated, trained, or found because he does not and *cannot* exist.

Furthermore, even if you could find a perfect leader, it would be dangerous to rely on a genius. Why? Because let's face it, geniuses appear very, very seldomly. Any corporation that depended solely upon the talents of one individual, even if that individual were outstandingly competent, would be extraordinarily limited. There is a military expression that illuminates this point: "Organizations should be organized by a genius so that even an idiot can run them, rather than organized by an idiot so that only a genius can run them." There simply are not enough geniuses to staff all organizations and all the positions in them.

Suppose an organization did have a manager who was so superior to everybody else that he naturally assumed all the decision-making power. If that person made a mistake, he could easily point the organization in the wrong direction. Even geniuses make at least one mistake once in a while. In the book *Corporate Management in Crisis: Why the Mighty Fall*, Joel Ross and Michael Kami[12] suggest that "what causes big corporations to fail is the one-man rule," even though it is also true that the one-man rule has often been the key to a start-up company's initial success.

The problem is that if no evolution to a longer-term style occurs over time, eventually the company grows so complex that no individual manager can fill all the essential roles — nor is he likely to let go of them — and the collapse of such conglomerates has often been swift and dramatic.

Origins of the Species

The paradigm of *individuals* as perfect managers is the fundamental error from which all management schools' derive their flaws.

12. Kami and Ross, *Corporate Management in Crisis*.

How did this come about? Why are millions being spent by corporations to train into being a creature who could not possibly fit the definition — and still be human?

There are several causes. A simple one is that management theory has primarily been developed in the United States, where the culture is individualistic and (E)ntrepreneuring. It is a logical manifestation of American culture to personalize the process of management into one individual, called the "manager" or the "leader."

If you take a chronological look at the development of management theory, you can actually see the PAEI code emerging, bit by bit, while the emerging theories continue to focus on one individual and his behavior and effectiveness rather than on a management team. For example, Frederick W. Taylor, a pioneer in the field, was concerned primarily with (P)roducing and specialization, the (P) role.[13] Both Henri Fayol and L. F. Urwick, on the other hand, were concerned with organizational structure, authority, span of control, delegation of authority, and staff-line relationships — the (A) role.[14] Mathematician, engineer, and social philosopher Norbert Wiener focused on the dynamics of change (E) and introduced the theory of cybernetics, which he defined as the science of communication and control in the animal and the machine.[15]

Elton Mayo, a sociologist at Harvard, did groundbreaking studies on behavioral science in the workplace and developed the human relations movement, which emphasizes the (I) role and has become the heart of contemporary management theory.[16]

13. Frederick W. Taylor, *The Principles of Scientific Management* (New York: Harper Bros., 1911).

14. Henri Fayol, *General and Industrial Management* (London: Sir Isaac Pitman and Sons, 1949); and Edward F. L. Brech and L. F. Urwick, *The Making of Scientific Management* (three-volume set, London: MPT, 1945, 1946, 1948).

15. Norbert Wiener, *Cybernetics; or Control and Communication in the Animal and the Machine* (New York: Technology Press/John Wiley, 1948).

16. Elton Mayo, *The Human Problems of an Industrial Civilization* (New York: Macmillan, 1933).

Psychologists, too, focus on behavior. In their case, why people have the styles they have: what needs motivate them. However, while understanding the why of behavior is interesting, it does not tell you what to do about it.

Whatever their ideas happened to be, all these theorists had one thing in common — they concentrated exclusively on the individual manager — claiming, in essence, that one or two fingers equals a hand.

More recently, general management theoreticians including Peter Drucker,[17] William Harold Newman,[18] and Harold Koontz,[19] have changed the definitions somewhat — putting result orientation, the (P) role; structure, the (A) role; change, the (E) role; and the human element, the (I) role; together into a whole that they call the "process" or "functions" of management. However, they stop short of challenging the old paradigm, where all these roles are meant to be performed by a single manager.

Most or all research and documenting of management theory has been flawed for this reason. It's true that some management theorists have attempted to correct this error, by basing their own studies on the observation of real managers functioning in real situations. But because the premise behind the classic definition of management has never been challenged, the results of these descriptive studies are liable to be misapplied. Henry Mintzberg's ten roles of management may be more specific than Fayol's four roles, but the individual who tries to master all ten roles is still attempting the impossible.

What than is the new paradigm?

17. Peter Ferdinand Drucker, *The Essential Drucker: In One Volume, the Best of Sixty Years of Peter Drucker's Essential Writings on Management* (New York: Harper Business, 2001).
18. William Harold Newman, *Process of Management: Strategy, Action, Results* (New Jersey: Prentice Hall, 1982).
19. Harold Koontz and Heinz Weihrich, *Essentials of Management* (New York: McGraw Hill International, 1986).

PART III

Building the Complementary Team

CHAPTER 10

The PAEI Team

If the ideal manager, executive, or leader is nonexistent, then what can organizations do to provide the four management roles that need to be performed to keep the organization healthy?

The roles of (P)roducing, (A)dministrating, (E)ntrepreneuring, and (I)ntegrating must be fulfilled by a *complementary* team, because no one person can perform and excel in all four roles simultaneously.

Let me repeat — and emphasize — *complementary* does not mean "the same." What is needed is a team of leaders (managers, executives) whose styles are *different* but complement each other — who can work together and balance one another's biases, who each excel in at least one of the four roles and are above the minimum threshold of competence in the remaining roles.

When a leader hires several more people like himself, that is not a team. That is cloning.

We need to engage people who complement us where we are weak, and we are all weak in some area!

Furthermore, when I use the word "team" in terms of people whose styles are different, I'm not talking about hiring one who *knows* marketing and one who *knows* finance and one who *knows* accounting. These are differences in knowledge. I'm talking about a diversity of *styles*, of behavior, and not of religion, color, gender or race.

If a team is composed of people whose judgments are all the same, the team is very vulnerable. If the team is completely incompatible, it's also vulnerable. What makes a team strong and viable is when it has people with different styles who work well together.[1]

If you analyze the history of any successful organization, you will see that its success was due to a team of people whose styles, behavior, and needs were different yet worked well together. Although organizational success is usually attributed to one person, there is almost always a team behind that person that enables him or her to perform well.

Consider the case of Warren Buffett and Charlie Munger. Munger told CNBC in 2016 that he and Buffett "don't agree totally on everything, and yet we're quite respectful of one another." There are "not too many people I listen to," Buffett told CNBC. "But Charlie, he's given me a lot of good advice over time. . . . When I met Charlie, I knew instantly he was the kind of guy that I was going to learn from."[2]

Which countries, over the course of history, have failed or had a disastrous regime? Those ruled by a dictatorship. And, by definition, a dictatorship negates any diversity. No one is allowed to disagree.

Think about Hitler, Stalin, Mussolini, or Romania's Ceausescu: Who was their complementary team? Who dared to disagree with them?

Now notice that democracy is an institutionalized complementary system. Research from the University of Toronto shows that political

1. On teamwork, see Rensis Likert, *The Human Organization: Its Management and Value* (New York: McGraw-Hill, 1967).
2. CNBC, *Make It*, January 31, 2019, and CNBC June 30, 2021.

affiliation is related to a personality style.[3] The liberal party is supported more by (E) types and the conservative party is supported more by (A) types.

The problem with a system of governance based on diversity of styles, outlooks, and judgements is that it produces conflict, which can become destructive. Democracy can deteriorate into chaos, anarchy, and give birth to dictatorship, which eliminates diversity. The challenge then, is to have a complementary team but without destructive conflict. In other words, to have a functioning team and not a debating committee.

In the following pages we will cover how to build a complementary team: Who should be on the team. How they should work together constructively. And which combinations are best, which are only acceptable, and which will not work at all

A complementary team can occur successfully at all levels of an organizational hierarchy, but it does not evolve naturally all by itself. In an ideal managerial mix, each individual team member must possess specific qualities. Then, the team itself must be capable of achieving certain goals.

What are the necessary characteristics for each member of such a team? Let's find out.

3. Jacob B. Hirsh, et al., "Compassionate Liberals and Polite Conservatives," *Personality and Social Psychology Bulletin*, 36, no. 5 (May 2010): 655–64.

CHAPTER 11

Team Membership Characteristics

First things first: Team members cannot have *any dashes* in their PAEI codes and should excel at one or more of the four roles. Dashes mean that their capability in that role is below the threshold needed by the task they need to perform and by the demands related to where the organization is on the lifecycle.[1]

Thus, team members with:

(P---)

(-A--)

(--E-)

or (---I)

or even those with a single dash in their code, like:

1. Adizes, Op. cit.

(PAE-)

(pA-I)

or (-aE-)

will not work.

Any manager with even one blank in his code will be incapable of working well with the person who excels in that role on the team. He will be inflexible and will have difficulty developing and inspiring mutual trust and respect with that person.

No blanks in the PAEI code means that the manager or leader *must* realize that they themselves are *imperfect*. They understand and appreciate the value of their strengths and the cost of their weaknesses, are familiar with and capable of recognizing excellence in areas in which they are relatively weak, and accept and appreciate other people's differences.

Let's say a prospective team member is a (Paei) type. He is strong at (P)roducing, but he can perform whatever other combination of managerial roles may be required, although he won't excel in them. He'll meet the necessary minimum required by the task and location of the company on the lifecycle. But if none of the other team members excels at (I)ntegrating, as in the above example, the team as an entity will be weak in the (I) role and unsuccessful. They will need external (I)ntegrating help — a (paeI) style.

Look at your hand. Every finger is different. The four extended fingers complement each other. The pointing finger is the most flexible and versatile; few would consider the fourth finger, the "ring finger," to be as functional. But can you imagine a hand composed of five pointing fingers? It would not work as well. What makes a hand functional is that every finger is different, and they complement each other.

What the pointing finger can do, the pinky cannot and vice versa. But the pinky cannot work with the middle finger. Try doing that and see

how awkward it is. That is what the thumb is for. It can touch and work with each and every finger. That is why in a certain language (and with all my traveling I have forgotten which language) the thumb is not called a finger but a "hand maker." Your thumb is the Integrator of your hand. Take the thumb out and the hand does not work. In Hebrew a thumb is an *agudâl* (pronounced *ah-goo-DAHL)*, which comes from "*aguda*," which means "bringing together." In Chinese the thumb character is 大拇指（拇指，拇）。The character 姆 is composed by 手 (hand) and 母 (mother). The role of the mother is to bring and keep the family together, so like the "hand mother," the thumb brings the fingers together.

Go to any church or house of prayer in India and look at the saints. Notice they all have a hand extended, palm out, and fingers together. The message is: be different and together. That is the blessing.

In the Middle East the extended hand with united fingers is called a *Hamsa*, and it is used in jewelry or as decoration at the entrance to a home. But when a hand is extended, palm out, with fingers separated, the same symbol becomes a curse: Be different and *not* together. This applies not only to businesses but also to countries and marriages, etc.

Every morning, religious Jews put a tefillin on their forehead and on their non dominant hand. Attached to the head-tefillah is a box. In it are four separate compartments, each with a different prayer scroll. The arm-tefillah is a leather strap that is wrapped from the upper arm down to the middle finger.

The message is: in our head we are different but in action, which the hand represents, we are united.

The message is united differences.

The book of Deuteronomy, in the Hebrew Bible, when dealing with the tribes, describes the four institutions (powers) of government necessary for the proper functioning of the Jewish state. These are (with my PAEI code interpretation): the King, performs the (P) role; the Judge, performs the (A) role; the Priest, performs the (I) role; and the Prophet, performs the (E) role. It is God who performs the big (I) role.

Such a system is similar to the hand, where the four fingers correspond to the four above powers, and the thumb refers to God, the grand (I). The Sufi branch of Islam sees God in everything. Spinoza saw God as Nature, in everything.

In the Middle East when they want to curse you, they extend their palm towards you with the fingers separated from each other. The message is: May you be different and not together.

The difference between a curse and a blessing is insignificant but the repercussions are very significant. Are we different together or different not together?

Difference creates conflict and one way to avoid conflict is to prohibit differences. All have to be the same. I am referring to nationalism, fanatic religions, racism, communism. And what happens when diversity is prohibited and persecuted? There is no synergy. There is no growth, or as Churchill said: "Capitalism is the unequal distribution of affluence; socialism is the equal distribution of poverty."

Look at a desert. All the same. A sea of sand. Nothing grows there. Now, add a bit of diversity, a new and different element, water, and what do you get? An oasis.

Look at a jungle. Diversity galore and what do you see? Incredible growth.

There are innumerable combinations of skills and personality traits that can add up to a PAEI team.

It might be composed of:

(Paei)

(pAei)

(paEi)

and (paeI)

Even better would be a team composed of:

(PaeI)

(pAeI)

and (paEI)

since all will perform well when it comes to (I)ntegrating.

In the latter configuration, since each team member excels at (I)ntegrating just as well as the others, they all transcend good management, and all are leaders. It is a leadership team. Each can lead but with a different focus.

These teams lead to an effective and efficient organization in the short and long run.

A successful organizational team does not have to be composed of four people — there could be three or even two.

One traditional model of a complementary team — the typical mom-and-pop store — consists of a (PaEi) and a (pAeI). The "poppa" (PaEi) opens new stores, finds new products, and sets prices, while the "momma" (pAeI) takes care of the books and deals with the customers service quality.

But this team doesn't have to be a store. It could be a multinational company with billions of dollars in revenues. Years ago, I lectured to the top management of Philip Morris. The CEO approached me afterward and said, pointing to the gentleman next to him, "Dr. Adizes, I would like to introduce you to Momma."

Why don't you ever hear of a "momma store" or a "poppa store?" It is always the mom-and-pop store, and notice who is mentioned first. Momma. Why momma? Because the *how* is more important than the *what*. Because there is no successful poppa without a successful momma! It takes a complementary team to build a store (or, for that matter, a family). Show me any successful organization, and I'll show you a complementary team. The macho expression, "Behind every successful man stands a surprised wife," should be changed to, "Beside every successful person stands a supportive spouse."

A mom-and-pop store where one is a of (PAei) style and the other is a (paEI) style will not work well, because one is mostly focused on the long run and the other mostly on the short run. They will clash.

A (PaEi) style with a (pAeI) style will work better. Instead of being focused on one to the exclusion of the other, each of these managers makes decisions based on a consideration for both short- and long-term goals. The (PaEi)'s role should be to look at what to do in both the short run, the (P) role, and the long run, the (E) role; these two roles cause external integration of the company. The (pAeI) on the other hand, should concentrate on how it should be done, mechanistically, in the short run, the (A) role; and organically, for the long run, the (I) role. These two roles cause internal integration. One focuses on external short- and long-term integration and the other focuses on internal integration in the short and long term. The first one, the (PaEi), is results-oriented, while the (pAeI) is process-oriented. They complement each other in multiple ways.

Is there a CEO?

We have established that we need a complementary team. And if all are high on the (I) role, they are all leaders. However, the question remains, who leads those leaders? Is there a chair? Is someone the CEO?

One member of the team should be *primus inter pares*, first among equals, who integrates the team to consensus. And if a consensus cannot be reached, the decision is elevated to the board, who has the final word. Who that person is — the (PaeI) or the (pAeI) or the (paEI) — depends where the company is on the lifecycle.[2] For a start-up and a Go-Go, a fast growing company, most probably a (PaEI), style of leadership should lead. For a company in transition from entrepreneurial company to professional leadership, a (pAeI) will be most appropriate. In an aging company or one in danger of becoming bureaucratized, a (PaEi) is called for.

Beyond the impact that the lifecycle location has on selecting who the first among equals is, the nature of the industry has a say, too.

---

2. Adizes, *Op.cit.*

Hospitals, operas, theaters, all fine arts organizations, and universities are all run by with complementary team at the helm, with the artistic director performing the (PaEi) roles and the administrative director taking care of the (pAeI) roles. And the same applies now to high tec companies. There must be a chief technology officer and a chief business officer. If there is no complementary team most probably the company will be short lived.

The Pitfall

By now it must be obvious that creating and sustaining a complementary team comes with its share of pitfalls: We need each other, but can we stand each other's differences? Differing styles, though they are both complementary and essential, aren't necessarily compatible. Fundamentally, working together means accepting variations in style and opinion — acknowledging that those variations will lead to conflict and recognizing that conflict is an inevitable and even desirable facet of managing. "To find out how to make conflict constructive, keep reading.

I'm not telling you anything you don't know. Consider your spouse, for example. I'll bet that their style is very different from yours.[3] If you are creative and excitable, you've probably chosen a partner who pours cold water on your head from time to time to bring you back to reality — someone who thinks the details through.

We fall in love with or at least appreciate our partner's strengths, which represent our own weaknesses. But after we get married, we begin to resent it when our spouse fails in the things we ourselves are good at, and we start to criticize them. Instead of appreciating the strengths they *do* have, which we do not possess, we want them to have our strengths, too, and begin to reject their weaknesses even though we have a full set of our own. Ready for conflict? Ready for divorce? The

3. Adizes with Madanes, *Power of Opposites.*

reasons one person marries another might just turn out to be the same reasons they later contemplate leaving them.

The typical couple is incompatible in a hundred ways. Peter Blumenthal once listed the ways in which he and his wife, Laura, see and do things differently. Peter is quiet; Laura is talkative. He is undemonstrative; she is effusive. He hates to talk problems out; she likes to shout her way through them. He prefers a quiet night at home; she likes a big party. He is thorough and meticulous; she hates details. He likes to plan things in advance; she is spontaneous and impulsive. He tends to be indecisive, but when he makes a decision, it is after a thorough review of the facts and he sticks to it. She is quick to decide but may change her mind tomorrow. When purchasing a new car or determining a color for their home décor, he prefers the staid and conservative; she wants color and pizzazz. When they collaborate on a project around the house, he works at a slow, consistent pace; she is quick but erratic. His spending is governed by a carefully constructed budget and savings plan; she is more of an impulse buyer. He tends to be firm and consistent with their children; she is spontaneous and warm, gives them lots of freedom, and often does clandestine favors. What is his style? (PAei), right? How about her? (paEI), right? Not an easy marriage but livable. If one of them had a dash in their code, they would be divorced.

Here is an example from my own family. On a trip to the Far East, we bought a new camera, a digital type that none of us knew how to operate.

The (P) style in the family, my wife, tried right away to operate it through trial and error. The (A) style, one of my sons, immediately got upset. "Read the manual!" he insisted.

The (E) style, that would be me, was totally uninterested in the manual or even in operating the camera. I, the big (E), wanted to decide on the appropriate angle, direct who was going to stand where, and choose which person would shoot the photo. And I wanted to make absolutely sure I was in the picture. In the meantime, Shoham, my big (I) son, was watching the commotion and said "C'mon guys, stop fighting."

The Inevitability of Conflict

Why do opposites attract? It's such a peculiar phenomenon. But the truth is, it only *seems* peculiar. In actuality, to attract your opposite is natural and even necessary.

In order to raise children, a family requires both "feminine" and "masculine" (yin and yang) energies. The child needs you both. Even in same-sex partnerships, it is still a complementary team, there is a difference in styles between the partners.

It's difficult to raise a child as a single parent, whether you are a man or a woman. No matter which sex is involved, both energies are necessary for raising healthy children. But this does not apply only to families. It applies to companies and to countries as well. For a healthy, well-operating country, there is a need for both a conservative (A) party and a liberal (E) party. And the same applies to every healthy individual. We have in ourselves both feminine and masculine energies.

When you have a problem, whether it's business-related or personal, you often choose someone who is different from you to consult with, don't you? You want someone who's going to see the holes in your argument, who's going to make you think about what you're saying. We always look for thecomplementarity.

In the Bible, the "perfect" spouse is defined as *Ezer Kenegdo*, which literally means "helpful against." Rabbis have argued about this phrase for centuries. How can a spouse be helpful if they are against? If they are against, then they're not helpful; if they're helpful, they're not against.

My explanation is that a spouse is helpful precisely by being against. That's exactly what we're looking for because we cannot embrace the total argument all by ourselves. It's too difficult to do. We need someone who's going to complement us and most probably disagree with us. In fact, the bigger our (E)ntrepreneuring spirit, the bigger the (A)dministering style we will be attracted to. Try pushing something. If it does not push back, you will fall.

Most of us behave as if peace and harmony are normal, and conflict is abnormal. In actuality, the opposite is true. Organizational conflict emerges naturally from the diverse styles of its members, so it is normal and inevitable that they are going to have difficulty communicating and reaching agreement. In fact, there will be conflict even if the goal, the information, and the reward system are clearly defined and understood (i.e., the three factors that Nobel economics laureate Herbert A. Simon believed to be the causes of conflict).

If a decision is to be fully analyzed in order to bring about a good decision, it must reflect all four roles. In other words, there must be conflict.

An organization can operate totally without conflict if it is composed of one individual who makes all the decisions himself and implements them alone. In that case, there is no organization. However, since the four roles still need to be performed, and they are still incompatible, he will conflict with himself.

Interesting research was done by Adizes Institute's Senior Associate Nebojsa Caric of the Southeastern Europe office. He measured the PAEI styles of thirty-six random people and compared them to the PAEI-style results of people recognized by MENSA as having superior intelligence.

He found that the common denominator to the MENSA people was that their PAEI code differentiations were low. In other words, none of the PAEI roles was far from the other ones in their size. They were not perfect (not excelling in all roles), but they scored just above average in all four roles.

Question: is there a relationship between being average in everything and being super intelligent?

My hypothesis is that when there are no extremes in the PAEI code, there is more peace in the human mind, and there is no wasted energy between the ears. The higher the internal differences in the code, the more internal conflicts the person will have. This impacts the level of energy required for the person to process information. With no wasted energy, a person can excel and is considered MENSA material.

Conflict could be avoided in an organization in which all the members of the managerial team have the same style: if they are all are (A)s or all (P)s. Such managers would have the same outlook and play the same role, and thus have no conflict.

An organization composed of Deadwood could conceivably operate without conflict, too. In such an environment, every decision would be programmed and predetermined, and no one member would want to change anything. No one would complain, but no one would care either.

In both of the above cases, however, the organizations would experience significant problems meeting their goals in a changing environment. They would become stale or stuck, without synergy,and no growth would be experienced, no change. As the saying goes: "Change fast or die slowly." These companies would die.

We need and want a complementary team. And we recognize the fact that the diversity will generate conflict. The problem is that the conflict can be destructive, consume all the fixed energy available of the parties involved leaving little energy if any to deal with the clients it needs to serve.

So, part of our new paradigm should include the notion that conflict is a necessary and indispensable component of good management and, like any other component, must be understood and legitimized. We need constructive conflict.

If you are a manager and don't like to mediate between people, if you are upset by friction and differences of opinion, then you're in the wrong profession. Imagine a person saying, "I want to be a doctor, but I can't stand the sight of blood and I don't like sick people." Then treating patients isn't for you. Go do research, or as President Truman said: "If you can't stand the heat, get out of the kitchen."

The challenge is to prevent conflict from becoming *destructive*. The challenge we will address in the coming pages is, how do we make it *constructive* — like couples who, after having an argument, come out the other side with a stronger relationship

Before we discuss how to make conflict which is inevitable, constructive rather than destructive, we need to look at another source of conflict that must be harnessed: the issue of implementation.

CHAPTER 12

Implementation

Leadership is the process of solving problems that emerge because of change. The purpose of leadership and management is to have a healthy organization, which means the company is effective and efficient in the short and long run. For that, all four PAEI roles need to be performed; and to perform them, a complementary team is needed.

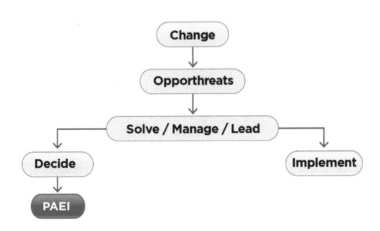

Deciding what to do, though, is not enough. A healthy system must make healthy decisions and then implement them.

To implement a decision, we need more than clarity (what to do, the decision making imperative of the (P) role); a gameplan (how to do it, the (A) role); a timeline (when to do it, the (E) role); and assignments (who should do it, the decision making imperative of the (I) role). Those are the ingredients, but they aren't enough To assure implementation, energy is required.

The three sources of managerial energy

authority power influence

Authority

Authority is the *formal* right to make a decision. Marketing, for instance, has the right to make the decision what kind of advertising to do.

Usually "to make a decision" is defined as the right to say "yes" *or* "no." The word "or" in this sentence means that someone might have the right to say "yes" but not "no." This, however, is rare. Someone else might have the right to say "no" but not "yes," and this is very prevalent.

How did that happen?

When the company was a start-up or young in its behavior, the founder had the authority to say "yes" *and* "no." He or she was the one and only.

As the company grew bigger and bigger, the founder had to delegate.

What was delegated? The right to say "no" to change, but not the right to say "yes," which the founders typically kept for themselves. And as the company grew even bigger, the right to say "yes" ascended further and further up in the hierarchy, and layers upon layers below them filed the organization with naysayers. The "yes" and the "no" got bifurcated. This is what creates the phenomena called *bureaucracy*. And that is why, if change is attempted, one needs to go all the way to the top of the organization to get agreement. This explains why consultants insist on working for the CEO. It's the only place where they can get a "yes" answer to their recommendations.

In the Adizes methodology, authority is defined as the *right* to say "yes" *and* "no." If you cannot say "yes," you are not allowed to say "no." You must pass the problem up until it reaches someone who can say "yes." The problem must migrate to the level where the "yes" can be obtained.

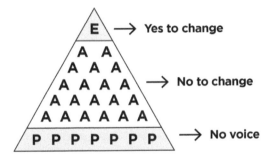

Below, I have depicted authority as a circle because there is a limit to your right to say "yes" and "no." Inside the circle you have authority. Outside the circle you do not have authority. If you decide or authorize any change beyond the border of the circle, you are abusing your authority.

Sometimes it is not sufficient to simply invoke authority in an attempt to make other people cooperate and help you implement your solution. If invoking your authority has failed, you may be tempted to look to the second source of energy to get the cooperation you need: power.

Power

Power is the *capability*, not the right, to punish and/or reward. If I can grant you what you want or cherish, it is a reward. Conversely, withholding what you want and expect is a punishment; You expect something, you believe you have earned it. You deserve it. If it is denied, you feel punished.

Power, then, is the capability to grant or withhold expected rewards. One of them is cooperation. You need something done and need someone's cooperation for it to be done. If that person will not cooperate then, de facto, that person is using power over you, he or she is punishing you.

How much power anyone has over you is a function of how much you need and expect from them, and how much of a monopoly they have over what you need. This explains why falling in love is such a powerful experience and why it hurts so much if the feeling is threatened. We say, *you* are the *only one*, and I *need* you very, very much, and I cannot live without you. Imagine the pain you will experience any time there is a sign your loved one might leave you. They have monopoly over what you desperately need. . . .

To avoid the pain, some people avoid falling in love. But in so doing, they are also avoiding the reward, the pleasure of feeling love. Pain and pleasure are two sides of the same coin.

My mantra:

Speak without offending,
      listen without defending,
           live without pretending, and . . .
                love without depending.

The more you expect from others, the more disempowered *you will feel.*

When you expect, you give power to those you expect from. The more you expect, the more miserable you because your happiness depends on what others will or won't do.

We live in a world of increasing interdependency. In agricultural societies, people were happier because they were less dependent on others. Their dependency was mostly on sunshine and rain. In contrast, we depend on an infinity of variables. Our standard of living has gone up, but our quality of life has gone down. The more developed the country, the more interdependencies there are, and the more of a sensation of disempowerment — thus, the higher the rates of depression, anxiety, and panic attacks.

Power is the second source of energy for implementation, but its use is not recommended. The problem with power is that the more it is used, the less effective it becomes, and the stronger the measures you need to progressively take to obtain the same results. Along the way, you destroy your relationships with the very people you need cooperation from.

This highlights the need for a third energy component, *influence.*

Influence

Influence happens when we convince the person we need cooperation from to do something — without using either authority or power

Influence happens when the focal person — the person you are trying to persuade — has a true choice to follow or not to follow your inputs. That's why when we want to influence, we say, "For your consideration. Up to you."

Imagine telling somebody what to do, assuming no one else is in the room and that there are no recordings. Imagine also that as soon as you finished talking, you had a heart attack and died. So, nobody knows what you told this person to do. Would that person do it? They may say, "Thank God, he died. I don't have to do this now. I am free." Or the person may say, "I am sorry he died, but I am going to do this anyway. I believe he was right."

In the second case influence worked.

In my work, when we finish designing a new organizational chart, I sometimes test the client's commitment to the decision by criticizing the decision. I start enumerating all the deficiencies I see and all the reasons why the structure may not work. This is never too difficult to do because nothing is perfect. Often my client's response is, "Please, Dr. Adizes, we worked on this long enough. We believe in it, so please let it go."

What happened? It's *their* chart now. Influence happened and they own their decisions.

Authorance

The three circles of energy overlap. We now have:

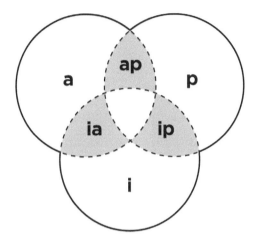

In the *authority* part of the circle, notice the section where you have authority but without power and influence. It's the weakest source of energy. You have authority but no power to enforce and no influence to convince. People might follow your decisions once or twice but eventually they might not follow them anymore.

How about power without authority? A subordinate can withhold cooperation — like not providing the information you need — and there is nothing you can do about it. I was once told that in Argentina some mail carriers pick up the mail, but instead of distributing it to homes, they just dump it in a garbage can. This is difficult to catch because people do not know that their mail did not arrive, and even if they did know, they would have no idea where it got stuck or lost.

With pure *influence*, you can recommend but that's it, and if it doesn't happen, there is nothing you can do.

Two sources of managerial energy can overlap.

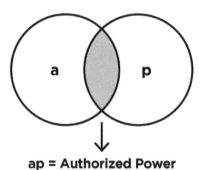

ap = Authorized Power

**The legal right
to punish or reward**

Authorized power (ap) is when you have both *authority* and *power*, you have the legal right to punish or reward. You have the right to say "yes" and "no" and to expect implementation. Some examples are the right to fire, to give a bonus, to provide information, etc.

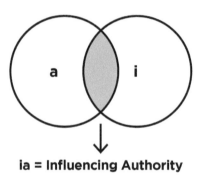

ia = Influencing Authority

**The right to make a decision
coupled with the capability
to convince that it is the
tight decision.**

Influencing authority (ia) (also called accepted authority or professional authority) is the overlap of *authority* and *influence*. You have the authority to decide, and the decision is acceptable by those you made the decision for. They believe in your decision.

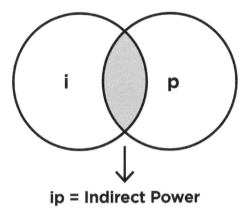

ip = Indirect Power

**Occurs when one person thinks he
is influencing, but other person reads
power "in between the lines"**

Indirect power (ip) is a treacherous combination: *influence* and *power*.

This happens when a person with power, but not in direct line of authority (such as a VP), makes a "recommendation." The focal person, however, reads power between the lines and, fearing the potential consequences of not listening to the person in power, acts on the recommendation — in spite of not believing in the recommendation. Why is this dangerous? Because it's not clear who is accountable. If the recommendation turns out to be a disaster, the plant manager, when asked why he did it, will reply, "The VP told me to do it." The VP, if asked, will say, "No, I was just recommending."

Nobody takes responsibility because no one *feels* accountable.

In *indirect power*, you are not really free to chose whether to follow the recommendation or not, and at the same time, you are scared not to follow it.

The three sources of energy can coalesce.

capi = coalesced authority power and influence

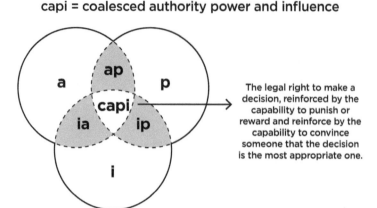

The legal right to make a decision, reinforced by the capability to punish or reward and reinforce by the capability to convince someone that the decision is the most appropriate one.

When authority, power, and influence overlap, you get a new combination which I call CAPI. The "c" stands for "coalesced." When you have CAPI, you have *coalesced authority, power,* and *influence.* You have the authority to tell people what to do. You can also influence them as to the validity of what you want done, and if their actions are delayed or they do not listen well, you have the power to punish or reward to cause compliance.

capi = control

When you have CAPI, there is no reason why people would not follow your decisions and implement them. They are convinced and, if in doubt, they would be concerned about not following the instructions. You have control.

For some decisions, the manager or leader has CAPI. Nobody challenges that.

In most cases, in modern time, because of the high level of interdependency, the CAPI is shared by multiple people. Authority is with management, power is with those managed, and influence might be with some professional consultants. Most people believe that power increases the higher you climb in the hierarchy. Those reporting to you have the capability to cooperate or withdraw cooperation. They can make your life as a manager or leader miserable if they don't cooperate. This is especially true with millennials. They grew up in a relatively easy time. They never went through depression or war. Many were born with a silver spoon in their mouth. They only do what they love doing. Where is the power? In them, because you need them, and they can chose what to do or not to do.

Inexperienced managers work hard to climb the organizational pyramid to get to power. And when they get to the top there is a sign: "Power is down there."

Authorance combines the *seven sources of energy* that cause implementation to happen. Here is an example of how *authorance* is used: Look at the managerial task of a mother trying to convince her toddler child to eat spinach. First, she says, "Eat. It's good for you. Popeye eats it. Look how strong he is. If you each spinach, you'll be strong like Popeye."

Total Managerial Energy

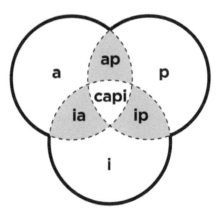

Authorance = a + p + i + ap + ip + ia + capi

Where is she on the authorance diagram? What part of authorance is she using? Influence.

But the child says, "Noooo! I hate spinach."

So, the mother tries again, saying, '"When Daddy comes home, I'm going to tell him you were a good boy. And if you eat your spinach, he'll take you to the zoo." By referring to the potential rewards or dangers, she has moved out of influence and is now using *influencing power*. Still, the child refuses to eat.

If the mother gets very upset and punishes the child — for instance, no dessert — what is she using? *Authorized power*.

But if the husband comes home and says, "What have you done? What are you punishing the kid for? If he doesn't want to eat spinach, he doesn't have to." Then she was using just *power*.

This is likely to happen in modem families in which parents share authority, or it is not real clear who has the final word.

The kid still refuses to eat spinach, and the mother is very stressed about raising him. "Listen to me. I'm your mother!"

Now she's using authority, but doesn't the child already know that she's his mother? The day you have to remind people of your authority, when it should be obvious, is the day you are in managerial overreach. The fact that you have authority should not be used; it should be *known*. Never use it. The moment you make it explicit, you've lost it. The day you tell your employees, "Do it because I'm your boss," what are you reminding them of? Don't they know you're the boss? If you have to remind them of such an obvious fact, you're in trouble. When somebody says, "But I'm your husband," or "I'm your wife," he or she is saying something equally obvious. It means that all sources of authorance, of managerial energy, have been exhausted. The person is down to the last gasp of breath. This is very dangerous because certain facts should never be spoken. After you say them aloud, you're left with nothing.

Authority by itself is very weak unless it's backed with power and influence. You probably can't use just authority alone more than once or twice. If you plead repeatedly with your children, "But I'm your parent," they eventually might say, "So what!" In that case there is really nothing else you can do.

The strongest combination is CAPI. How does one get CAPI?

The three sources of energy have different interests.

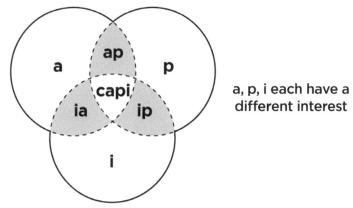

a, p, i each have a different interest

Owners usually have the ultimate authority to decide. They might want more profits, more growth.

Power, usually the workers, want better conditions and pay.

Influence, usually the technocrats, want more professional improvement and challenge.

In order to get CAPI a manager or a leader has to develop a common interest if he or she wants to assure cooperation and thus swift and rapid implementation.

Success Indicators

Managerial effectiveness is a function of authorance in relation to responsibilities. Managers are effective when they have sufficient authority and/or power and/or influence for their responsibility.

$$\text{Managerial effectiveness} = f\{\text{authorance/responsibility}\}$$

Managerial efficiency is a function of the amount of CAPI held by the managers out of the total authorance they have. The more CAPI, the less energy they have to spend to get things done.

$$\text{Managerial efficiency} = f\{\text{CAPI/authorance}\}$$

$$\textit{Managerial Efficacy} = f\{\textit{ CAPI/responsibility}\}$$

An efficant (one that produces efficacy) manager or leader has full CAPI over his responsibility, he or she is both effective — can get the job done — and is efficient in using his or her limited energy.

These are the dictators. They are efficant but for a short time. This is due to the power component of CAPI." Since they have full power over the task, their natural tendency will be to use power to get the task done. The issue with power is the more you use, the less effective it is. Since they use mostly power — albeit authorized to start with, and because it is the most effective and produces results the fastest results — eventually they lose power, and ultimately their authority, and they are removed from power.

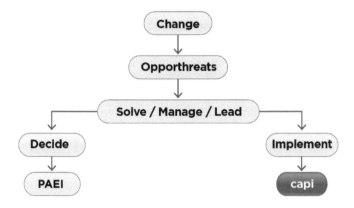

For effective implementation, *authorance* is necessary. For efficient implementation, CAPI is necessary.

When CAPI is possessed by one single individual, it is an authoritarian or dictatorial style of leadership. It's very dysfunctional because a single individual, by definition, has weaknesses, and this single all-powerful leader can take the company over the cliff. What is needed is *team CAPI*, a complementary team that shares a common interest.

Whether the implementation will be effective in the short or long run and whether it will be efficient in the short or long run depends on the energies used for implementation and by whom.

If power and/or just authority is used, the implementation will be effective only in the short run. If influence and authority are used, the implementation will be effective in the long run.

If individual CAPI is used, implementation will be efficient but only in the short run. If team CAPI is used, implementation will be efficient in the short and long run.

Summary

When you have CAPI, decisions will be implemented efficiently and fast.

When you have *authorance* but with limited CAPI, decisions will be implemented but with a certain struggle.

When you don't have *authorance*, decisions will get shelved and won't be implemented, or they will only be partially implemented.

To coalesce CAPI, leaders must develop a common interest, common vision, common benefit, and perceived symbiosis. A symbiotic relationship, a mutually beneficial relationship, provides for the common interest.

In a symbiotic relationship, there is a time lag between when you contribute energy and when you benefit from the system you are contributing to. Things will get done when there is mutual trust. Without trusting the system, there will be no contribution to it and, thus, no symbiosis.

Take the example of paying taxes. If you do not trust the government, if you believe your taxes are wasted or syphoned to benefit crooked politicians, you won't be eager to honestly calculate your taxes and pay.

But if there is no corruption — you trust and believe in the elected officials to use your money most effectively and efficiently, and that you will benefit from a better system — you will contribute your taxes more willingly.

When there is mutual trust, conflicts of interest can be channeled into being constructive, collaboration will take place, and implementation will be swift and accurately correspond to the decision that was made.

CHAPTER 13

Managing Conflict

Change is here to stay, and it is accelerating. It poses challenges that could be problems or opportunities, depending on how we approach them.

Healthy systems handle change better than sick systems. A healthy organization will succeed in competing in a changing environment better than a dysfunctional, sick organization. It does not waste its fixed energy on handling internal dysfunctionalities. It focuses all its energies on external integration.

Healthy systems make effective decisions that are implemented efficiently.

If we make bad decisions and or implement them inefficiently, the problems generated by change will grow and become a crisis. Thus, making effective decisions and implementing them efficiently is what the process — whether we call it management, leadership, governing, or parenting — is all about. Whether it is to manage ourselves, our family, our business, or society, we need to manage change. We need to manage life. We need to make good decisions and implement them using minimum energy and resources.

The main role of management, leadership, government, and parenting is to see to it that the system being managed is *healthy*. If the system is a business, the by-product of being healthy is being profitable in the short and long run — or to have a well-integrated functioning family, if we are talking about a family, or a sustainable healthy society and economy,if we are looking at a country.

An effective decision requires an answer to four imperatives, which we call roles. They are the (P) role, (P)roducing the needed service that clients want and for which the organization exists; the (A) role, (A)dministering for efficient delivery of needs and satisfaction; the (E)ntrepreneuring role, positioning the company to address the changing future; and the (I) role, (I)ntegrating the organization because disintegration is the by-product of change (and change cannot be stopped).

For implementation we need CAPI or at least authorance in which the contributors to CAPI or authorance share a common interest.

The way to lead, govern, or parent to manage change, is to have a team composed of the correct composition of diversified styles who share a common interest: diversity of styles but commonality of interests.

Easier said than done.

Change causes conflicts among styles and interests. Different styles handle change differently, and interests change over time, too.

Good Conflict, Bad Conflict

We have said that conflict is inevitable for managing change, for making effective decisions that will be implemented efficiently. Yet conflict can be constructive or it can be destructive. It can be functional or dysfunctional.

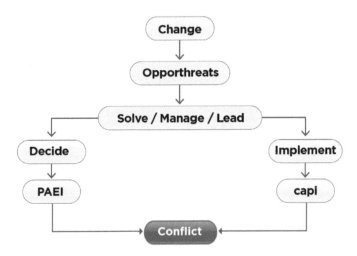

Dysfunctional conflict is dangerous to any organization. It can stymie an organization, sap its energy, and even destroy it. When managers are at odds with each other, the energy that should be conserved for building the company is gobbled up by internal conflicts.

An organization that wastes precious energy on internal conflicts will necessarily be handicapped. I believe this factor alone can determine whether the company succeeds or fails. In fact, if the ratio between external and internal energies spent is known, I believe we can predict the success of any system. External energies are spent to integrate the company with its market. Internal energies are spent to get the organization subsystems aligned, so the organization can deliver efficiently what the market desires and is willing to pay for.

So the next ingredient in our new paradigm for management and leadership is a formula for success that discourages wasted energy, leaving the fixed disposable energy available for building the company. Leadership needs to build managerial teams in which the team members are different from each other yet work together. A team leader must be able to harness the natural tensions of styles and interests that inevitably surface in any diverse group.

How do we ensure that those differences will work *for* us instead of against us?

The key lies in how we as managers or leaders deal with conflict. First, we must legitimize conflict. Next, we must make it an opportunity for learning and thus growing; we need to channel the energy of conflict to be constructive.

Note that I did not say we must *resolve* conflict. this would, in fact, be exactly the wrong attitude. Those who try to *resolve* conflict are, again, barking up the wrong tree and working from the mistaken assumption that conflict is inappropriate or wrong and should be avoided: "We *should not* have disagreement." "We *should not* have differences of opinion and differences of interest." But this common perception ignores the reality, which is that differences — and thus conflict — are natural and normal. Before we can start to reap the benefits of our differences, we must accept that conflict is appropriate and necessary, and we must render it functional.

Now, how do we do that? Leadership (whether it is a parent, an executive in a company, or a leader of a country) needs to create an environment of mutual trust and respect (see illustration on next page).

On Mutual Respect

First, let us see how we transform a conflict that stems from differences in style into constructive energy.

Differences in style means differences in perspective, in judgement: What is right and what is wrong, etc. Let's define *respect* as the willingness to listen to and learn from anyone who disagrees with us but has something to contribute.

In a learning environment, differences of opinion are seen as opportunities to gain new perspectives, rather than as threats or challenges or annoyances. We grow *through* disagreement rather than in spite of

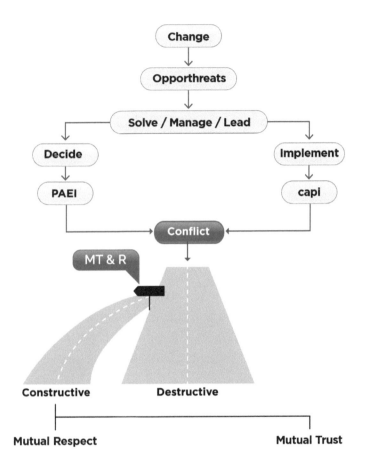

it. When someone has a point of view that I don't have, I might feel uncomfortable with that and I might not like it, but when I respect those differences, I might learn something that I had not previously thought about.

> *If two people agree on everything, one of them*
> *is not necessary.* — Popular saying

Immanuel Kant, the philosopher, said that respect is when we recognize each other's sovereignty to think differently. My contribution is that we recognize each other's sovereignty to think differently because we appreciate the difference, as we learn from them.

In Hebrew the word respect has two translations: honor and appreciation (*kavod* and *haaracha*) I suggest looking at respect as appreciation — that we have a chance to learn something. Thus, to respect someone is to appreciate that their differences will enrich us somehow.

What would happen if you spent a lot of time listening to someone's opinions, but found in the end that nothing they said had made you change your position — that your thinking had not expanded into new perspectives? Over time, you would lose respect for that person and stop listening to them.

> *Some people have something to say. Some people have to say something.*
> *Avoid the second group.* — Anonymous

On the other hand, if two people agree on everything, one of them is dispensable. So, we need to find people whose opinions diverge from ours and who retain our respect. These people, if we are lucky enough to find them, are called "colleagues," and they are essential to making good decisions.

A colleague is *not* someone who agrees with you. A colleague is someone who *disagrees* with you but for whom you have respect because you learn from their disagreement. You don't learn from those who agree with you. Notice how academics handle each other: "May I respectfully disagree with my learned colleague . . ."

Why this respectful behavior? To create a relaxed learning environment so we can learn from each other. . . . And this behavior should not be reserved only for the academia. . . .

Learning from differences is painful, but we also enrich ourselves through being different. In other words, we may start with different points of view, but by interacting we can arrive at the same conclusion.

For good decision-making, team members who both respect and disagree with one another — colleagues — are essential.

*"Great minds don't think alike. They challenge each other to think differ-
ently. The people who teach you the most are the ones who share
your principles but not your thought processes. Converging values draw
you to similar questions. Diverging views introduce you to new answers."*
— Adam Grant

On Mutual Trust

If mutual respect is necessary for good decision-making and efficient
implementation, a commonality of interests is needed among all those
whose cooperation is necessary to implement the decision. But permanent common interest isn't a realistic goal. People eventually develop
different and often conflicting interests, depending on their positions
and sphere of responsibility in the organization as well as their personal styles and conditions. People's interests change over time.

Recognizing this as reality, we need to come up with a reasonable and
viable alternative that will achieve the same goal: Decisions will be efficiently implemented, in spite of the lack of common interest at the time.

How?

Although there may be no common interest in the short run, this does
not mean the organization cannot have a *perception* of common interest in the long run. And for that, a culture of mutual trust must be
established and nurtured

Trust is the long-term belief and hope that even if we do not have common interests in the short run, we still share the same basic interest
over the long run. Having that mindset, we trust that our cooperation
in implementing a decision is not an isolated case. We have faith that
others will also do their best for the betterment of the system, and
eventually we will all benefit from the contribution we made.

Analyze a good marriage: There might be a conflict of interests between the partners, but if there is a common interest to keep the family

together for the long run and there is trust that all parties will do their best to overcome their short-term interests, then the marriage will survive and over time gratify each partner with a happy marriage.

In English, we say, "Life is give and take."

In other languages, like Arabic, Turkish, and even Modern Greek, it is said differently: "Life is take and give."

There is a difference.

In "give and take" there is trust. You "give" and believe, you trust, that the benefit will come back for you to "take."

When you say "life is take and give" you "take" first (to be sure you get your share), and only then do you give. There is no trust.

And this describes the problem of certain countries or regions like the Middle East. The language used suggests there is little trust and respect among the different branches of Islam, between the different tribes and countries.

When there is mutual trust and each interdependent component of the system contributes to the system, there is symbiosis.

One of the ways to transform potentially destructive conflict into constructive conflict is to create a nurturing, symbiotic environment. In such an environment, there is a perceived win–win climate. People trust that the short-term imbalances or conflicts of interest should be overcome so that all can benefit from the cooperation in the long run.

In a distrustful environment, especially in an era of rapid change, no one can predict what might happen in the long run. One result is that people only feel comfortable with short-term thinking and planning, and each member of the group will protect its interests at the cost of hurting the interests of the totality.

Those with the power can undermine those with the authority; they can "pocket-veto" decisions by simply not implementing them, later claiming that they misunderstood the decision.

I have come across a dysfunctional organizational behavior called "malicious compliance." A person whose cooperation is needed (i.e., a person who has power) says, "Sure. Will do," making everyone believe that a decision will be implemented. In reality this person does nothing whatsoever — or does just enough to not get into trouble but not enough to successfully implement the plan. In one organization this person was called the "snake in the bushes." Quiet. Looks dormant. Take it in your hands and it will bite you, maybe mortally.

When we have major decisions to make — new situations, new conditions, new complexities — we like to get other people's advice, preferably from people whose perspectives are different from ours. But would you go for advice to just *anyone* who disagrees with you? Of course not. You would only approach someone for whom you have respect, who is different from you but whose differences you appreciate and can learn from. If *this* person disagrees with you, he or she will be able to show you the holes in your argument and make you think harder about what you're saying. Moreover it is a person whom you trust and you believe they care for your interests and do not have their own interests that compete with yours.

Now, note that we say "mutual trust and respect" and not the reverse: respect ahead of trust. There is a reason for this.

Intuitively, we must first trust a person before we can listen to their difference of opinion. Without trust, respect cannot play a role. Trust is the precondition for respect and it has repercussions. As we analyze and try to provide solutions for, let's just say, the ongoing conflict in the Middle East, I would claim there will be no peace between the Jewish people and the Palestinians, no matter how the two states' borders are designed, until there is mutual trust and respect.

There is a difference between Bosnia and Switzerland. In Switzerland live French, Italians, and Germans in peace, although their nations had been at war with each other for generations. In Bosnia there is non-stop fighting between the Serbs and the Muslim Bosnians.

What is the difference?

Mutual Trust and Respect.

How to build it? Start with trust. Start by finding common interests. Follow with mutual respect for each other's culture.

The United States was founded on a fundamental appreciation for diversity based on mutual trust and respect. "Live and let live" is an expression that points to mutual trust. Recognizing the different cultures is a sign of mutual respect. Irish and Latin celebrations. Gay Pride parades. I believe these cultural acknowledgements and celebrations account at least in part, for America's enormous success and prosperity.

People often credit America's vast resources for its economic success but that alone cannot be the whole answer. After all, other countries are also rich in resources. What America has in addition to resources is its climate of mutual trust and respect. We still recognize and honor the differences among us. When the natural order presumes respect for differences — instead of discriminating by creed, religion, color, or gender — then the sky's the limit. The result is an environment in which freedom of expression is the ideal we constantly strive for. And through diversity based on mutual trust and respect we cross-pollinate and develop the economy and the country. Without it the market economy will not work out well at all. The hidden hand of Adam Smith will be crooked or in chains. It is this freedom based on mutual trust and respect that attracts so many people who seek to come to America from all over the world.

The Collaborative Leader[1]

A collaborative leader creates an environment that nurtures mutual respect (which is necessary for making good decisions) and mutual trust (which allows those decisions to be implemented efficiently). Both elements contribute to collaboration in decision-making and cooperation in implementation. Mutual trust and respect creates the conditions for symbiosis and synergy. The Adizes Methodology is Symbergetic. It promotes a symbergetic organization (Symbergy is a combination of the words symb(iosis) and (Syn)ergetic.), led by a symbergetic leader.)

For decision-making we need colleagues. For implementation, on the other hand, we need friends. A friend is someone who shares our interests. In Hebrew a friend is a *Haver*, from the root of "to be connected," *HVR*. Since you are connected, what happens to you happens to your friend as well. Francis Bacon defined a friend as a person who halves your sorrow and doubles your happiness. By empathy. By sharing your interests. That is why we say a friend is someone you can turn your back to. They will not stab you because that would hurt them as much. Implementation is swift when working with friends, who care for each other as if they were one.

You should surround yourself at work with people who are your colleagues and at the same time your friends. They may disagree with you, but you will learn from those disagreements, and they share your interests, so those disagreements will benefit both of you. This applies also to choosing a spouse. Or a partner.

Symbergy

To predict whether a decision will be a good one, we have to determine whether it was devised by a complementary PAEI team that worked *synergetically* with mutual respect.

1. I am using the word collaborative leader as a title of this book because symbergetic leader might be too strange for readers to remember but they are synonymous.

To implement decisions, we need CAPI: coalesced authority, power, and influence. We need to build a coalition of the different interests of the different people necessary to implement the decision. Implementation is always faster if there is a perception of the existence of symbiosis. This can only happen if there is a perceived win-win climate of mutual trust.

A healthy system then is *symbergetic*: (**symb**)iotic and syn(**ergetic**). It is based on synergy that is driven by mutually respectful and complementary diversity, and symbiosis driven by common interests and based on mutual trust.

The leaders of symbergetic organizations are able to:

- Integrate the different PAEI styles for effective decision-making (the left side of the map).

- Coalesce interests, so these decisions are implemented efficiently (the right side of the map).

In PAEI the (I) role integrates the styles.

In CAPI, the "c" letter that stands for "coalesced" is another form of integration. It's the integration of *interests*.

What keeps an organization integrated and *symbergetic* overall is that both (I) and (C) perform up to par. I call this *Symbergetic Integration*.

Interestingly, this model replicates the French Revolution's slogan: *liberté, égalité, fraternité*.

Liberté is freedom of speech, which is based on mutual respect. It is the value on which the (I) role of PAEI is based. *Égalité* is the foundation for common interest, for which the (C) of CAPI is necessary. *Fraternité* is the Symbergy, it is how humanity should be: different yet together (see illustration on next page).

To integrate the different styles is not easy. They have different ways and speeds of processing information. Integrating interests is not less

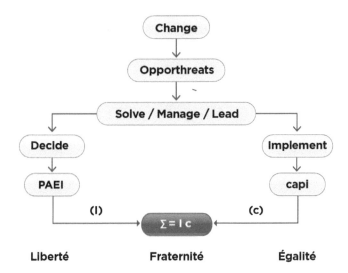

complex. The idea of a win-win climate is wonderful, but it is not easy to create and maintain a lasting win-win climate, is it? Win-win situations don't always happen, even in families, so why should they happen in an impersonal organization? The reason why win-win is not sustainable is because of change. Even if you achieve a win-win climate now, the situation will change.

So, there are actually two sources of conflict: miscommunication (because we follow different PAEI decision-making processes, which creates problems of collaboration), and divergent interests (which lead to a lack of cooperation).

So, what should we do?

There are four factors, or categories of factors, that determine whether a culture of mutual trust and respect can thrive in a given organization.

As shown on the following map on the next page, these factors (which correspond to the PAEI roles that need to be performed) are:

- Collaborative decision-*making*, (P) role

- A complementary and diversified organizational *structure*, (A) role

- Common mission, *vision*, and values, (E) role

- Leaders who command and grant *trust and respect*, (I) role

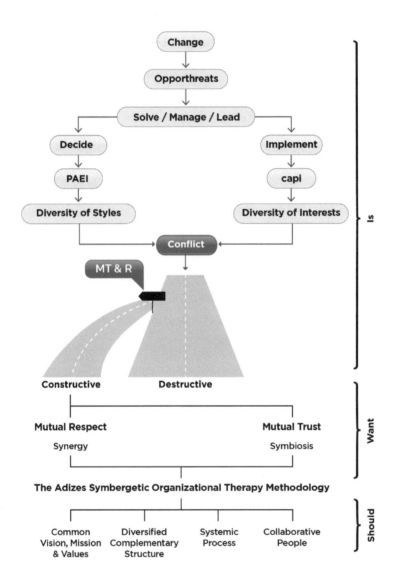

Those four factors, when accomplished, develop mutual respect first. Next, we start developing trust by developing a reward system that benefit all contributors, an outcome one of my clients, Ricardo Salinas of Mexico calls *prosperidad incluyente*, inclusive prosperity.[2]

We start with respect, although the theory says trust should be developed. If you trust the person you are interacting with, you will be open to listening to their points of disagreement and learn from them. If you suspect that the other person has a different interest, a different agenda from you, you will not be as open to listening to their disagreement.

The mistake of putting respect before trust was made by Gorbachev during the transformation of the Soviet Union. Bob Haldeman (who was chief of staff for the White House under then-President Nixon, and after the Watergate event joined the Adizes Institute) and I wrote a white paper warning Gorbachev that he was starting the transformation from the wrong end.[3] What was the mistake?

Mutual respect means an openness to hearing a diversity of opinions and honoring them. In Gorbachev's model, this practice was called *glasnost*. Mutual trust happens when there is common interest. For that, on the macro level, he wanted to restructure the economic system from the central-planned economy to a market-driven economy, and that was his *perestroika*.

Gorbachev started with glasnost and then followed it with perestroika. Respect ahead of trust.

And what happened? As he brought in political freedom, he lost political power and could not implement the perestroika for which power is necessary — and he was ousted.

---

2. As we learn from the other person, and gain knowledge we did not have — making better decisions that keep us from making a mistake — we start developing trust.
3. Ichak Adizes and H. R. Haldeman, White Paper: "Why Gorbachev Might Fail" (Santa Barbara, CA: The Adizes Institute, January 1988).

Even common language tells us that trust should precede respect As part of our vernacular we say, "mutual trust and respect" rather than "mutual respect and trust." The latter way does not roll off the tongue as easily.

A Jewish sage[4] once preached on how to behave: "*kabdehu ve hashdehu*," which translates to "respect and suspect." Respect people but always watch for the interests that hide behind all their arguments. I think he had it in the wrong sequence.

If trust should be developed first, why does the Adizes program for Organizational Transformation start with respect first?

I have trust issues because I survived the Holocaust. I struggle with trusting others, and until I solve a problem for myself, I have trouble developing it for others. Maybe one of the readers will make the transition.

To manage change well, we need to make effective decisions and implement them efficiently. For decision-making, we need a complementary team: diversity. For implementation, we need common interests. Both diversity of styles and diversity of interests generate conflict. To make the process constructive, we need mutual trust and respect.

Summary

Let's see where we are so far:

- Change causes "opporthreats": threats or opportunities, depending on how we handle them.
- Change causes disintegration that wastes energy.
- Healthy companies do not waste energy and handle change better than the unhealthy ones.

4. Talmud, *Derekh Eretz.*

- A healthy company is one that is effective and efficient in both the short and long run.

- To be effective and efficient in the short and long run, a company needs to fulfill the (PAEI) roles and have CAPI.

- To have the (PAEI) roles performed, the organization needs to be led by a complementary team.

- The diversity of styles found in a complementary team can cause conflict.

- For efficient implementation (i.e., to coalesce CAPI), there must be common interest among those with the authority to decide; those who are needed to implement the decision and thus have the power not to fully cooperate; and those who are knowledgeable about the subject and thus have influence.

- Conflict of interests is another source of conflict. This is because those with authority do not necessarily have the same interest as those with the power not to cooperate and those who have professional interest in the subject.

- Conflict of styles and interests can be destructive.

- To make conflict constructive, an organization needs a culture of mutual trust and respect.

Now we discuss how to build mutual trust and respect.

In my fifty years of experimenting in fieldwork I have developed a formula for achieving this, and it involves four factors:

1. Collaborative decision-making

2. A complementary diversified organizational structure

3. Common mission, vision and values

4. Leadership that commands and grants mutual trust and respect

Let's discuss each one of these elements.

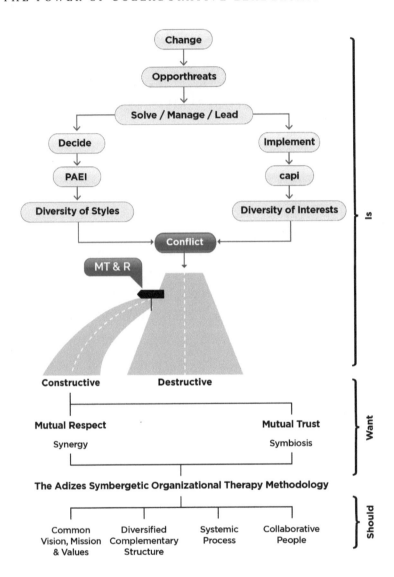

PART IV

Building Mutual Trust and Respect

CHAPTER 14

Collaborative Decision-Making

In order to decide collaboratively, we need to communicate. First, we will discuss one-on-one communication and what can go wrong and what to do to make it right. Then we will proceed to how to manage meetings, team decision-making, where there are multiple styles, the whole complementary team, and how strategies applied in one-on-one communication may not always apply to the team.

ONE-ON-ONE COMMUNICATION

One of the causes for loss of respect is bad communication. When we are not understood, or when what we say gets misinterpreted, it might annoy us to the point that we even attribute bad intentions of the recipient of our communication. We might assume that he or she does not want to understand us, and that leads to erosion in trust.

Let us first discuss what causes miscommunication and give some examples. Then let us proceed with the prescription for how we should communicate in order to avoid loss of respect and trust.

The Meaning of "Yes" and "No"

Different personality styles assign different meanings to the same word. As an example, the meaning of the words "yes," "no," and "maybe."

I remember a situation that exemplifies how a word might have different meanings to different people.

My two sons, as children, were in the kitchen, and I was eavesdropping on their conversation. One said, "they (referring to my wife and I, his parents) said "no."

"Who said 'no'?" asked the other one. "Mom or Pop?"

In other words, if it was Mom, we better listen. If it was Pop, well, we can dance around it.

In politics we need to interpret what is being said by analyzing who said it. For instance when President Trump said "yes," it had a totally different meaning than when JFK said "yes". I analyze Trump's (E) to be way much bigger than JFLKs whose (A) was bigger than Trumps. I make this judgement based on watching their style as presented in the media. Even a small change in the relative magnitude of each role changes a style.

For the (E)ntrepreneuring type, "yes" actually means "maybe" or "Hmmm, why not." They are very open-minded, and everything is possible, so *why not*? That is what their "yes" means. It is not a definite, finalized decision because (E) types change their minds frequently and without advanced notice.

How about "no"?

If an (E) says "no," it is final, final, final, and I strongly suggest not raising the issue with them again. For them "no" means "no" and it is final. Why?

They do not like to say "no" because it limits their freedom. Thus, they do not say "no" very often. Their rejection of an idea is expressed by the word "maybe." Thus, if an (E) says "maybe" he means "NO," but if he says "no," than it is a final "no" and coming back to discuss the subject will be at the requestors own risk. He may be shamefully rejected.

It is just the opposite with the (A) style. (A)s do not like change and uncertainty — or worse, a loss of control. So, for an (A)-style person to say "yes" to change is not an easy decision to make. Consequently, the first response to a request for a change is to say "no," but this "no" is a *provisional* "no" just to make the person making the recommended change understand that the (A) is in control. You might eventually get a "yes" if you can come back and support your argument well and convince him that there is minimum or no risk. Thus, the "no" of a type (A) is really a "maybe." When the (A) style however says "yes," it is a real yes! You can take the money to the bank. They are committed.

This difference in what yes and no means to different styles can be a source of stress and miscommunication. Take a marriage for instance:

An (E)-style person comes home late from work and complains about how tired he is.

"We should go on a vacation," he says.

"Do you really mean it?" his type (A) spouse asks, excitedly.

"Yes," he says.

For an (A)-style person, "yes" means a definite, black-and-white "yes!" So, she starts planning and packing.

"What are you doing?" he asks, surprised.

"You said we are going on vacation. I asked you if you meant it, and you said 'yes'."

"I did not say yes! I said, '*Yeeees*,'" he replies, saying the "yes" in a singing voice that sounds like "Why not?"

The (A) type loses all trust and probably all respect for the (E) type, deciding that the (E) type can not be trusted. The (E) type does not understand what all the commotion is about — the accusations, the put-downs.

 If you want to get a real "yes," a real commitment, from an (E)-style person, put it in writing and make him or her sign it.

Now imagine a reverse scenario. An (E) type comes home and says, "Let's go on vacation."

The (A) type says, "No, I can't."

The (E) type gets upset. "You are always negative. You won't move out of your chair. I cannot have any fun with you."

The (A) type is caught by surprise, and says,

"Why are you being so aggressive? You are always so upset and offensive. You have no respect for anyone but for yourself."

What the (E) type does not understand is that her "no" meant "Maybe, but right now I have no time for vacation. Let's talk about it and try to find a time."

For a (P)-style person, however, "yes" is "yes" and "no" is "no." These are the black-and-white people. No uncertainty. They do not understand what the (E) types and the (A) types are fighting about.

For an (I) style, everything is possible depending on how the political wind blows — "yes" is a "maybe," and "no" is a "maybe." For them there is no black and white. Everything is gray and there is always room for negotiation.

SAYS	MEANS			
Type	P	A	E	I
YES	Yes	Yes	Maybe	Maybe
NO	No	Maybe	No	Maybe

Here is an example, from the Watergate case, how words can be misinterpreted because of the style differences.

Years ago, Bob Haldeman — chief of staff at the White House during President Nixon's administration — and I diagnosed how the Watergate scandal happened, an event for which President Nixon had to resign and Haldeman went to prison. Here is the sequence of events as per my and Bob's interpretation:

Nixon said, in a typical (E) style, something like why don't we find out what the Democratic Party is up to.

Bob was a typical (PA) type who took this vague idea, this question, to mean it was a decision and ordered the person under him, Jeb Stuart Magruder — a typical (I) style — to find out what the Democratic Party was planning to do. Magruder's instructions, typical to an (I), were vague to reduce the chances that it might stir controversy which he communicated to two other (P) styles, Howard Hunt and Gordon Liddy, who both — in typical (P)-style mode — interpreted the vague instructions as "just do it" and broke into the Democratic Party headquarters and stole documents. Nixon had to resign the presidency, and Haldeman and others went to prison.

The Meaning of Silence

The (E) style often doesn't even bother to set up an appointment. The moment he has an idea, he wants to discuss it. He just shows up, impromptu, in the (A) type's office or on the phone or on WhatsApp.

But an (A)-style person hates surprises. He has his day organized, his desk organized, his files organized, and his year organized. When the unguided missile, the Entrepreneur, arrives, unannounced, he messes up the Administrator's carefully planned schedule. (A)-style people often complain that (E) styles mess up their lives.

On the way to the (A) type's office, the (E) style busily formulates plans, discards them, and formulates new plans. By the time he hits the (A) type's office, he's moving at 150 miles an hour. He hits the (A) type like a ton of bricks.

(A)-style people are slow not because they are stupid, but because they are thinking about the repercussions of the (E) style's ideas. It takes them time to process each idea. For an Administrator, listening to an Entrepreneur free-associate ideas is like drinking from a fire hose. For any single (E)-type idea there are at least ten repercussions that matter to the (A) type: *How* is this plan going to work? *What* are the details? *Who* will do it?

The Entrepreneur, however, never gets around to talking about such details. He really doesn't care about the *how* or the *when* or the *who* as much as he cares about the *why not*.

You can see that this is not going to turn out well. The Administrator can't handle the (E) type's load or the speed with which ideas flow. He is listening and is silent, which opens the door for a new kind of misunderstanding: the interpretation of silence.

For an (E), silence means agreement. If you did not agree you should have spoken up, and if you did not speak up it automatically means that you agree. In Hebrew (Jewish culture being very (E) by nature) there is even a saying that expresses this: *Shtika ke hodaya* (silence means agreement).

On the other hand, when an (A) type disagrees, his face freezes. Says no words. For an (A), silence means disagreement.

The (E) type says to the (A) type, "How about . . . ?" and expresses a revolutionary idea. The (A) type is silent. The (E) type takes the (A) type's silence for agreement. Later, if you ask the Entrepreneur, "How was the meeting?" He'll probably say, "It was fantastic! It was great! I totally convinced him. He didn't say a word."

But if you ask the Administrator, he'll tell you, "The guy's totally crazy! He's going to burn the company down! He came in here, dropped a hundred ideas, and left. I did not agree with his half-baked ideas and just let him talk. It is impossible to argue with this lunatic."

A year later the (E) type asks the (A) type what happened with the idea they discussed and that he agreed to. The (A) type says he did not agree at all. The (E) type becomes incensed. He considers the (A) type untrustworthy, a saboteur, etc. A decision was made and agreed, and it was not carried out.

The is-want-should Confusion

The three little words *is*, *want*, and *should* signify very different perspectives that create a tremendous amount of conflict and frustration in human life. Why? Because we often confuse *is* with *want* (believing that what we want is happening, although it is not); or *is* with *should*, (thinking that what should happen is happening, although it is not); and *want* with *should* (insisting that what we want should be, although it is not).

Let's define *is*, *want*, and *should*.

Is, is reality. It is what is going on right now. What you *want* is your wishful thinking and *should* is what your sense of obligation dictates.

The three words, I believe, correspond to Freud's theory of the ego (*is*), id (*want*) and superego (*should*). And — like Freud's ego, id, and superego — the *is*, *want*, and *should* are often in conflict. You *want* to eat a whole box of cookies, but you *are* overweight, and you *should* be on a diet.

That these perceptions of reality will conflict, even within a single person, is normal and actually helps us to reach decisions based on more than one perspective. What creates a problem is that people often use one word when they really mean another.

Here are some examples that I believe manifest the confusion.

"We hold these truths to be self-evident, that all men are created equal," America's founding fathers wrote in the Declaration of Independence. Let's look at that statement carefully. *Are* people, in fact, born equal, or *should* they be born equal, or do we just *want* them to be born equal?

Here's another example: for years we've heard that "America *is* the leader of the free world." Well, *is* it? *Should* it be? Do we still *want* it to be?" The answers to these questions would determine our foreign policy, yet we don't often attempt to clarify and differentiate our reality from our desires, and our desires from our obligations.

In organizations, if you sit in a meeting and listen to people talk, you'll find they continually misuse the three words. Instead of saying, "I *want* this," which sounds arrogant, they say, "We *should* do this." But if you carefully analyze their position, you will see that what is being labeled as necessary does not *have* to be done — it is not a *should* situation.

I often hear in meetings that "We *are* the leaders of our industry." Actually, they *aren't*. They just think they *should* be because they have invested enough money to become one.

Each of the four PAEI styles attaches a different meaning to the words *is, want,* and *should,* based on their own idiosyncratic worldview.

The Entrepreneur typically perceives events — and makes his decisions — through the prism of *want* and often confuses *want* with *is*: "Since I *want* it, it *is*." It is as if he believes in his own legend and sometimes in his own semi-truths.

For instance, an (E) type comes to work and says, "We *have* a million-dollar contract."

"Whoa," says the (A) type, "Where *is* the signed contract?"

"They will decide next week."

"So, we do not *have* a contract?" yells the (A) type.

"But they love it," says the (E) type. "They *want* our service."

In the meantime, the (P) style is getting emotional about how time is being wasted in meetings. "Come on, guys, *do* we have a sale or not?"

(E) types have difficulty with reality. Since they *want* it, it *is* already a reality for them. Often it is enough for them to imagine a reality, get satisfaction from just imagining it, and move on to the next project without doing much.

The Administrative style comes from the *should* direction. "Since it *should* be, it *is*." If you ask an Administrator, "Do we have a solution to this problem?" She might say, "Of course we do. We spent a million dollars on it, didn't we?" Well, perhaps it's true that we *should* have a solution because we spent a million dollars, but that's not the question. The question is, "*Do* we have a solution?"

Now, which style's perspective is this? "What is, *is*. Never mind the *want* and the *should*." That's the (P) style. He is very reality-oriented. He understands what *is*, and that's all that interests him. He is not concerned with what *should* be or what somebody might *want*. He is proud of the fact that his feet are planted solidly on the ground and that his decisions are practical, based on what *is* and not on what *isn't*.

And finally, who is continually moving around from one perception to the other? The (I) style. The (I) type is capable of understanding the differences because he doesn't have any single avenue through which he comes to reality. *Is*, *want*, and *should* are irrelevant to the (I) type. His views and his decision-making are determined by his concern for *other* people's opinions, not his own.

Let us focus now on how to communicate correctly.

On Patience, Pain, and Tolerance

On the highway of conflict, when you come to a fork in the road, where one road leads to destructive conflict and the other to constructive conflict, there is a very small sign that points in the direction of constructive conflict. Inscribed on it are these words: "mutual trust and respect." Unfortunately, the sign is so small that only people who *slow down* at this crossroad can read it. Those who speed up miss the sign and end up in destructive conflict.

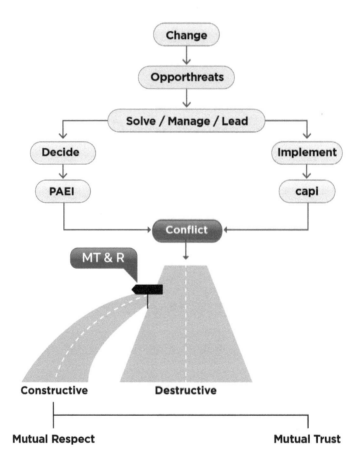

When people experience the pain of conflict, their usual tendency is to speed up the decision-making process. They start speaking faster. They raise their voices; start shouting and interrupting each other;

they pound the table; they become more entrenched in their own arguments.

The result? Destructive conflict. The more tense, angry, or strident someone's behavior, the less he will succeed to win the argument because the other party, feeling that they're being disrespected, will harden their position instead of trying to work out a compromise.

Working with the CEOs of many companies around the world, I have noticed that the best, most successful managers seem to grow increasingly relaxed as the conflict gets tougher and more difficult. From this observation, I derived my "duck theory" of management: on the surface, a duck looks calm and unperturbed as it floats along in the water; *under* the water its feet are working fast — *very* fast. In other words, a good manager stays calm in the midst of conflict. He does not lose his head or become emotional. He does not lose his objectivity. He is considerate and respectful of others, even those with whom he strongly disagrees.

In Hebrew there is an expression that sums up what I am trying to say: "Slow down so I can understand you fast." Whenever there is a conflict or misunderstanding, take a deep breath and slow down. In fact, the more pain you feel, the slower you should speak. Don't try to get *out* of it; try to get more deeply *into* it by slowing down. Take a deep, slow breath in and a slow one out. By taking slow breaths, you create the necessary condition for patience. And patience is a precondition to tolerance and tolerance is a precondition to being able to learn from someone who disagrees with you. And learning ends leads to respect.

In Hebrew, the root consonants of the word "tolerance" (*SoV- Lanut*) is "SVL." There are two other words that derive from that root: "patience" (*SaVLanut*) and "pain" (*SeVeL*). How are these three related? Think about it — tolerance cannot exist without patience. But to be tolerant of other people's opinions — and patient enough to listen to those opinions even when you strongly disagree — can be quite painful.

To develop mutual respect, leaders must learn to have patience to hear what others have to say and listen without interrupting them. With patience and tolerance of others, respect develops.

People who can listen patiently to people who disagree with them and tolerate being presented with ideas they might disagree with are, I believe, people with healthy self-esteem. One way to test if a person is material for a leadership position is to check how many times the person interrupts you when you speak. Do they have patience to listen to the end of what you say? Can they tolerate you making arguments they disagree with?

This might have implications for leadership development. Training should include a lot of opportunities for people to learn how to overcome the pain of controlling their ego and realize that someone else might have even better ideas than them.

Some companies hire MBAs right out of school and put them on a fast track to top management. These people have no experience, and have not yet learned how to take the pain of working with others who think differently. They manage numbers, the P&L, and not the people who create the P&L.

The Golden Rule of Management and Leadership

All religions — Buddhist, Jewish, Christian, Muslim — have a principle that is known in the West as the Golden Rule: "Don't do to others what you'd hate to be done to you." Its corollary "Do unto others as you would have them do unto you."

This may be a good rule in personal life but in organizations, communicating with others the way you wish they would communicate with you is definitely a mistake: If you are an (E) type and you speak to others as if they are also (E) types, unless they actually are (E) types, they are going to misunderstand you. Worse, they are probably going to resent and dislike you, and that's not very effective managing.

To manage well, you must convince others. In essence, management means selling your ideas. If you can't sell ideas, you can't manage and for sure you cannot lead.

Every salesman will tell you that to "sell" successfully you have to know your clients. If you don't know what they need and what they want, how will you be able to convince them to buy your idea?

Before you talk to people, it is important to ask yourself, "*Who* am I talking to?" When people talk to you, you have to ask yourself, "*Who* is talking to me?" Then you can correctly interpret what they are saying.

Thus, the prescription should be: "When in Rome speak Italian if you want to be understood." If you speak English, don't get upset if those Italians do not understand you. So, when you speak to a (P) style, speak in (P)-style language. Focus on the (P)-style way of processing information: fast, focused, structured, and result- and outcome-oriented.

And if you are speaking to an (E) style, do not speak about problems (which is typical of an (A) style). Speak about opportunities to improve something. It is the same thing, just packaged and communicated differently. Simply match your communication to the style of the person you're talking to.

It is equally important that you must be conscious of your own style, too. You must be able to answer the question: *Who am I?*

This question of "Who am I?" is not an easy one to answer. Many of us spend our whole lives asking this question and not finding a satisfactory answer.

Here is a simple hint for how to go about answering this question: Pay attention to the impact your behavior has on others.

When I am considering taking on a new client, I like to try to determine their style. I do this by watching their subordinates.

If they are all gofers, it's not too difficult to conclude the boss is a (P) style. If they are all silently clapping hands when he speaks, he is an (E) style. If they are informers, sharing info and rumors, he is an (I) style. If they arrive on time, leave on time, and make no waves . . . you know the answer.

One more point. The prescriptions below that address how to communicate with people who are different from us do not necessarily pertain to differences in personality — because we may not know the other person's personality. We cannot give every person we communicate with a test to identify their personality. Just watch their behavior at that moment. Watch their energy. The (E) is impatient. Not finishing a sentence and moving to a new subject before finishing the previous one. The (P) is also impatient but differently. He wants to finish the discussion. and get the hell out back to work. The (A) is phlegmatic. Slow and collected. And the (I) is very pleasant and non-confrontative.

If you don't know someone well and are not familiar with their typical working style, ask what job they perform. Look at the organizational chart — it can tell you a lot. If this person is in marketing, you can expect him to be an Entrepreneur. If he is in sales, he should be a Producer. An accountant will very likely be an Administrator. As already stated, behavior is impacted not only by personality but by the task a person performs, and also by the environment, the specific conditions of the moment.

You can also find telling clues by looking at their office, their desk, how they dress, their posture, their energy level. In other words, be sensitive to and observant of the other person. Watch their reactions to your comments and adapt your style to theirs so that you can communicate to them clearly.

The Jewish religious literature provides an interesting short cut for how to identify a personality. It says you know a person by their *coso, ciso, and caaso* (i.e., their drinking habits, how they handle pocket money, and how they behave when they get angry).

I do not think I can identify a personality by how someone drinks, but I can do so by how they handle money and how they behave when angry.

I suggest the (P) and the (E) are not as controlling of financial resource as the (A). (P) spends as needed and the (E) to fulfil his dreams. An (A), on the other hand, knows the cost of everything and the value of nothing. So, he will hoard money. An (I) will spend money to gain acceptance and popularity.

As for anger, the (P) can easily become (for a short time) a little dictator. "I do not want to discuss it anymore. Here is what I want you to do, and that is all. No more talk. Understand ?!!!"

The (A) will freeze. You can see his jaws grinding and when he says, "Never mind. It's fine," it means *You will hear from me when it suits me.* He is recording what is going on and will get back at you on his schedule. And he will keep a grudge.

The (I) will yield. Like a young tree in the wind, he will yield and make you believe he agrees with you — only to later find out that was not the case. Like the tree, he will straighten himself up and go back to the position which is most politically acceptable.

The most dangerous style when he or she gets angry is the (E). He will attack, and it could be a very vicious attack. They will attack you, your education, your personality, your appearance, religion, nationality, your mother and sister and your whole family . . . and then forget it the next day as if nothing happened. The one who will not forget is the (A). But they usually marry each other or are partners, because they are a complementary team.

Learning how to handle anger is critical for long-term relations. Discomfort should not undermine respect and trust. And this fact should be the North Star that guides all relationships.

What is important for clear communication is style or behavior in the moment. The situation in the moment might cause an (E) personality or style to behave like an (A), and if this happens you should relate to them as if they are an (A). To communicate effectively you must be present. Watch the person you are communicating with and adapt your style to fit their behavior in the moment.

Knowing whom you are talking to and how to communicate with them is essential for success in management and, I believe, life in general.

A collaborative leader, who by definition has a big (I) in their PAEI code, should be able to communicate with anyone, of any style. It is like speaking several languages.

Paei Languages

Different styles focus on different variables.

If the four styles of managers were looking out of a window, each would focus on something different. An (E) style would see the mountains and the horizon. An (A) style might only notice that the window frame was dirty. The (P) style would wonder how the window operates and how it opens and closes. And the (I) style would not be looking to the window at all. He would be looking at the other three people and wondering what they are looking at, or asking them to describe what they see.

Now, how can we communicate with people whose style is different from ours?

Look at the chart below.

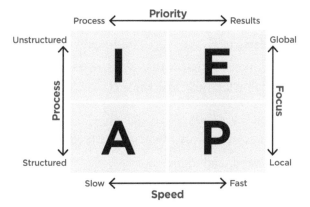

The four sides of the window give you the four variables of any individual's decision-making style: priorities, focus, speed and process. For each of those variables, there is a continuum.

On the horizontal line at the top, which measures priority, the continuum goes from being exclusively process-oriented to being exclusively task- or result-oriented. Does this manager attach more importance to the task (what we're doing and why) or to the process (who does it and how)?

Across the bottom of the window, we are measuring the speed at which people make decisions: from slow, on the left, to rapid, on the right. Some people are slow and methodical in their decision-making. A joke about Bureaucrats, for example, is that you should never tell a Bureaucrat a joke on Friday because he might burst out laughing on Sunday in church!

On the opposite end of this continuum is the Arsonist, who probably won't let you finish telling your joke. It reminds him of another joke, so he'll interrupt your joke to tell his.

The right side of the window addresses focus, from a global orientation at the top, to a local orientation at the bottom.

The left side of the window presents the last variable: the process by which people make decisions. Some managers address a problem in an unstructured way; others are structured. The unstructured type will start out talking about A, which reminds him of Z. Z reminds him of Q, which he relates to B, then to C, and finally to X. In his holistic view, everything is interrelated, thus there is no particular predetermined sequence in which the whole must be understood.

Structured thinkers are linear. They don't like to start talking about B until they fully understand A. They'll put off talking about C until B is fully understood, and so on.

Every person's typical perspective can be mapped somewhere on this chart.

The Entrepreneur (or Arsonist, depending upon how extreme his style is) has the global, or big-picture, perspective; he thinks and acts quickly and without structure; and he is result-oriented in his decision-making.

Administrators (or Bureaucrats) have a local perspective and a structured, slow-moving style focused on process and details. They pay attention to the *how*.

You will be mixing water and oil if you put these two people together to work. Their priorities are different; their speed of decision-making is different; their focus is different; the way they organize facts and draw conclusions and communicate those conclusions is different.

When an (A) type and an (E) type get together, the (E) type quickly becomes exasperated with the (A) type's incessant harping on details.

Sometimes he'll simply leave the room in the middle of a discussion. This causes the (A) type to feel ignored, abused, and abandoned. She's convinced no one cares about her problems. If she were the sort of person (she isn't) who understood and could communicate in metaphors, she might tell you she feels like she's working with a seagull. The (E) type appears from above out of nowhere, lets out a shriek, drops a shot on (A)'s boat, and disappears only to reappear later and upset why his less than half-cooked project that no one understood well is not complete yet.

The (P) and (I) styles don't like each other or get along any better than the (A) and (E) styles. Producers (or Lone Rangers) are fast, local, structured, and focused on tasks, details, and results. They are the railroad engineers. They are the ones who say, "Show me the tracks, give me the train, and get out of the way." In meetings they are the ones who interrupt the discussion to say, "Look, what do we need to do? Let's just go and do it. We have a business to run. What we *really* need is to talk less and do more."

Integrators (or SuperFollowers) are process-oriented, slow, and unstructured — which is why they are so politically astute. They have a global view; they see the big picture, and they can easily change and adapt.

Seen from this perspective, the potential conflicts are obvious. The task-oriented, quick Producer is not generally very personable or sensitive. This upsets the Integrator, who wants to slow down and pay attention to how people feel. The (I) style thinks the (P) style is an insensitive and "macho" "hatchet man," who steps all over people without regard to their feelings and needs.

The (P) type, on the other hand, thinks the (I) type is insensitive to what the *organization* needs. He perceives the (I) as weak and slow. This is not a gender issue. A woman can be a (P) type and a man can be an (I) type. In fact, I have observed a real flip-flop from traditional gender stereotypes in the United States over the last twenty years.

So, between these two types, there will often be hard feelings and a lack of mutual respect. They need each other, but at the same time they cannot work together without difficulty.

In communicating with people, keep this chart in mind. And now, here are some insights on how to work with each type of person that I have learned in my fifty years of working in the field. see Ichak Adizes: Leading the leaders op cit.

Dealing with (P) Types

A Producer is fast, doesn't have a lot of time, and is usually under pressure to deal with a crisis. He is generally highly structured and detail- and result-oriented.

Now, how does this affect his ability to communicate? And what is the communication style you should adopt to effectively connect with him?

Think about what would happen if you called a (P) type and said, "Bob, I need you for three hours to discuss a problem." Would that work? Obviously not. Your (P) style would almost certainly reply that he has so many crises he can't even tell you where he is going to be tomorrow!"

So, how much time can you realistically ask for? Five minutes. Ten minutes. Fifteen minutes at most. Try to be short. But first, you must get his attention, and to do that you will probably have to disguise your problem as a crisis rather than a mere problem — because the Producer is busy! Since he has more problems than he can solve, he deals only with crises. That means that if your problem is *not* a crisis, it's going to have to wait. He will tell you, "Put it on my desk," and you will not hear about it for some time; it will just sit there with 300 other problems he has on his desk. The ones that get attended have the squeakiest wheels. He goes for the most squeaking, which means, he goes for the crisis, and only everything else if there is any time left.

Next, when you get into his office, do not start your presentation with Adam and Eve. Start from the end instead of the beginning. In other words, first give him the bottom line. Tell him what your conclusions are. *Then* give him any supporting material he asks for and answer his questions. The most important thing is to start from the end, with the decision you have already come up with.

Next, you should tell him that you're *already working* on this problem and all you need from him is his approval: "Bob, we have a crisis, and we have very little time to deal with it, and because of that I've already come up with a solution. All I need is your approval."

Why phrase it like that? Because if there isn't any time pressure, or you are not already in the midst of implementing the solution, what will he say? "Put it on my desk."

And if you are dealing with a (P---), a Lone Ranger style, you will *really* have to take the initiative, because he's never going to delegate to you. You'll have to delegate to yourself. To avoid taking unnecessary risks, however, you'll still want him to approve what you're doing.

But imagine what would happen if you communicated this way with an (A) type. Let's say you called her and said the same thing: "There is a crisis, and I am already midway into implementing the solution." What's going to happen? You might get fired. "Who gave you the right to start implementing any solution?!" "How dare you take the initiative without getting approval first?" With an (A) type, you can't make any changes without getting permission first.

Dealing with (A) Types

What *is* her way? Well, the (A) type is more interested in the *how* than in the *what*. She confuses form with function, so you have to pay enormous attention to the form. She doesn't care if something is a crisis or not. She cares about whether or not you are following the correct procedure.

If you want to grab an (A) type's attention, you must show her that your problem is actually a violation of something that had previously been agreed upon: "A rule has been broken. We agreed, and guess what? They are not doing what we agreed upon. It's not working right." The word "right" is important.

Then, to prove the validity of your proposed solution, bring as much evidence as you can, the more, the better — with lots of details and footnotes. Show her that your solution has been tried already successfully by people or companies she looks up to, that it's been done before, and that there is no risk. Finally, end your presentation with a sentence that goes something like this: "This is my recommendation, and I take full responsibility for it."

Basically, an (A) type wants to avoid risk so you deal with her style in a way that she will feel comfortable.

How do you handle an (A) type under ordinary circumstances, in your day-to-day meetings and communications when there is no urgent matter to be dealt with? You must follow a protocol.

When you need to meet with an (A) type, always ask for an appointment. Don't surprise her. If you do, you'll lose the first half hour of the meeting because she won't be listening. She'll be obsessing about how you've caught her unprepared.

Next, use your "bias multiple," which is the term I use to measure and compensate for each style's idiosyncratic view of time. For instance, (E) and (P) styles move fast, while (A) and (I) styles can be very deliberate, even plodding, in their actions.

I have found that as an (E) type, my own bias multiple is six. When I tell my associates, "We can do this in an hour," how long does it really take? Six hours. If I tell them, "Ah, we can do that in a week," how long will it take? Six weeks.

We should perceive of an (E) type as an eagle up in the sky. With one move of his wings he can travel half a mile. In fact, the bigger the (E) style, the higher up in the clouds he will be, and the more impatient he will be with the people working for him. To cover the same distance the people on the ground, traversing that same territory might entail going up and down canyons, mountains, and rocks, and it might take them many hours. An (E) type tends to overlook that fact, which is why it's important to remember the bias multiple.

So, if you are an (E) type, and you need to meet with an (A) type for what you estimate will be half an hour, you'd better call and say, "I need a meeting with you hmmm . . . for three hours." You should calculate according to your bias multiple. An (A) type will be infuriated by a person who asks for a half-hour meeting and then stays for three hours. With an (A) type, you must ask for a specific amount of time, and you must keep to that schedule. It is always better to leave a meeting with an (A) type early, than to stay overtime.

When you schedule the appointment, you should also make sure to tell the (A) type what the agenda of the meeting is going to be so that she has time to prepare herself. And before the meeting, you should prepare *yourself* by breathing. Deep, slow, breathing. The more relaxed you are, the more slowly you'll make your presentation, and the more chance you'll have of being understood. In addition, the more relaxed you are, the better your decisions will be, because when you slow down, you can also be more observant of the person you are talking to. Watch their eyes, their eyebrows, their hand movements. Watch their body and synchronize what they say with how they say it. Body language can be the key that unlocks the meaning of what someone is trying to say. But you won't notice it if you are rushing. To become more observant, you need to slow down. And that means deep, slow breathing.

Entrepreneurs and Producers are not very good at breathing — they're always running out of breath. Why? Because they're going full speed ahead all the time. In countries like Mexico, they joke that in an argument, the first one who stops to take a breath is the loser of the argument. The most important technique for (P) and (E) styles to learn, especially when dealing with Administrators and Integrators, is to slow down.

Another reason why it's crucial to slow down to the (A) type's speed is that for every one of your ideas, she is going to think of ten or even a hundred ramifications. She needs time to process that information. *So slow down.*

Begin the meeting by telling her again what you are there to discuss. Confirm your agenda. Again, no surprises. Begin with item number one. (It's important to go in order, with the first item on your agenda broached first.)

As you present to an (A) type, it's very important to watch her eyes. When her eyes go "out to lunch," she's not listening anymore. She's thinking. What is she thinking? About the repercussions of your idea? Who is she listening to when her eyes are out to lunch? Herself. Is she listening to you? No.

What should you do while she's listening to herself? Stop talking. *Stop talking*! She is not listening to you. This is very difficult for an Entrepreneur, who cannot stop "selling" his idea, to do. But to effectively communicate with an (A) type, it's crucial to wait until she has finished processing the information you gave her before you continue and download more.

What should you do while you're quiet? If you're an (E) type, 300 new ideas will have crowded into your mind while you waited, and you'll want to say them all before you forget them. Don't. Write them on a piece of paper. You can get to them later. Once you write them down, you will immediately feel calmer because you'll know you can find them any time you want. One of the fears (E) types have is that their genius ideas will be ignored or lost. Calm down and put it in your notes. You will find and deal with it later.

Tom Moynihan, the founder of Domino Pizza, is one of the most creative executives I have worked with.[1] His (E) was somewhat controlled by his (A). He showed me a whole file cabinet with files filled with ideas. He just writes his ideas down and files them so he can stay focused. When he is ready for a new idea, he opens his files to choose which one is next.

When the (A) type comes back from processing what she heard from you, she will have a question. And what will that question be? It will be about some detail of implementation, which, especially if you are an Entrepreneur, will probably upset you. Here you are trying to save the world, and there is this (A) type asking you what time the train leaves the station.

Don't get upset. That is who she is, and you are not going to change her. Take another deep breath and then acknowledge the question: "Good question. Let me write it down." Even better, write it on a flip chart so the (A) type can see that you respect her question and are not ignoring it. Now say, "I would like to address it later, when I finish my presentation, if you don't mind, so that it can be discussed in the full context of what I am presenting." This serves two purposes: first, the (A) type will understand that you're acknowledging her concerns; second, you avoid being sidetracked. In this process the (A) type cannot veto your idea, or even argue against it. She cannot take you into a rat hole over a detail, discuss it at length, and leave no time for you to finish presenting your idea. You must not be drawn into discussing the *how* until you've communicated the *what* and the *why*.

When you finish explaining the big picture, summarize it for the (A) type, making sure she understands it, and conclude: "Now let me address your questions." Then it's time to deal with the details, one by one by one.

---

1. Thomas Monaghan and Robert Anderson, *Pizza Tiger* (New York: Random House 1986).

If you're ready with answers to the (A) type's questions then and there, go ahead and answer them. But beware — if you are not absolutely sure of your answer, it would be better to ask for time to consider. Make another appointment to come back and present your answers.

Addressing the (A) type's concerns might mean that you will have to change your original recommendation. So be it. If that is what happens, the important thing to remember is that by giving yourself extra time to reconsider the details, you avoided making some major mistake. Be thankful.

How long should you stay in a meeting with an (A)-style person? *Only the length of time that was allocated to you.* Don't say, "Ten more minutes, just ten more minutes and we'll be finished," which is what a (P) will tend to do because they need to finish. . . . The worst mistakes are usually made in the last ten minutes of an extended meeting. In the rush to the finish line you might ignore critical details.

There is one more important point to remember when communicating with an (A) type, especially if you yourself are an (E) type.

For an (E) type, numbers tend not to be meant literally. They're really only a magnitude. Thus, an (E) type might say, "We sold a million," when he really means a million *more or less* — somewhere between nine hundred thousand and a million and a quarter.

Now for an (A) type, a million is exactly a million. If it is 999,999, then it's not a million. This is a huge issue between (E) and (A) styles. It's one of the main reasons that (A) types mistrust (E) types.

(A) types are very literal-minded, so try to honor that. Be careful not to confuse ideas with facts because if you refer to something as a fact when it isn't, as soon as the (A) type catches your mistake, she won't trust you anymore. She will dismiss everything else you've said as if it has no value.

Dealing with (E) Types

It would be a waste of time to approach an Entrepreneur the way you would an Administrator — with a thirty-page report detailing a problem and its solution. An (E) type will not read your thirty-page report. He will put it on his desk and most probably never read it. President Trump actually said that he does not read any reports given to him.

Furthermore, an Entrepreneur resists any idea unless it is his own. If you walk into a meeting with an (E) type and say, "Bill, here is a problem. Here is the solution. I just need your approval" — a perfect approach for a (P) style — there is a good chance he's going to say, "Wrong problem, wrong solution." He's going to try to change it, he's going to attack it, he's going to look for a loophole, he's going to try to find out what's wrong with it. Why? Because he wants to put his stamp on it. He does not like finalized ideas that don't require his input. In fact, he feels threatened by them. For an (E) type, if you present an idea that's already finalized, it means you're charging ahead and leaving him behind, forgetting him, ignoring him, not consulting with him. He feels disrespected, and sooner or later, he's going to find a way to put you in your place.

So how should you approach an (E) type when you have a problem? First of all, don't call it a problem. An (E) type is not interested in problems. In fact, he gets annoyed when you talk about problems because solving problems is something he hired you for. Instead, figure out how to transform your presentation so the problem is presented as an opportunity. When you get to his office, instead of saying, "We have a problem," try saying, "We have an opportunity to do something better," or "We have an opportunity to change something for the better. What do you think?" Now notice, you did not lie nor manipulate because every problem, when solved, is an opportunity to improve the organization, the system. So instead of presenting the negative, "We have a problem," you present it as a positive, "We have an opportunity."

The second issue to think about is: "How do I make the solution *his* idea?" Here, it helps to use phrases such as "I suggest" or "May I suggest" or "I've been thinking" or "It appears that" or "What do you think?" instead of saying, "Here's what I think we should do." Or worse, "Here is what I think *you* should do." This is often a mistake (P) types fall into when talking to (E) types because it is how the (P) type talks.

Please note that I'm referring to communicating and handling not just the person you report to. I'm talking about the people who report to you as well. If you treat an (E)-type subordinate as a subordinate — "This is what you need to do. Here is how I want you to do it. This is when I want it done — now go do it!" — he's going to be unhappy and resentful. The reason is that you aren't giving him a chance to use his creativity. (E) types like to design the train. They even like to design the route the train is going to follow, not to just run it. So whether they are above you in the hierarchy, a peer, or a subordinate, you have to talk to them in (E)-type language: "What do you think?" "What would you suggest?" "How would you improve this?"

You know you've succeeded in selling your idea when the (E) type gets excited and says, "Yes, that's good, but what if we also . . . ?" and begins to add his own thoughts to the mix. All you need to do at that point is find a way to incorporate his ideas so that he can own the solution.

Here's another technique: explain the problem and your solution but intentionally leave an obvious detail out, at the very beginning of your presentation. An (E) type will see it immediately and correct it, and in correcting it he will feel ownership toward the solution.

In the advertising business, this is called "the hairy arm" strategy: When the storyboard is designed for a TV ad, the artist will deliberately draw excessively hairy arms on one character in the ad. The minute he sees the storyboard, the (E)-type client will notice the hairy arms, point them out, and say, "That's wrong. Fix it." This accomplishes two goals: the client feels he has contributed to the process and, thus, "owns" the result of that process; at the same time his attention has been redirected from other aspects of the project that he might have felt like changing.

Finally, how do you give an (E) type bad news?

If there is any hint in your presentation that he, the (E) type, is somehow to blame for the problem, he will attack you: "I don't know what the hell you're talking about!" "You have completely messed this up!" The key is that the bad news must not reflect badly on him.

If he denies what you're telling him, you have no choice but to retreat. If he replies, "That's interesting, but don't worry about it," trying to dismiss you, you can press a little harder: "Well, but it appears that. . . ." But be very careful, because if he interprets the bad news as making *him* look bad, he will look for a scapegoat, and you will be the most convenient target.

I find that (E) types always have someone in the penalty box — someone they accuse of not being good enough. If that person is fired or resigns, they immediately turn around and find a new scapegoat to put in the penalty box. It is as if they need someone to take the blame for the frustrations they feel over not being able to reach their ambitious goals at the speed they want.

Dealing with (I) Types

What is an Integrator, or in extreme cases a SuperFollower, looking for? His highest priority is agreement. In other words, "Is there a consensus?"

Thus, if you go to an (I) type and say, "Jack, here is the problem and here is the solution, and we want your authorization," what is he going to say? "It's not time yet, we are not ready, have you talked to Rudy, have you talked to Paul, have you talked to Denise?" He's going to want to assess the political climate before approving anything.

So, before you approach him with a problem, cover all of your bases. Talk to Rudy and Paul and Denise and Nancy and find out where they stand. Then you can go to the (I) type and say, "Jack, *we* have a problem, *we* have discussed it, *we* all agree, *we* think this is the solution, and we want your approval." The (I) type will immediately want to know: "Who are the people who agree or don't agree with this solution? And what about Joe? Did you talk to Joe?"

If Joe is very important to him, and you haven't talked to Joe, he's going to say, "Well, I just don't think we're ready yet."

If you say, "Yes, we talked to Joe and he's going to resign unless we implement this solution," then the (I) type will probably reply, "Then what are we waiting for? Let's do it."

This strategy can easily backfire if you misread the style of the person you're talking to.

Imagine that your style is one of an (I) type reporting to an (E) type. When a problem comes up, what do you do? You go and talk to all the relevant people, you resolve all the conflicts, and then you go to your (E)-style boss and say, "Bill, *we* had a problem, *we* all met, *we* all agreed what the problem is, and *we* all agreed what the solution should be. Now *we* need you to approve it."

How is the (E) type going to feel? He's probably going to think *This guy is building a revolution behind my back. He's trying to execute a coup d'état against me. They never told me about the problem, they just went into a back room and discussed it without my input. They came up with a solution, and now they're trying to force me to approve it! And this guy organized it all.* An (E)-style boss will never forgive you for solving a problem without him, and he will never forget. He might even fire you. (I) types try to build a consensus, encourage participatory management — and they end up getting fired by (E) bosses who feel threatened by that style of management. Be sure never to give an (E) a final product. There must be always a space for them to make changes and put their fingerprints on it.

Now we come to another problem. If adopting the "language" of the person we're talking to is the only way to communicate effectively, then how should we behave when we're dealing with several different styles simultaneously? How do we manage meetings?

TEAM PROBLEM-SOLVING

Definitions, Definitions, Definitions

What happens when you try to speak to several people at once, as in a meeting, where some or all the basic managerial styles are represented?

If you speak in (P)-style language, an (A) type might misunderstand it or resent it. And the same applies if you speak any other PAEI language. The problem is even further accentuated in global companies, where multiple cultures work side by side. For a German, whose style is likely to be (A), a budget is a policy that cannot be violated. For an Israeli, probably an (E), a budget is at best a guideline. For a Brit, who is often an (A) type, a delivery date is sacred. Whereas for a Mexican, mañana (tomorrow) might mean anything from next week to next year.

Trying to communicate as a team while each participant attaches different meanings to the words being spoken is like trying to play a team sport in which one player is following the rules for ping-pong, another the rules for water polo, and a third the rules for rugby. How in the world could that team ever play together, much less win a game?

Thus, it is no surprise that such meetings are very frustrating and end with misunderstandings.

In my work with organizations, I insist that we first define the terms we will use because we cannot move forward effectively until everyone understands what is being discussed, what they are being asked to agree or disagree with, and what their colleagues are saying when they make comments.

My clients often have difficulty with this protocol. The (P) types are very uncomfortable: "Oh, so we are paying you to teach us English now?"

To illustrate how essential it is to have identical understanding of what a word means, I tell them a joke about a 23-year-old man who goes to a surgeon and says he wants a castration. "Why on earth would you want to do that at your age?" the concerned doctor says.

"It is my religious conviction, and that's that," the young man replies.

So, the surgeon, reluctant to challenge the man's religious convictions, makes him sign a release form, wheels him into surgery, and castrates him.

When the young man wakes up in the recovery room, he finds another young man lying next to him.

"What are you here for?" he asks.

"For a circumcision."

"Argh!" screams our castrated young man. "*That* is what I meant to say!"

So, in a meeting when the participants give me a hard time about defining what a word means, I ask them, "Are we talking about castration or circumcision, please?"

Defining Terms: "Policies," "Rules," and "Guidelines"

Guidelines are instructions that can be ignored at will. They are the accumulation of a body of knowledge and experience, either written down or in someone's head, and whoever is supposed to implement them is free to do so or not. That's why they're called guidelines.

Rules are instructions that you can violate if conditions warrant it. When you're in the field and must decide whether to follow a rule or not, you are free to violate the rule if you judge that the situation you are looking at constitutes an exception to it. However, if you violate a rule, you must inform your superior, who will need to do damage control or might reconsider the wisdom of the rule itself and decide, "Ah, this rule really should not be a rule, it should be a guideline."

A *policy* cannot be violated without getting an approval *up front*.

There should be very few policies. That's why the biblical tradition names only Ten ((absolute) Commandments, no more, because more would be too difficult to follow. We have a hard time with even ten. There can be more rules and many guidelines, both written and un-written. But everyone in the company should know which is a policy, which is a guideline, and which is a rule. And knowing if something is a policy, a guideline, or a rule will depend solely on the style of the leader who made the decision.

In organizations led by big (E) types, they may claim a particular de-cision is a policy and threaten to fire anyone who violates it. Despite this, the (E) type may violate that very same policy the next morning. What he claims is a policy, de facto, is just a guideline.

What (A)-style leaders present as recommendations, subordinates in-terpret as policies. "You better follow this 'guideline,' or you will be in trouble" they warn each other. So, de facto, the (A)s recommendation is a policy.

A (P) style will be totally confused. If he works for an (A) style he will become paralyzed, and if he works for an (E) style he will get so frustrated that he'll lose confidence in his decisions.

Another reason to periodically review the company's regulations — and strictly label each one as a policy, rule, or guideline — is that com-panies tend to accumulate policies over time without being aware that it is happening. And when that happens, the company is getting bureaucratized by default. This happens because if a decision is made and it survives and impacts how the organization is run, over time it becomes a policy: It is like if you smoke just one cigarette and stop, it does not do too much damage, but if you continue to smoke, it becomes a habit and eventually you develop the personality of a heavy smoker. Tactical decisions that a manager made in the past, if they survive and continue to be applied, eventually become policy.

Here is an example. In a company I consulted for we were reviewing actual vs. budget, and I noted a very high number for photography (this was before the digital camera). I found this strange because the company was a food broker: they represent food and beverage companies in selling their products to supermarkets.

Research found that years ago someone took a picture of a merchandizing campaign to show the supermarket headquarters. it was a successful initiative and other salespeople copied the practice. After few years no one remembered why salesman have cameras. But they did and were taking pictures of whatever. It had become a policy that salespeople would carry cameras and document their work, but the pictures were just kept in archives, useless.

In a company, when you ask someone why they are doing something and they respond, "I do not know, but it's company policy," you have come across a tactical decision that was not reviewed and became a policy over time.

Often managers make a temporary decision but if, a year later, they want to change the decision they might have difficulty. People have built processes around this decision, and now they will have difficulty dismantling the system or practice. What the manager planted developed deep roots and pulling this tree out of the ground now will not be a simple effort.

Here is a story from the military. I could not verify if it is a true story or a military joke, but I would not be surprised if it is a true story.

At the Pentagon, one young staffer got sick and tired from the multitude of reports he had to file daily. So, out of mischief, he developed an official looking form for people to report how many cups of coffee they drank each day. His department started filling out this report and sending it to the administration. Days pass. No reaction no commentary from the administration, he put a stop to them. The joke was not working, or so he thought. But the next day he got a message: "Where are your reports on coffee consumption? Please submit immediately." And to his surprise, he discovered the report was now required from all departments

Policies and rules should have expiration dates or if they survive, over time, a policy becomes like a religion and a guideline a policy.

The difference between a young organization (behaviorally, not chronologically) and an aging one is that in a growing, flexible organization — generally speaking — everything is allowed unless specifically forbidden. In an aging, bureaucratized, inflexible organization, everything is forbidden unless specifically permitted. This happens when there are too many manuals, policies, and at a certain point the organizational culture changes, and employees start to assume that everything they want to do differently must be forbidden somewhere — and hold back in taking initiative unless it's specifically permitted. In such organizations, the written word becomes the dominant driver of behavior.

So everybody asks for permission instead of forgiveness. Eventually, the climate becomes so moribund that even when something obvious needs to be done, people are afraid to take responsibility for it, thinking, *I'd better not do this unless I get specific permission because who knows if somewhere there is a policy prohibiting it*. And if they ask permission, often it is denied because the manager who must decide is burdened by the same concern: *Why take chances?* At this point, people are no longer managing according the policy book. The policy book is managing the people.

Hard Rules

We want teamwork. Granted. But getting people with different styles and interests into the room to jointly make decisions can turn into chaos or at least a very bad experience. Actually, research shows that in committee meetings, often the decisions made by the committee are much worse than if they had been made by just one person.

How do we differentiate between decision-making by committee and decision-making by teamwork?

There are several differences:

First, a committee is not necessarily composed of participants with complementary styles.

Second difference, committees do not necessarily have CAPI, so they can turn into mere debate forums where people get frustrated making a decision they have no authority to implement. They have to recommend but who knows what will happen. . . .

Third: Committees do not necessarily have rules of conduct on how to lead the discussion in a manner that nourishes mutual trust and respect. True, there are Robert's Rules of Order,[2] but I find them insufficient to create an atmosphere of mutual trust and respect, which is necessary for creating a symbergetic environment for better decision-making and efficient implementation.

Below are some pointers on managing team problem-solving:

1. Meetings start on time. Whoever is late gets a penalty: some push-ups for each minute he was late or some money per minute — or whatever people can agree to without resentment.

2. Robert, H. *Robert's Rules of Order* (New York: Hachette, 12th edition, 2020).

2. When the penalty is exercised, all participants clap hands in appreciation.

Let me explain the reasons for rule one.

Starting on time is a way to show respect for each other. Our time is precious. Do not waste it. Imagine people show up to a meeting on time but they have to wait, maybe half an hour, for another participant to arrive — or the meeting starts anyway, but when the late one appears it is as if you are adding a new raw potato to a dish that has been cooked and is ready to be served. We have to start from the beginning to get this newcomer on board. It really annoys everyone. He might have an excuse but we can have a valid one too but we showed up on time

We also end on time, again, out of respect. Maybe some participants have other appointments. Forcing them to stay forces their body to stay, but their mind is already on the next meeting, so what is the use.

We clap hands when a person pays the penalty or does the push-ups to communicate that this is not a punishment. We appreciate the person acknowledging that they broke the rules and accepting a penalty for that.

Often when people arrive to a meeting, their body actually arrives but not their mind. It is still somewhere else, wherever they came from. Since we want the brain in the room, we need to help them bring it to the present moment. So, we start the meeting by asking everyone to briefly share how they feel about the agenda of the meeting. This forces them to bring the brain to where the body is.

In meetings (which we call sessions, to remind everyone it's not a committee meeting but a class session where we will learn something new as we solve our problems), no cellphone use is allowed. No reading or signing of papers. All papers needed for the session must be distributed in advance and read in advance. No leaving the session early, either. If someone does leave, he is barred from returning to that session. The purpose of these rules is to get the full attention of the participants.

The sessions should have a mandatory break every hour and twenty minutes, which I have found is the maximum time people can stay in a meeting and remain alert and productive.

In the session the person speaking can talk for as long as he wants to, and nobody can interrupt him or even use body language that shows impatience. Anyone who interrupts must pay a penalty, which is donated to a charity chosen by the participants.

When the person who is talking stops, that doesn't necessarily mean he's said everything he wants to say. It often means that he's processing what he's just said, running the "transcript" back to see if he's said what he actually meant to say. So, we wait. Usually he will start talking again, then stop again, think about what he has said, and resume talking again. The only person who knows whether he's said everything he wanted to say is the person who's talking. Sometimes he repeats himself three or four times. When he's truly finished, he demonstrates that he is finished by looking to the right — not to the left, but to the right.

To look to the left is effortless. That is how the clock turns. That is how, in agricultural societies, the seeds were dispersed by hand in the field. Because it is natural to turn to the left, there is a chance the speaker will do so and pass the speaking privilege to the next person before he is actually finished saying what he has to say. Only when you have stopped thinking about what you want to say, and said it as adequately as possible, should you consciously turn to the right and elect the next speaker.

The moment the speaker turns his head to the right, that's a signal for anyone else who wants to talk to raise his hand. The previous speaker then will call on the *first person to his right whose hand is raised*. He must call him by his first name.

To call on someone by their first name reduces tension and potential conflict. In contrast, for example, when you are upset with your child, you might address him by his last name: "*Mr.* Adizes, it's time to go to sleep." That is how you distance yourself and assert your authority.

If you call someone by their nickname or last name in a tense situation, you might inject a tone of voice that is condescending or a put-down, or you might be misinterpreted as injecting that tone. But the moment you call someone by their first name, the aggressive voice disappears. I do not know why, but I have now tested this in fifty-two countries, and it works. Even if you've spoken very passionately and said some very strong things, when you're ready to yield the right to give speaking privileges to the next person, if you call the person you select by their first name it will always come off in a relaxed, unemotional tone, without any animosity. It will effectively convert the atmosphere to neutral.

It's even more important that you call on the first person to your right *whose hand is lifted, not* the person who lifted their hand first. You must call the first person with a lifted hand on your right even if they lifted their hand last. That means that the people who lifted their hands earlier have to wait. Slowly, this forces them to develop patience and tolerance, and behaviorally it is interpreted as trust and respect for other people who are talking.

This method keeps the (E) type from dominating the meeting. An (E) type can, and often does, start talking before he's finalized in his head what he's going to say. (E) types interrupt others, whereas (A)-style people wait their turn. So, if there are no rules of conduct in the meeting, (A) types will never get a word in and the (E) types will look down on the (A) types for not participating — and pat themselves on the shoulder for being the smartest ones in the crowd and dominating the meeting.

We do not want that. Again. A threat to mutual respect. This rule guarantees that everybody participates.

Enforcing "hard rules" isn't easy. Some managers resent them. Knowing that, before I lay out the rules I usually initiate a group discussion: "What destroys meetings?" If you ask people why they hate meetings, they will tell you for sure that meetings are not effective because people come and go, they interrupt the flow of discussion, they do not listen, etc. I present the Adizes rules of conduct and write them on the board for everyone to see and discuss how those rules will address their concerns.

It's crucial to enforce the rules as well as the penalties. If you don't strictly enforce the penalties, people will soon lose respect for the rules — and for you.

To generate acceptance of the rules and penalties, I often take the role of being the first person to violate the rules, and I am the first one to pay the penalty. I set the example and all follow.

Sometimes there is somebody — often a (P) type — who will refuse to pay the penalty for breaking a rule. Often, he will arrive late (too much to do), and when you ask him to pay the fine or do the push-ups, he is offended: "I was *selling*, and I resent that I have to pay a penalty when I was only doing what the company needs and pays me for."

In that situation, I do not argue. I explain that if we start accepting excuses for why rules have been broken, then where will it end? And how much time will be wasted in deciding which explanations are acceptable and which are not? I simply take out my wallet and pay the fine for him or do the push-ups for him, which embarrasses him and, in my experience, ensures he won't break the rule again.

Accepting rules is especially difficult for companies in the Infant and Go-Go stages of the organizational lifecycle, when the (P) role and, thus, (P)-style managers dominate. But I have found that there is no mutual trust and no mutual respect without rules of conduct. Example: When you offend someone of a different culture unintentionally, or unconsciously, notice that you have broken a cultural rule that you did not know existed.

Once people accept the principle of hard rules that was imposed during these sessions, their respect for rules and boundaries tends to carry over into their decision-making and other situations such as their ability to adhere to budgets, follow up on decisions, and honor commitments.

Decision-Making and Paei Styles

Let us now explore how a team composed of different styles should work together in arriving at a decision they all support. There are eight steps to making a decision.

People of varying PAEI styles move differently across the eight steps: the (P) types take a decision without making it. The (E) types are continuously making and remaking their decision by nonstop changing their mind, and the (I) types look for ways to make the decision acceptable, whatever it is.

An (A) person (a detail-oriented and overly organized bureaucrat type) will start out by *accumulating* information, and when he tries to *deliberate that information,* he will think: "Ahhh, I need more information." And more information. And even more. He will see the complexity of the problem, want to do a deep analysis, and will come down with "paralysis from over analysis."

The (E) person, upon the slightest *accumulation* of information, will jump straight into *Illumination.* An (E) type may jump too prematurely into *illuminating* without really understanding what the problem is (that is, without true prior *accumulation* and *deliberation).* And if another person *accommodates* their "solution" by telling them, "Perhaps this is not the best idea. Have you thought about this or that?" instead of adapting the idea based on this new advice or suggestion, an (E) type might just move on to *another* idea. And another one. That's why, when it comes to decision-making, (E) types may have lots of ideas and *illuminations,* but people can end up confused over which decision to actually implement.

And who hates this eight-step process with a passion? That's the (P) type. She just wants to *finalize* and get out of there. "We are wasting our own time, let's do something, we can worry about this later." They jump straight to the seventh step, *Finalization.* All the previous steps are perceived as a waste of time. They just want to deal with the issue quickly and move on.

Making a decision is a creative process. Creativity requires lots of energy. It uses the brain extensively, and we know that most of the calories we consume go to operate the brain. So, one top-notch problem can exhaust you in no time. Since problem solving is exhausting and somewhat intellectually stressful or very demanding, people that cannot take intellectual pain well — usually the (P) style, they want a fast and short meeting. So, there is no defreeze (a term I will explain in the next pages) nor accommodation. It is shoot first, ask questions later.

Conflicts develop because of these differing speed preferences in the process of deciding. Arguments arise. The (A) is trying to analyze the problem or the solution thoroughly; the (E) has a series of suggestions for what to do, not analyzed in depth; and the (P) wants a decision, any decision and wants out of the room as soon as possible. And the (I) types want to make sure, often to a fault, that everyone is on board, that there is no conflict *at all* during a decision-making process, and that we all agree. They want harmony. So, they get stuck in step six, *Accommodation.*

The way to arrive at a team decision-making and taking to which all agree, the team has to advance together each step of the decision-making process. To quote the popular song, "Do not walk ahead of me, I might not follow. Do not walk behind me, I may not lead. Walk besides me and be my friend."

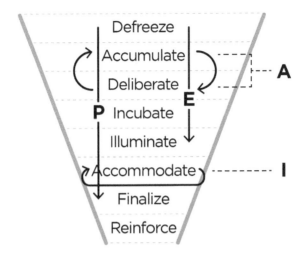

The Eight-Step Decision-Making Process

For good decision-making, we need a complementary team: The (P) type will naturally focus on reality: what is, *is*; the (E) type will provide the *want* elements of the discussion, the ambition; while the (A) type will keep reminding everyone of which rules and policies *should* be adhered to, or they will remind everyone of the details that will make or break the solution.

Integrated and motivated by the (I) style, and properly managed, a complementary team will be able to reach a strategy that is based on reality (*is*); reflects the company's goals (*want*); and also takes into account its limitations, obligations, and responsibilities (*should*).

To make a decision, the team needs to follow a process. This process is like a funnel. At the beginning there is a lot of uncertainty and we really don't have an idea what to do. Through the process and its eight distinctive steps — from *defreeze* to reinforce — we reduce the uncertainty, one step at a time, until the decision is finalized and reinforced. There is still some uncertainty left but not as much as there was when we began the process.

Interestingly, in the English language we say "decision-making." In Spanish and French, it is "decision taking," and in Hebrew it is "decision accepting." Who is right? All. But each is referring to a different part of the decision-making process. Let me explain the steps and why they are all valuable distinctions.

First Step: Defreeze

I have created the word *defreeze*. It's a word that doesn't exist in the dictionary. I am not using *unfreeze* because Kurt Levin already used it for something else.

We each have a left side to our brain and a right side to our brain.[3] We create, the (E) role, and feel, the (I) role, with the right side of our brain. When we act, we perform the (P) role, and when we logically process information, we act on the (A) role, and we do these with the left side of our brain.

We spend most of our time on the left side of our brain. When we need to make a decision, which is a creative process (EI), we need to stop the action and the activity that is happening on the left side of our brain (PA) and move to the right side (EI). This is because when we make a decision and think in terms of options and problem solving, we need the creativity of our right-side brain.

This doesn't happen automatically. It's like a train changing tracks; you have to slow down to change tracks and move from the left side to the right side where you need to be thinking and feeling.

Intuitively, you already know this. Anytime you have to make a major decision you probably go home, shut the door, mute the smartphone, and take a deep breath. Some people take off their shoes and pour a

---

3. This is at best an approximation of how the brain functions. It's simplified here to make the point.

drink. Those that light a cigarette do so, in my opinion, to take a deep breath — as if this will relax them and slow them down.

Those that can't find a quiet time during the day, safe from interruptions, will have insomnia during the night. They fall asleep but wake up soon thereafter and start thinking. What happened? When they fell asleep, they were defreezing, slowing down. And now they are awake and creatively thinking about what, why, how, etc., to do.

So when the team gets together, and absolutely on time, we sit in a semicircle. The first five minutes are used either for a meditation or each member says how they feel about the meeting we are going to have. Either of these two activities brings the mind to where the body is and slows the mind to prepare it to deal with the issues of the meeting creatively and peacefully.

Second Step: Accumulate

Now you can start accumulating information. You ask, if it is a diagnostic decision-making session, "What are all the problems we are having here?"

If it is a diagnostic session, you accumulate what the issues, the problems, are; and if it is a problem-solving session, you accumulate what your options are, etc.

Third Step: Deliberate

Once you have *accumulated*, you can start *deliberating* the information. You take all the information you have accumulated and try to narrow it down into patterns because a mind can only handle a limited amount of information at any point in time. When you have too much information, you cannot make a decision. One way to identify patterns is to organize them around the PAEI roles: the (P) role pattern — *what* are the problems; the (A) role pattern — *how* they were created; the

(E) role pattern — *when* is it happening; and last, the (I) role pattern — *who* is involved.

It is similar to a diagnosis you might receive when you visit a medical doctor and tell her you have pain. She will ask you, *"Is it* (P), sharp or dull?" *"How* (A), painful is it, from one to ten?" Then she will ask, *"When* does it happen?" (E). And her last question, if it applies, might be, "Who else in your family has had this problem?" (I)

Fourth Step: Incubate

This is where you say, "I cannot think about this anymore. I have to sleep on it." It's a sort of "catching your breath." You have exhausted yourself. You have used up all of your energy, and now you have to sleep on it. In Spanish they say, *tengo que consultar con la almohada,* "I have to consult my pillow." You need to step back from the problem a little bit. Take a little distance from it. You've been too close to it for too long. You ran out of your "mental batteries" and need to recharge.

Fifth Step: Illuminate

Then comes the stage that psychologists call the aha experience. It's like having a flash of insight that results in you realizing what the problem is or finding the solution to your problem. This has also been called the "eureka effect." You suddenly understand a previously unsolved or incomprehensible problem. All the patterns of the puzzle fall into place, and you see just *one* pattern. "That's it. That is the problem or that's the solution."

Sixth Step: Accommodate

What happens after that? You get cold feet. You say, "Yeah . . . but . . . however . . ." You accommodate. You say, "It's not exactly that, you see." Like a baby, when it's born, needs to be washed. An idea, when it is born, is the same: it needs to be worked out to make it realistic. To understand it, we have to accommodate, to think of the "why nots." This is the step where you think, "Maybe I should wait. Maybe I should try another day." This is the step minutes before tying the knot, when the groom or the bride get cold feet. That is why, I believe, in Jewish weddings they hold the groom from both sides, holding him tight, actually carrying him to the *chuppa*, the site where he will make his oath.

How should you accommodate your *illumination* and handle your "cold feet"? How can you manage this step? For that, use the QDD process, which is as follows:

In a meeting, when we finally reach an illumination, a working idea, everyone takes a piece of paper and divides it into three parts by drawing two horizontal lines across it. We label the upper part "questions," the middle part "doubts," and the lower part "disagreements."

Let me define each.

"Questions" mean you're seeking more information. "What is this?" "What is that?" "What happened to this?" "What happened to that?" "How will this work?" "How will that work?" You aren't expressing an opinion and don't necessarily have one; you're simply asking for more details.

"Doubts" mean you have all the information you need, but you're in doubt about whether you really agree, or feel comfortable, with the illumination. Here you list your concerns.

"Disagreements" mean you're not in any doubt. You disagree with the illumination.

We spell out the diagnosis or the solution in detail, and everybody writes down their questions, doubts, and disagreements in the appropriate sections of the page.

Then we gather *only* the questions — not the doubts and not the disagreements — and the group tries to answer them. Nobody feels threatened or gets upset because we've already established that a question is not a disagreement. We take the questions one by one, and we try to answer them together until they are all addressed.

As we deal with the questions, and the questions are often very legitimate, we change and adapt the proposed diagnosis or solution.

When all the questions have been answered, we again accumulate questions, doubts, and disagreements (I call it the QDD list) ignoring the previous list. What will happen is that the doubts from the previous list will move up to become questions in the new list, and the disagreements will move up to become doubts. And we start the process again. We deal only with the questions until they are all answered.

Next, we do another new QDD list, and now the original disagreements have moved up to become questions. We repeat the process until when I ask, "Any new questions?" There are none. "Any doubts?" There will be none because they have all been dealt with. "Any disagreements?" None as well.

I assume readers will find this hard to believe but working with coalition governments using the methodology I am describing here, I succeeded in resolving issues they were struggling for months and could not resolve.

On the rare occasion that we reach an impasse, I postpone the discussion until the next meeting. Usually, what happens is that after they sleep on it, the group comes back much more relaxed and much more willing to change. Time is a good healer. What people cannot agree about today, they will get used to by the time we meet next week or next month.

Seventh Step: Finalize

When we have cleared the questions, doubts, and disagreements raised in the *Accommodation* step, we are ready to *Finalize*, which means . . . to bite the bullet.

This brings us to the difference between decision-making and decision taking.

Up to now, using the previous six steps, we have been *making* the decision. Now we are ready for *taking* the decision. Moving on. Done. Finished. To finalize your decision, you must have all four imperatives addressed: *what, how, by when,* and *who.*

Sometime people jump from illumination to finalization, skipping accommodation. They accommodate after finalizing. But by then it is too late. The decision was taken. All questions, doubts, and disagreements should be done before finalizing. Otherwise, do not be surprised if you do not feel at all good about the decision you made or took.

Eighth Step: Reinforcement

So, is our decision-making process finished? The answer is no. There is one more step. To accept the decision, the people on the team must say how they feel about the decision that was finalized.

It is okay if someone feels still uncomfortable during the reinforcement step, although all QDDs were done faithfully in the accommodation step before finalization. Wait till the next session and see if the discomfort continues. If it does, treat the finalization you arrived at in the previous session as if it was not a finalization but an illumination. Re-accumulate any questions, doubts, and disagreements, and deal with them like you did before. Some decisions need long cooking before being served. The way to arrive at a team decision-making and taking to which all agree, the team has to advance together each step of the decision-making process

Let's summarize the main points for making, taking, and finalizing a decision in a team decision-making process:

- When faced with a problem, calm the team down. Defreeze. Give yourself and each member of your team some time to bring their mind to where their gut is. Avoid any rush.

- Next, the team should accumulate every aspect of the problem. No discussion. No analysis. Just an accumulation of ideas or observations.

- Now look for a pattern. If you identify more than one pattern, try to see if they create an overall pattern. Can you put them into a sequence, and does that reveal the grand pattern of the problem at hand?

- Now ask the team, "Do we have any questions, doubts, or disagreements pertaining to the illumination?"

- Answer any questions and amend the conclusion as you go along. Continue answering questions until there are none left.

- By now the team should have a defined problem and can start the same sequence for defining the solution.

Team decision-making is highly disciplined. All participative activities, not only games but even wars, have rules of conduct.

Without discipline and rules of conduct, we might jump from *accumulate* to *illuminate*, back to *accumulate*, *finalize* in haste, end up feeling bad about our decision, and then realize we have to start *illuminating* again. It is always better to practice self-restraint and advance through the decision-making process only in an organized fashion. You must finish each step *completely* before moving to the next one.

Summing It Up

Meetings can be frustrating and unproductive because of the different styles and interests of those present. It is not enough, even for a strong manager, to simply "run" a meeting according to his or her own style and expect good decisions or good follow-through. Inevitably, someone will be misunderstood and resentment, resistance, or confusion will result. When that happens, what's missing is a set of rules. Every participative endeavor must have agreed-upon rules of conduct. Without them you get either anarchy or dictatorship.

Well-functioning groups can develop their own rules for effective participation, but it's best to have a group leader who can bring order and efficiency to meetings. More important, by promoting a spirit of mutual trust and respect, the group leader can help the management team make effective decisions together.[4]

---

4. For professional training on how to integrate team problem-solving, apply to academy@adizes.com.

CHAPTER 15

Complementary Diversified Structure

So far, we have covered the first factor necessary for having a culture of mutual trust and respect: disciplined communication and a constructive decision-making process. We now move to the second factor: organizational structure.

> "Good fences make for good neighbors." — Robert Frost

We have discussed why a complementary team is necessary, but that is only part of the picture.

Staffing an organization with well-trained, well-rounded managers with complementary styles — who have no zeros in their PAEI codes, are suited to their tasks, and even work together admirably — will not necessarily make an organization well managed. That is a starting point and a necessary condition, but it is not sufficient.

The organization must be structured to attract and nurture those complementary managerial styles. In other words, we need a structure that is going to enable the PAEI functions to be performed. If a structure is designed only for the (P) and (A) roles, those with (E) and (I) styles will have no chance to perform their (E) and (I) functions.

Think of this process as a kind of organizational ecology. Organizations must be structured so that there is an environment in which the diversity of styles — (A), (E), (P), and (I) — can thrive in a way that nourishes the (P), (A), (E), and (I) subsystems. Without that essential supportive structure, even an ideal complementary team will eventually become twisted and distorted by the biases of the existing structure.

I had this insight many years ago when my second son, who is now an associate of the institute, was a small child. I had bought him a globe. He looked and looked at it and then asked, "Dad, why is the globe inclined? Why is it not this way [he put it into a horizontal position] or that way [he turned the globe into a straight vertical position]?"

"Because if the Lord had made the globe vertical or horizontal instead of inclined," I replied, "we would not have different climates."

"Imagine what would happen if the whole world were subject to one long, forever winter," I continued. "Only the polar bears would survive. If a camel wandered by mistake into this North Pole weather, it would have very few choices. It would try hard to get the hell out of there, fast, while it was still alive. Or it could die, or adapt and grow polar bear fur in a hurry."

When you look at people working for an organization that has become bureaucratized to the core, you might think you're looking at bureaucrats (polar bears), when you are really seeing camels in polar bear fur. In other words, the Bureaucrats who manage bureaucracies may actually be Entrepreneurs in their personalities, but have, somewhere along the way, given up fighting a losing war. They were hired to be Entrepreneurs, but when they came in and started learning the ropes, they discovered that the company would not change its culture to accommodate their entrepreneurial style, so they had to change their style to fit into the culture. And guess what happened? Eventually, even hard-core Entrepreneurs behave like Bureaucrats. Outside of their workplace, these managers might be very entrepreneurial. They might even have a business on the side. But when they come to work, they mirror the behavior expected in that organizational climate.

How can you get those camels in polar bear drag to start acting like camels again? Many organizational development facilitators teach Bureaucrats entrepreneurial skills experientially, by taking them on a weekend retreat. There, they practice wall climbing and falling backward into each other's arms and group creativity, etc.

But even if these managers truly want to change, even if they remain enthusiastic throughout their training, what are they going to see when they return to work on Monday? It's freezing cold and snowing all day, just as before. They retreat back into their polar bear drag. They experience a painful disillusionment. Yes, they participated in a wonderful, heartwarming weekend, but in reality, in the company culture *nothing has changed*. So, they pull on their polar bear fur and (even worse) lose all hope that change can come. The next time a change is attempted, they are not very responsive.

The only effective way to change a polar bear into a camel is to tilt the globe, to change the environment by changing the organizational structure — and that means changing the responsibility structure, creating organizational units to perform the (E) and the (I) functions — and to change the authority structure toward decentralization which encourages (E) and changes the reward system to reward taking risks.

That will change the culture and make the (E)s productive. Tilt the globe and the true camels will migrate to the Sahara and true polar bears will stay at the North Pole. This structural change should create areas that are cold and areas that are hot — every kind of animal should have a place to live and survive. There must be areas in an organization that have structured responsibility — discretion in decision-making and rewards wise — for each of the (P), (A), (E), and (I) styles. Each one of them requires a different type of responsibility, a different type of discretion in decision-making, and different type of reward structure.

To change organizational behavior — a.k.a culture — you need to change organizational structure and that involves more than just an organizational chart which defines responsibilities. You need also to design the authority structure who decides what and the reward structure who gets rewarded how and for what.

If you want to change the direction of a cruise ship, there is no use of standing on the deck, studying the map, and deciding the ship should change direction — or gently speaking to the crew about how valuable it would be to turn the ship to the left. You need to change the engine's powers.

WHY STRUCTURE MATTERS

Designing an organizational structure is unique to each company. It must take into account diverse factors such as the company's product mix and market segments; its geographical distribution; its available managerial resources; the degree of innovation it needs to generate in the marketplace; as well as its phase in the organizational lifecycle.

So, it's important to read the following chapter as no more than a basic template, a platform composed of broad strokes that should be adapted according to many variables.[1]

1. For a deeper look, see Ichak Adizes, *Managing Corporate Lifecycles: Why and How Organizations Grow Age and Die and What to Do About It* (Santa Barbara, CA: Adizes Institute Publications, 2004); and Ichak Adizes, *Mastering Change* (Santa Barbara, CA: Adizes Institute Publications, 2016). If you are interested in being

Good structure is necessary for fostering mutual trust and respect. Why? Because good structure provides boundaries, which we all need to focus our energies appropriately. Unless you know what you have to do, vs, what I have to do, where our responsibilities intersect, and where they conflict — how our jobs affect each other — we're bound to interfere with each other's decisions and create a confusion and lack of accountability.

When I come into an organization where people are accused of being interfering, micromanaging, or being "empire builders," I know that the company's managers lack a clear idea of where their job ends, and someone else's job begins.

An effective structure would set clear limits around each manager's responsibilities. Ironically, it is precisely within the narrow confines of a detailed job description that managers become free to focus their energies appropriately. When the boundaries are poorly defined, a manager cannot rely on others to carry out specific tasks — he cannot even figure out who, if anyone, is responsible for getting them done. So, he is hostage to every little detail of implementation, leaving him with less time and freedom to make decisions and act on them.

Is Restructuring always Necessary?

Sometimes it's possible to make valuable changes in an organization without redesigning its structure. If the prevailing environment is already relatively accepting of change, we can sometimes deal with issues such as motivation, strategy, vision, and information flow *without* touching the structure.

But if what you want is a paradigm shift, a change in the company's mission and direction, then a structural adjustment is crucial. Organizations are like motorboats: they have a power system, engines, etc. If

---

trained and/or certified in the methodology, please email academy@adizes.com or ltd@adizes.com.

you tell me what the engine settings are, I can tell you which direction the boat will take. To change the direction, you need to change the settings.

For example, companies that traditionally made money producing electronic devices for the military started rethinking their mission when military budgets dwindled with the end of the cold war.

Let's suppose such a company decided to venture into consumer electronics. Simply designing a new strategy would not work. Why? Because the organization's power structure was historically based on its managers' ability to produce military electronics. A change in the organization's primary mission sets up an inherent conflict of interest. Those in the company with power, who must initiate the change, are precisely the people with the most to lose when the company's direction changes, and new skills and technologies are needed. Naturally, they would obstruct any change that would shift power away from them.

In one company I counseled, they would bring in some newly minted MBA and make him a project manager in charge of consumer electronics. He would write lots of reports, plead, explain a lot, smoke a lot, cough a lot, but very little would happen. Eventually he'd leave or be fired, and they'd bring in the next victim of their ignorance, and then the next one, and the next.

The problem was that the project manager position, as it was conceived, had no clout. The MBA manager could talk as much as he liked, but he had no crew behind him to enforce his decisions. The ship's engines were going to the right. To turn the boat to the left, the company was using a very, very small engine (the newly minted MBA) that hardly could move a bicycle — much less a cruise ship — to turn it to the left.

My solution was to transfer the entire engineering group, which in this company had been under military electronics, to consumer electronics. This was a radical organizational change, which forced a shift in direction.

Now, that was not an easy thing to do. The military guys did not like it at all. Structural change is painful change. As an analogy, I sometimes describe myself as a chiropractor of organizations rather than a masseur. Why? A masseur works with your muscles; a chiropractor deals with the alignment of your bones. My task is to realign organization's bones so that it function much better, which, granted, is a much more painful process than getting a massage.

If the organization is not structured properly, you might end up placing camels at the North Pole or polar bears in the Sahara Desert. Lacking a compatible structure, you could start out with all the right people in place to create a complementary team, but eventually they will have to adapt their styles to bend to the existing structure — and that complementary team will be lost.

Elements of a Good Organizational Structure

A well-designed organizational structure contains three distinct elements:

1. the structure of responsibility
2. the structure of authority, power, and influence
3. the structure of rewards

Each of these subsystems is necessary, and together they are sufficient to provide an effective and efficient structure. Why? Because they ensure that every person can be held accountable for his role in the organization.

People often interpret being accountable and being responsible as meaning the same thing, but there is actually a big difference between the two concepts.

I define responsibility as the result a person is *expected by the organization* to deliver for the task assigned. Accountability is what people consider is reasonable to expect of them, what they feel they can be held responsible for. For that, they need to know what they are responsible for, have enough authorance to carry out that responsibility, and feel sufficiently gratified by a reward structure they believe they deserve.

It is crucial that the boundaries of each person's authority and power be defined. How far should his authority be valid? How much power can, or should, he use? (Influence, which relies on persuasion and is available to everyone, does not require boundaries.)

The third component involves structuring a system of rewards that will motivate the person to use the authority he's been given to accomplish his assigned tasks. The rewards should correspond logically with the task and also be satisfying to the particular managerial style of the individual performing that task.

To demonstrate this point, let me tell you about my experience consulting for a fast-food restaurant chain.

One day, the founder/CEO complained to me that the company lacked entrepreneurial spirit. His employees were content to just do what they were told, he said, but that was not good enough for him. He wanted people like himself, who would take initiative and help build the company.

I happened to know that this CEO was adamantly opposed to giving any ownership or profit sharing to his employees, so I asked him how he would feel about working for a straight salary.

"Absolutely not," he said, "I want equity. I want to benefit from the growth of the company I contributed to building."

"Exactly!" I responded. "Don't you see that the rewards system you've established attracts the wrong kind of people? If you want

Entrepreneurs, you have to entice them with entrepreneurial rein-forcements, otherwise they won't come to you. In fact, if you *did* man-age to hire any Entrepreneurs, they would soon leave you because what you're offering is not what they want. If you want to have lions, why do you feed them vegetables?"

Accountability, then, cannot be assumed until all three requirements have been met: the person knows what he is responsible for; he has sufficient authority, power, and/or influence to carry out those respon-sibilities; and he feels he will be adequately rewarded for doing so, with a reward that is right for his style.

Once all three criteria are met, a person can and should held account-able: they knew *what* to do, they *could* do it, and they were *rewarded appropriately* for doing it.

In this book we will cover only the principles for designing the right structure of responsibility. That is all we can do, taking into account the limitations of how long a book can be. For the structure of author-ity and rewards please apply to academy@adizes.com.

Structuring for Responsibility

This form of structuring separates long-term responsibilities — the (E) and (I) roles — from short-term responsibilities. If the (P) and (E) roles are put in the same box, most probably the (P) role will win over time, and the (E) role (instead of *driving* the (P) role) will be *driven by* the (P) role. Take a vice president for sales and marketing as an ex-ample. Marketing should perform the (E) role and sales the (P) role. When put together, marketing is reduced to sales support activity. And if you put production and engineering together, engineering will end up performing maintenance, rather than continually improving, the production system or the product.

A perfect demonstration of disastrous structuring can be found in the phenomenon of the CFO, a position that's been embraced with almost religious fervor among American industries. The treasury, investor relations, budgeting, controlling, and bookkeeping (accounting) functions all report to the CFO. In many organizations the CFO also supervises the administrative functions: the legal department, HR, and even IT.

This structure puts control of all the company's financial data in the CFO's hands. The CFO — having also all administrative roles under them as well as controlling the financial resources — has enormous power and can put the brakes on any change they find undesirable. If they are the (A) type, which is very conservative, the company might be stymied and not change fast enough because of the CFO's too powerful position.

Instead of a CFO, two people — a finance VP and a corporate controller — should report directly to the CEO. The finance VP should determine whether the company is getting a good enough return on its investment, how best to handle cash flow, and what the company should do with its money. The corporate controller's focus should be on collecting adequate and precise financial information and ensuring its integrity. Naturally, these two will be in conflict. Finance will constantly challenge the information that the corporate controller provides, and the corporate controller will disagree with how finance is interpreting the data. It is precisely through such conflict that the CEO will hear a variety of perspectives and be able to judge them for herself. CEO accountability will derive from structuring the information hierarchy to ensure that she receives dissenting information, which will enable her to judge the merits of different opinions and make decisions.

When the Tail Wags the Dog

Ideally, an organization's strategy should direct its structure. That is what Alfred Chandler taught in 1969, and it became the guiding light of all consultants: strategy precedes structure. As in the architecture example above, once an organization has set the functions it wants or must perform, it can determine the structure that will best support those objectives. If the strategy is to move to the right, for instance, then we need to change the engine settings, reducing the power on the right and increasing it on the left. That is what *should* happen, but it is not what *is* happening.

More often than not, it is the other way around: the structure determines the strategy. The frozen engines that are already set are steering the boat, regardless of how much you shout that the new strategy dictates a change in direction. Basically, the form is leading the function to behave in a certain way.

Why does this occur? One reason is that changing the power structure is extremely difficult and painful in any organization — and risky to those who initiate or support it. Some people's power positions will inevitably be challenged, and anyone who gets into that crossfire could get hurt. Any time you want to decrease power on the right and increase it on the left, the left side will be delighted, but the right side is will fight tooth and nail not to lose control. That is why Machiavelli said, "It must be remembered that there is nothing more difficult to plan, more doubtful of success, nor more dangerous to manage, than the creation of a new system. For the initiator has the enmity of all who would profit by the preservation of the old institutions, and merely lukewarm defenders in those who would gain by the new ones."

By contrast, changing strategy is relatively easy. You look at the environment, and you make a decision. The bottom line, however, is that changing the strategy — standing on the deck and shouting new instructions into the wind — is not going to change the boat's course by even one degree. The only effective way to change the direction of the boat is to change the power settings. For that you need first to unfreeze the engines. Make them willing to change first.

Designing a strategy without following up with the right structure is the equivalent of doing a rain dance in the Sahara. Unless you change the power structure — unless you tilt the globe to bring rain into your area — the desert is going to remain a desert. All this talk about process, teamwork, quality of people, vision, values — it's all useless if the power settings are stuck in one place.

How and why do those power settings get stuck? When the same process is repeated and repeated and repeated, it becomes a habit. Eventually, after more repetition, the habit becomes a form. If the form isn't regularly examined and analyzed and tweaked or changed, it becomes petrified. And when this happens, structure (form) and process (function) exchange places. In the beginning, process dictated structure. By the end, when structure becomes petrified, it takes over and impacts process.

Picture water trickling down a mountain. Slowly, gradually, it is sculpting the river trail. As it repeats itself, working deeper and deeper into the ground, it slowly becomes a canyon. At that point, it is no longer the water that influences how the river bends. It is the riversides that direct how the water flows.

> "Sow a thought, reap an action; sow an action, reap a habit; sow
> a habit, reap a character; sow a character, reap a destiny."
> — Anonymous

The Adizes program for organizational transformation always starts with relaxing the engines. Creating an environment in which the CAPI group themselves ask for change. This is done with a three-day workshop called Syndag (which stands for Synergetic Diagnosis). In the first two days of the workshop, the CAPI group is sequestered and guided through a very systematic and controlled process during which they self-diagnose where the company is on the lifecycle. They also identify which of its problems are normal vs. abnormal, until they arrive at the conclusion that the company needs to change

Thereafter there is another multi-day workshop on where the company should advance to — what is changing in the environment that calls for them to change — and thus what is their new mission, new purpose Based on that, we guide the CAPI group to redesign the company's organizational chart.

A Template for Good Structure

A structure should be customized for each company's unique goals, resources, and current phase in the corporate lifecycle. In this section a basic template is presented.

To emphasize the critical driving role for each task, I have listed only one PAEI role for each. The other roles, although not presented in the chart, must also be present, at least at a threshold level of competence. In fact, it is much better if *two* roles are performed well. For instance, marketing should ideally be (PaEi), sales (PAei), and new product development/engineering should be (PaEi).

I have oversimplified the chart shown here to emphasize a point: in order to have the diversity of styles necessary for a complementary team, you must also have a complementary structure that nourishes the right diversity. To start, let's talk about how to organize small start-up companies that cannot afford many vice presidents.

Structure for Young Companies

In a small company managed by its founder, there will probably be a salesman to do the selling or help the founder do the selling. But for what to *produce* and which markets to go after (the (E) role), as well as how much to charge, and how to promote (product, place, price, promotion — the famous "four Ps" of marketing), it is the founder who calls the shots.

The founder might hire someone to supervise *production* or assembly or operations. But who decides what technology should be used, where to locate the plant, how big the industrial park will be? Again, the founder makes these decisions for the production subsystem, performing his (E) role.

What about finance? Even if the company has a VP of finance, even if she is called the CFO, who *really* decides whether to take loans, what kind of loans, and what amount? Who woos investors? Once again, it is the founder, the CEO.

If there is a human resources department, it might have a vice president. However, this person is usually one level above a secretary and would not normally attend the executive committee meetings. As to human resources *development* (HRD on the chart), it probably does not exist.

Now, how would this structure look?

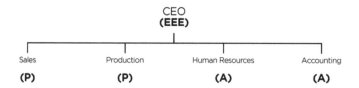

As you can see, in a start-up company the (E) role is monopolized by the founder or CEO.

The danger, which I call the "founder's trap," is that when the founder leaves or dies, the company's (E) role dies with him — and the aging of the company starts toward its demise.

In a Prime organization, where it is both flexible and controllable, the best in its health it can be, there is a complementary PAEI structure aligned with a complementary PAEI team — a marketing job with an (E)-style person; a sales jobs with a (P)-style person; an accounting job with an (A)-style person. This would be a complementary structure with a complementary team.

The structure for a Prime organization should have Marketing, Engineering, R&D, Finance, Human Resource Development — all (E) functions reporting directly to the CEO, or to the head of Development if the company is big enough to afford one, in which case the CEO is not doing as much (E) but more of the (I) function.

Also reporting to the CEO should be the COO who has all the (P) functions: production, supply chain management, service, quality assurance and control, maintenance, etc.

Last reporting to the CEO is the CAO who is in charge of the (A) functions: administration, accounting, Human Resource Management, etc.

The company should also have someone who is in charge of change management, someone who continuously handles the processes of change the company should be going through ongoingly. I strongly recommend that this function be outsourced. Managing change causes resentment and an internal agent of change will be criticized by his peers and not be able to do his or her job well. You need a trained and certified change-management expert who does not fear being fired for doing their job.

The Board's role is to (I) the (E). In other words, the board needs to integrate the entrepreneurial spirit: Where is the company going? Which companies are we going to buy? In what ways can the culture be improved? Where is the organization going, and how can we go there *together*? If the board doesn't fulfill this mission, people will predictably complain that the board not doing enough strategic planning.[2]

2. The Adizes Institute has professional certification programs, training, and organizational architects. Contact academy@adizes.com

To get a complementary team that can perform the PAEI roles well, there must be correctly diversified organizational structure staffed with the right complementary leadership styles.

STAFFING THE ORGANIZATION

Diagnosing a Style

We all have default personality styles, probably driven by physiological variables,[3] but we can perform differently, if not quite as competently, when necessary. Most people can perform all the roles if needed and when needed, although they prefer some roles better than others. I'm a (P) style when I set the table, I'm an (A) style when I'm in the office, I'm an (E) style when I'm with my clients, and I'm an (I) style when I'm with my kids. All of us have all the PAEI capabilities to some degree, but which one dominates will shift depending on the situation. Which one we prefer is determined genetically.

People often ask me if there are tests that can determine a person's style.

There *is* a test available at www.adizes.com that identifies a PAEI style. It's called the Adizes Leadership Indicators Suite (ALIS).[4] The test allows you to classify your job duties in the PAEI code and find out your preferred PAEI style to see if the two match.

Careful though.

Before you can do a good match well the PAEI personality of a candidate to the PAEI code that he will have to lead in the company, the organizational structure must be designed correctly. It is useless to

---

3. Elliot Abravanel. and Elizabeth King.: *Dr. Abravanel's Body Type Program for Health, Fitness and Nutrition* (New York: Bantam Books, Inc., 1985).
4. For more information on ALIS please visit Adizes.com

match a person to a task in a wrong structure, like in the case of hiring a VP of sales and marketing. No matter whom you hire either marketing or sales will suffer.

Leadership Style

An understanding where the organization is on the lifecycle[5] is needed to determine what should be the PAEI code of the leader.

For a start-up, you need the leader to be (PaEi). When the company is big enough and needs to be institutionalized and led by a professional manager, this calls for a (pAeI) leader who will systematize and organize a company that grew wild.

In a Prime company, when the organization is at its top of capabilities and health, the leadership should be (paEI). The (pAeI) leader, then, will either need to change their style or need to replace themselves.

Every system has a lifecycle, and that includes corporations as well as families.[6] A parent's techniques and disciplinary methods should change as they adapt to a child's growing emotional maturity. You should not parent a baby as if it is an adult, and you should not treat an adult as if he is a baby. The same applies to leading an organization.

Task Demands

Each team member should be placed in a position in which their respective style can be most useful. Finding someone whose style already fits the task will obviate the need for expensive development and permit immediate job training.

---

5. For readers who are interested in a thorough discussion of the lifecycle phases, see Adizes, I. *Managing Corporate Lifecycles: How Organizations Grow, Age, and Die.* (Santa Barbara, CA: Adizes Institute Publications, 2014).
6. See Adizes, ibid and Adizes, I. with Y. & R. Madanes. *The Power of Opposites.* (Santa Barbara, CA: Adizes Institute Publications, 2015).

So before filling any position, the first step is to do a job description and codify it into a PAEI code that will indicate the PAEI code of the personality needed for that job.

Exercise: What should be the PAEI code for:

Marketing_____.	Quality Assurance_____	Finance_____
Sales_____.	Quality Control _____.	Treasurer_____
Production_____.	Supply Chain M_____.	Marketing Res_
R&D_____.	Controller_____.	Purchasing____
Prod. Dev_____.	Project Man_____.	Audit_____
Gene Man_____.	HR_____.	Public Rel____

Most are obvious. Notice that there is a difference between Research and Development. Research should have bigger (E) and a smaller (P) than Development, assuming it conducts basic research and Development is applying the research to develop something profitable.

Notice that Quality Assurance is to (E) the (A), to develop the system of quality control. Quality control is to (A) the (P), accept or reject the output.

Project Management depends where is the project in the lifecycle. It is similar to being a General Manager. As the project or the unit being managed matures, so must the style of the Product Manager.

Audit is similar to Quality Assurance and Control. An audit needs to be designed and executed. Preferably, this will be handled by two different units: one to design. the other to execute. The required styles of each are different. We can say the same for the IT department. Here we might need a whole slate of styles: The system designers are the (E) of the (A); those running the systems need lots of (P); and those that audit the system need yet another style, and on it goes . . .

One more example: Public Relations is different from Advertising: Advertising needs to (E) their (P), while Public Relations needs to (I) their (P)."Finance

> *I differentiate between finance and accounting. Finance should look into the future toward the coming financial needs of the company: what cash flow and what resources will be necessary so the company can finance what it wants to do?*

The clients of the finance department are those who have invested in the company. The company works to give those who took the risk and gave the company their financial resources a return on their investment. The finance department's responsibilities include overseeing investor relations, relations with banks and the investment community, and the analysis of financial results. Its main functions are planning the company's financial needs (E), and ROI as the (P) output Finance should be free to challenge marketing and new product development by asking whether the new product is worth the investment. The (A) and (I) roles are less important here. Its code, therefore, should be (PaEi).

Accounting - Controller

While finance is looking into the future, accounting has to look from the past into the present and supply financial reports, provide a picture of the financial flow from the past to the present day, and inform leadership the value of the company as of a certain date (and how it was created or lost). Accounting concerns itself with accuracy and following the rules; in other words: its function is, first and foremost, an enormous (A); and its (P) is to satisfy the needs of those who request the information.

There are accounting departments that are only (A), and they will give you a very accurate report, but it will be totally useless.

A story: A small firm was going to hire an accountant. Three people showed up for an interview, and each was asked the same question.

The first candidate was a young graduate with a brand-new degree. When they asked him, "What is two plus two?" he said. "Four, absolutely, without question." People without experience are usually very confident and self-assured.

The second candidate came from a large accounting firm. His answer was, "I'll have to call the home office first." The larger the company you work for, the less discretionary authority you have, so this *apparatchik* would not take any chances. He wanted to follow company policy and be safe.

The third person had a lot of street experience and came from the school of hard knocks. When he was asked, "What is two plus two?" he answered, "It depends. Are you buying or are you selling?" Accounting should be (A) for (P) and the (P) is to give information and not just data.

Information is data organized for making decisions. The accounting department should be able to give you information, not just data that you are not sure how to interpret. Accounting should be able to organize the data for those that need information so that they can make decisions. The department's job is not only to collect information for the IRS. Accounting should be able to tell production, for example, what it costs to produce each of its products or services.

The code for accounting should be (pAei), with the (E) role in the third place and the (I) role last — a style that many nicknamed the "pain in the neck". Whenever you try to make strategic changes, a good accountant should show you where the costs are and why you should be careful. On the other hand, if you do not often initiate change, the same accountant should challenge your propensity for staying in place, which could do damage to the company over time. Basically, a good accountant is a good contrarian.

Human Resources

I differentiate between human resources *administration* and human resources development (HDR), which is charged with developing *new* capabilities. Most human resources departments are now called human talent. They were once called personnel, but their name was changed because personnel made the department seem boring and maintenance-oriented. Human resources implied some kind of exploitative connotation, and capital seemed good, but now the competition is for talent — how to find it, nourish it, and keep it. Thus, the new name. Human talent, however, doesn't change the fact that companies continue to need human resources *administrations* for better *performance*, such as performance reviews and training for its people. So, I code human resources administration as (PAei).

There is a new need that is emerging, known as *change management*, which in my judgement is erroneously assigned to the human talent department. Could you see managing change assigned to a (PA) department? The human resources department — or whatever the company choses to call it — wants peace and not the turbulence that change causes.

If you want to see frustrated people — people who are hardly ever recognized for their contribution and value to the company, people who are politically astute, i.e., paying attention to the political currents and adapting to them — look at the people in human resources. Although the department is called HRD which is what its members were trained in (EI), they in fact are doing *administration*. The fact is that many of them are not trusted inside the organization. They talk like (I)s but function as (A)s. They promote teamwork but they are the ones given the task of firing a person. For human resources *administration*, I recommend hiring a person whose background is in labor law. And in parallel, place someone from Human Resources Development in charge of leadership development (not job training, that is for the Human Resources Administration department) and also change management and/or culture change.

My belief is that change management should be outsourced. It is a profession, and it requires professionals who are not bound to follow in company politics. When a person in charge of managing company change is an employee and a member of the company's team — seeing his colleagues daily in meetings and in the corridor — he or she cannot implement strategic changes in the company because they will be subject to rejection and political pressures. Even the best heart surgeon cannot operate on his or her own family, and no psychologist or psychiatrist will provide services to his family or close friends. The style expected here is (paEI), if it is to be done well, not (PaEi). Successful change should be participative.[7]

The tasks of the production department are assembly, manufacturing, and other operations. Their client is the sales department, and what do the salespeople want? They want the product (or service), on time, at the quality and quantity that was agreed upon. That is the (P) role: what are you going to *produce* for me? The next priority for them is the (A) role: they want to *produce* the product for the least possible expense, with no waste.

Naturally, for the department to run smoothly, its manager must ensure that people work together, which is the (I) role. So (I) would be the third priority. There is typically the least amount of focus on the (E) orientation, change, and innovation. The reason is that to achieve results, many variables must be kept under control for extended periods of time. So those who work in production typically resent changes, which require painful adaptations on their part. The focus is on effective and efficient operations, and the expected role to be performed is (PAei).

7. If you are interested in being trained and/or certified in the methodology, email academy@adizes.com or ltd@adizes.com.

Engineering

In engineering, the four roles have the following sequence: The (E), creativity of engineering is directed toward (P)roducing results — whether that involves creating new products (if we are talking about new product development engineering), designing new processes (new process engineering), or searching for disruptive technologies not yet commercialized (new technology).

The (I) role is important, but not so important that it is allowed to interfere with the (E) or (P) roles. And the (A) role, which hinders creativity and replaces it with routine, is the least significant of all.

R&D

When R&D is lumped with production/manufacturing under the same vice president, the (E) role will be lost. R&D should be (E)-oriented, of course, while production/manufacturing is focused on the (P) role. When thrown in with (P), R&D's priorities will be crushed by the (P) urgencies. Instead of doing some real disruptive research, they will end up doing continuous improvement and calling it research.

Similarly, if engineering and production are combined, the engineering department will end up doing maintenance work for production. The (E) role will be sacrificed for the benefit of the short-term (P) role.

Marketing vs Sales

You rarely find a "vice president for marketing and sales." It is invariably the other way around: "vice president for sales and marketing." This is not happenstance.

Let us codify marketing in PAEI terms. First, it must analyze what changes are likely to occur in the market over the long run. That is the (E) role. Then, it has to recommend a course of action for the company in response to those changes, the (P) role. The marketing department must also have some (A) and (I) abilities so it will work well with other departments, but those roles can be met at the threshold level only. So, the PAEI code for marketing is (PaEi).

Now, how about sales? Above all, the sales department must see to it that sales happen, that revenues come in, that clients are satisfied. That is the (P) role.

Second, these sales efforts had better be efficient. We want maximum bucks for minimum bang. This requires training and allocation of sales territories, which is the (A) role.

The sales department's code then is (Paei): results-oriented and efficient.

In marketing, where the most important role is (E), the focus is on the long run. For sales it's (P), which has a short-run perspective.

Herbert Simon and James March pointed out many years ago in their book *Organizations*,[8] that short-term orientation always squeezes out long-term orientation. It's human nature, after all, for the expedient to squeeze out the significant.

When you have a VP for sales and marketing, he is very likely to be sales-focused, and the marketing staff will be consigned to doing sales-support activities such as analyzing which products were sold and measuring how many more were sold compared to previous years. Instead of analyzing and driving what changes the company should make in its product line and market segments, the marketing department just follows along, measuring the effectiveness and efficiency of the sales effort already in use.

8. James G. March and Herbert A. Simon, *Organizations* (New York: John Wiley and Sons, 1993).

Discretion in Decision-Making

The higher a person ascends in a hierarchical organization, the more power, authority, and influence he is expected to have, and therefore, the more discretion in decision-making he *should* have.

On the other hand, if the organization is relatively decentralized, some of that decision-making discretion will be granted to lower levels of the organization.

Thus, in two organizations, where one is centralized and the other is decentralized, the same task will require two different styles of management. The more decentralized an organization, the more initiative it will expect and the greater its (E) and (I) roles should be.

Needs

Each of the styles has certain psychological needs that must be met in order to have job satisfaction. Intuitively, we would not expect someone who is very comfortable in his accounting job to be excited about a transfer into sales, or vice versa. A Producer, who likes functional involvement, will resent the time he spends on administration. This is a complaint frequently made by people who have been promoted to administrative jobs from positions in which they were expected to produce. For example, there are many artistic directors who would much prefer to direct productions themselves instead of engaging others to do it. Senior architects may suffer at having to Administer, solicit new projects, and motivate others to do the designing that they would love to do themselves. Becoming the chairperson of a university department can be personally costly to those who love research. On the other hand, there are those department chairs in academia who love Administration and have a difficult time getting back to research and publishing.

PAEI styles have different needs but the predominant need for each style, I believe is:

- Need to achieve_____(P)
- Need to control_____(A)
- Need to affiliate_____(I)
- Need to self-actualize_(E)

THE UBIQUITOUSNESS OF THE PAEI ROLES

It's important to understand that the roles within PAEI — P, A, E, and I — each requires *their own PAEI* to function properly and stay balanced. In other words, each PAEI system has its own PAEI subsystem. Each of these subsystems, in turn, has its own subsystems and sub-subsystems.

Each P A E I system has it's own P A E I subsystem

For example, within a company the marketing department provides the (E) role: analyzing future trends. To do the (E) role well, the (P) role is needed to write the reports and conduct the research, and the (A) role is needed to keep (E) organized and deliver the output on time and accurately. And (E) needs to (E) its (E) role; in other words, it needs to consider how to improve its function from time to time.

According to Marilyn Monk,[9] every subsystem always serves a bigger system. This holds true for unicellular organisms like the amoeba to multicellular ones, like humans.

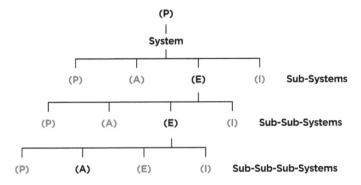

Accordingly, marketing should be made up mostly of (E) personalities, but not only (E). Too much (E) style brings lots of ideas, but nothing will happen without a (P)roducing-style focus. Furthermore, ideas and implementation will run amok if (A) is lacking, which may cause collateral damage rather than add value.

We should codify the desired style of the head of the department, but in large companies that can afford it, we should staff the remaining roles, too.

PAEI can also be applied when seeking to understand why and how organizations grow, age, and die because the PAEI roles develop over time and in a predictable manner.[10]

9. Marilyn Monk, "A Hierarchy of Consciousness," *Heartfulness* magazine, February 2020, 57–66, https://www.heartfulnessmagazine.com/issue/heartfulness-emagazine-february-2020/.
10. Adizes, *Managing Corporate Lifecycles. Op cit*

CHAPTER 16

People

In the prior chapters we learned that to cultivate a culture of mutual trust and respect, we must have disciplined communication and a constructive decision-making process (first factor) and a correctly diversified organizational structure (second factor). We now move to the third required factor: *people.* This factor focuses not on the organization and its processes, but on the humans who run it and the culture that they themselves create and operate within

What kind of people do we want? Those who will command and grant mutual trust and respect. And what should we do with a person who works for us but who does not grant nor command trust and respect? The usual answer I get is, "Fire him!" I disagree. Instead, I say, "Recommend that person to your competition." Why should you be the only one to suffer? As the competition gets entangled in the internal intrigues and fights that this kind of person will start, as they turn their energies inward, you can take their market away.

What should you do with a person who is extremely knowledgeable, such as an indispensable engineer, but who trusts no one and shows no respect for anyone. He demands respect but does not grant it. (There are many geniuses like this.) You should treat them like monkeys: You keep them in their cages, and whenever you need information, you give them a banana and extract the information. But you don't let them out into the corridors, and you never promote them to a managerial position. They are not managers — they never can and never *should* be managers. They are only there to provide the professional know-how that you need in order to manage. Call them whatever their expertise is: Chief Technology Officer, Chief Innovation Officer, Chief Evangelist, Chief . . . what they are called is not critical. What is critical is that they manage no one because they hardly can manage themselves.

Producing a culture of mutual trust and respect goes beyond hiring people we trust, respect, and can learn from. It is like cooking a gourmet dish — it takes more than just outstanding ingredients. You can destroy a dish despite having excellent ingredients if you do not know how to cook them together. Bringing the right ingredients together and knowing how to combine them is the role of the leader.

THE ROLE OF COLLABORATIVE LEADERSHIP

Having a complementary team does not mean all are equal. Someone has to lead.

Is the character of a team leader substantially different from the rest of the team? I suggest that it is not. All good managers should command and grant mutual respect and trust. If they cannot, they should not be on a complementary team to begin with.

But how do you get divergent personalities to effectively communicate and ultimately come together around important decisions? That is the leader's role. A leader, then, is a person who not only excels at certain roles but is also energized by the process of collaborative decision-making. He can build a climate — a system of shared vision and values — that encourages everyone to work together so that no one is indispensable, change the consciousness of the organization from mechanistic to organic, and turn individual *entrepreneurship* into group *entrepreneurship*.

Thus, to identify the leaders, or those with the potential to become leaders, in our organizations, there are certain qualities we should be looking for.

Leadership is Being a Thumb

The best things in life are sometimes discovered in their absence. You don't know the value of love until you don't have it. You can't realize the value of health until you've been sick. You don't know the value of democracy until you've lived under a dictatorship.

A good leader may also be revealed by what happens — or doesn't happen — in her absence. That's when her staff notices that everything is running as if she's around, even though she is not. As Ralph Ablon has said, "A good manager creates an environment in which the most desirable thing will most probably happen."

Many people visualize leadership as a pointing finger. "Do this, do that!" My view is that a complementary team is like a hand composed of fingers of different lengths and capabilities, and its leader is like a thumb: the only finger that "works" with any or all of them, enabling them all to perform as a hand.

The difference between good management and the next level, leadership, is that a leader must excel in at least two of the managerial roles, one of which must be (I)ntegrating. Without that ability to *integrate*, which enables four fingers to perform like a hand, there can be no teamwork.

Understanding that no one can be the ideal, perfect manager who excels in all PAEI roles as described in management school textbooks, what general characteristics should we be looking for instead?

A good member of a complementary leadership team sees herself as a servant. She's there to serve the organization so that the people that comprise it can get their job done. She creates an environment in which people can shine.

And a good leader assumes that her people are doing their best. As K. H. Blanchard said, "Catch them doing it right. Don't catch them doing it wrong. Reinforce the positive." If someone is not doing his best, a leader will sense that, figure out what is blocking his capabilities, and help him to improve. If that proves to be impossible, a leader will find another place for that person to work that better fits his capabilities and style. Eventually, with the help of the leader, that person will shine somewhere.

A good leader comes from the University of Hard Knocks and has experience that includes failures. But I suggest that winners are those who do not accept the failures.

Success is not how infrequently you fall but how fast you get up. As the late Mary Kay Ash said when she was asked the secret of her success, "Do you want to see the scars on my knees?"

Elon Musk went almost broke twice in his career. He was asked, "Did you ever think to quit?" His answer was, "Never!"

Show me a person who knows how to lose and come out a winner (by acquiring some wisdom in the process), and I will show you a good leader because the road to heaven is through hell. That person knows her weaknesses and has learned to be humble. She's learned to seek the assistance and support of others.

A good leader creates an environment in which the most desirable outcome will probably happen. She *integrates*. She is a thumb, not only a pointing finger.

I am aware that many of the attributes I ascribe to a leader are traditionally thought to be feminine rather than masculine traits. The role of the Integrator in a complementary team is analogous to that of one parent — usually the mother — in a family. What makes a house a home if not the feminine energy? What integrates a family, with its multiple needs and personalities, into a cohesive entity if not the feminine energy? But please notice I did not say "a woman" or "a man" because the so-called feminine energies can be possessed by either.

"A leader is best
When people barely know that he exists;
Not so good when people obey and acclaim him;
Worst when they despise him.
Fail to honor people,
They fail to honor you.
But of a good leader, who talks little,
When his work is done, his aim fulfilled,
They will all say, "We did this ourselves." — Lao Tzu

Can the elements of good team leadership be broken down and generalized? In working with leaders of organizations all over the world, I have found that good leaders do have certain characteristics in common:

Self-Awareness

Most people do not know themselves. All of us tend to be a bit deluded about ourselves, believing that we are excellent Producers, fine Administrators, creative Entrepreneurs, and good at being Integrators. We rarely have an accurate picture of ourselves. We are either favorably or unfavorably biased toward ourselves.

A collaborative leader must be aware of what he is doing, aware of his style, his PAEI code. Can you monitor yourself the way you monitor others? It may sound simple, but it isn't. When I describe mismanagement styles in my lectures, people in the audience laugh because they immediately start identifying their bosses, their peers, their subordinates. They say, "Bob is a big (P)," or "Lucille is a big (A)," etc.

But when they try to categorize their own style, it's more difficult. Why? Because most people are not aware of how they behave. "It takes two to know one," as the social scientist Gregory Bateson once said. Being aware means being cognizant of your and other people's reactions and emotions. Can you *feel* what is going on?

At the Adizes Institute Anna Gurariy developed a program to teach PAEI in kindergarten classes.[1] The children became aware of when they were in the (P), (A), (E), or (I) modes. They became aware of their style.

Consciousness

What is the difference between being aware and being conscious? They are not synonyms. Consciousness, to me, means, "I am aware of the *consequences* and *meaning* of what I am aware of. I understand cause and effect. I am cognizant of my effect on others — the impact *my* behavior has on *other people's* behavior."

You might think that you are a wonderful Integrator what counts is not how *you* feel but *how you make others feel.*

One way to be conscious of your behavior and its effects is to watch how people react to your words and actions.

But that is not as simple as just *seeing* what happens; you have to *notice* it, *understand* it, and *evaluate* it. This requires, first of all, that you have the ability to intuit other people's feelings by observing their body language and behavior, their words, and their silences.

Second, you must be conscious enough of what you have said and done, and how it might have been experienced.

1. For more information, contact info@adizes.com

For example, let us say you are a big (P)-style manager, and you tend to order people around very brusquely when you're tense. After an episode of that kind, it wouldn't do you much good to notice that your staff people seem angry or subdued — *unless* you are also aware that you behaved brusquely and might have hurt some feelings.

None of this is simple. This is multitasking in the inscrutable arena of human relations, where knowing all the facts does not necessarily make you wise.

But this awareness beyond yourself of the meaning and impact of what you do is part of what defines us as human beings. Have you ever seen an animal build a temple or worship a god or make symbols? We are the only living creatures who assign meaning to symbols. We even die and kill for symbols. Animals are aware, but they do not attempt to construct a bigger picture, to derive meaning from their acquired knowledge. Humans do so with our consciousness, which goes beyond awareness.

In order to be conscious, you have to be *integrated* in the world and understand that there is a larger meaning beyond yourself. There must be an intention behind your actions, a purpose for what you do that transcends yourself.

Awareness is short-term; consciousness is long-term. Unless you are conscious, you will not try to build a learning environment, you will not try to be tolerant or patient. You will just do whatever you want to do because you're not thinking beyond yourself and your short-term desires.

We are what we do to others; we are how we behave. This existentialist, behavioral approach implies that to know ourselves, we must realize what effect we have on others. We can do this best if we are open enough to hear and accept what people have to say about us — even if what they say is inconsistent with our own beliefs about ourselves.

Can you see yourself through the eyes of others? If you really want to know who you are, go ask your subordinates. They know who you are. If you cannot bring yourself to ask, or you cannot credit what people tell you when you *do* ask, you're almost certainly going to be living with some illusions about yourself. (Be careful, though, whom you ask. Some have their own problems, and they will load them onto you. So, instead of being an honest mirror they will show you a badly screwed and twisted window. Ignore them.)

A conscious leader knows how his style affects the team as a whole. Thus, being conscious, means you must first hear and then *listen* to and *feel* what you hear — rather than just hearing without listening, or listening without feeling. This brings me to a personal story:

Many years ago, I was lecturing in Mexico, speaking in English with a simultaneous translation. And I was getting tired of the simultaneous translation because the audience always laughed at my jokes a minute or two after I said the punch line; it was all out of sync. So, I asked them whether they would mind if I spoke to them in fifteenth-century Spanish, or Ladino, which, as a Sephardic Jew, I had spoken as a child. (It was the only language in which my grandmother and I could communicate. We were the descendants of the Jewish people who were expelled from Spain in 1492 for refusing to convert to Christianity, who kept the language of that time for over five hundred years.) The audience agreed.

So, I began speaking in Ladino and something very interesting happened. At a certain point when I asked them, in fifteenth-century Spanish, "Did you hear me?" they looked as if they did not understand me. So, I asked them in English, "What did I say? You seem confused?"

"Well, you asked us if we *feel* you."

"No, no, no, no," I said. "I did not ask you if you *feel* me, I asked you if you can *hear* me."

And they said, "Oh no, the word 'to hear' in modern Spanish is *es-cuchar*, and you were using the word *sentir*, which is 'to feel.'" (It's interesting, however, that in modern Spanish the source of the word remains: a person who is hard of hearing is called *"mal de sentido."*)

I had a big illumination. Five hundred years ago, the verbs "to feel," "to hear," and "to listen" were one and the same word: *sentir*. It really meant "to sense." (That is why in languages that developed from the same root, the word *sentir* today has different meanings. In Spanish it means "to feel," in Italian "to hear," in French "to smell.")

What has civilization, development, and sophistication brought us? Three words instead of one. Now I can hear and not listen: *"I heard you!"* (but I did not listen to what you said). I can repeat every word of what was said (but it went in one ear and out the other). Nothing was absorbed because I did not *listen*. Then there is the next level of disintegration, in which a person listens to what he hears but he does not *feel* it.

Five hundred years ago, people *felt* what they were saying to each other; they were more in touch with each other. Life was more primitive but more connected. My dog, for instance, can hear, listen, and feel me just by smelling me. When I come home, it senses whether I am in the mood to play or if I am so upset that he'd better keep out of the way. I do not have to say a word. He *feels* me.

With some people, on the other hand, it might take time and effort for them to make the transition from hearing to listening and finally to feeling what I want to say. The modern world with its rapid change has caused disintegration, disengagement, separation, tuning out. It is much more difficult to communicate.

Here is another example. One day I was in Chicago, driving a rental car from a client's office to the airport. There was a blizzard outside, and it was freezing.

Of course, I did not feel the cold. I was in a heated car. I was an inch or two from a freezing situation, yet I felt none of it.

This is emblematic of the new, bold world we live in. The person working for us may be falling apart emotionally, but we do not feel it.

So, in essence, what I am saying is that a good leader has to *feel*, not just think and analyze and rationalize. He must try to understand less in his head and more in his heart.[2]

What makes you a good manager or leader is not what you know, but what you *are*. What you know gets obsolete over time. What you are is forever. Thus:

> *It is easier to hire a person who IS,*
> *and teach him to know,*
> *than to hire someone who knows*
> *and teach him to BE.*
> *Ichak Adizes*

Well-Rounded: No Zeros in the Paei Code

Every manager and leader has their strengths and weaknesses. In other words, they are human. There are no perfect PAEI managers, and it is useless to go looking for one.

On the other hand, a manager who has any blanks, or zeros, in his code is doomed to be a mismanager. Each zero signifies a blind spot in his perspective, which leaves him unable to properly fit any position. It is as if he is a pilot who must distinguish among different-colored signals, and yet he is colorblind.

---

2. In other words, leaders need to possess not only good mental and analytical abilities, but also emotional intelligence. According to Daniel Goleman, emotional intelligence is the capability to manage feelings so that those feelings are expressed appropriately and effectively, as well as the ability to understand other's emotions and empathize.

What would happen if you were missing one of the four roles but had a surplus of another? Could you make up for your lack of the (E) role, for example, by throwing lots of extra (P) style into the mix? No, because (P)'s ability to contribute to the totality is limited by the deficiency of the other roles, all of which are necessary for the team. You can carry that (P) role only so far, and how far depends on the deficiency of the other letters.

This same principle can be seen in chemistry, in the concept of limiting regions: If the reaction mixture contains one of the reactants in greater quantity than is required by the equation, the excess reagent simply does not react. The quantities of the products obtained are determined by the reagent(s) not in excess.

If a manager has no competence in, or understanding of, a particular role, then his collaboration with the person whose major task it is to perform that role, might be not be optimal. If you are blind to the hardships of the (A) role, on what basis can you learn to respect an (A)-style person? But if you can perform each one of the (A) person's tasks, at least minimally, then you can appreciate what the (A) style excels in, and probably the (A)-style person.

Knows Strengths and Weaknesses, Knows his Uniqueness

It is important to have a balanced view of yourself. Some people only identify their strengths while denying their weaknesses. Some magnify their weaknesses and underestimate their strengths.

A balanced view means, "I know what I'm good at; I know what I'm weak at. I don't overestimate my strengths and underestimate my weaknesses, and I don't underestimate my strengths and overestimate my weaknesses. I'm aware of both and I am also aware that I am unique in my strengths and weaknesses."

Why are you unique? Because if you take the PAEI roles and score each one from zero to one hundred, you will get more permutations than there are people on this globe. We are all alike, and we are all different at the same time. There are no two people who are the same. There is nobody like you, nobody in the whole world.

How do we reach an understanding of our unique capabilities and limitations? By being in regular communication with others, by being open to the assessments that others make of us. In these ways we can help determine our place as managers on the PAEI map.

This knowledge is particularly important for working well in a team. You must know who you are so that you can find out what kind of people you'll need to complement yourself.

Accepts Strengths, Weaknesses, and Uniqueness

A collaborative leader knows his weaknesses and his strengths, but he also accepts them.

Accepting oneself does not come from taking tests. It is part of becoming mature. An adolescent may act out his dreams, but adults accept reality. As adults, we know our limitations and like ourselves despite them.

Accepting oneself does not mean giving up any effort to improve. Acknowledging that I will never be a perfect PAEI leader doesn't mean I should fatalistically accept all my flaws and give up the hope of learning to be better.

The question is better in what?

Usually, people try to improve and remove their weaknesses.

That is not the equivalent to accepting oneself.

One has to learn to live with their weaknesses. If the weakness is dysfunctional, meaning it interrupts your marriage or work or being a parent, then by all means work on improving it. And improving means to bring oneself to a point where the weakness is not dysfunctional. It must be at least at the minimum threshold level.

What one should work on is improving what one is strong in and complementing oneself with another person who is strong where we are weak. Perfection, absolute excellence, should not be what any one person strives to achieve. This requires a complementary team

Accepting yourself is important, because unless you accept who you are already, you cannot effectively change. Your energy is a limited resource. If it is spent on rejecting who you are, it will not be available when you try to adapt and change yourself into the person you want to be. Furthermore, by accepting your weaknesses you will be open to complementing yourself and accepting and appreciating people who are much better than you are in the areas where you are weak.

In my professional practice, I do not try to change the leadership style of the leaders or managers I advise. I try to *enrich* the style so that a manager or a leader can communicate and work more effectively with others. I teach and train people to know how to work together — not in spite of being different but *because* they are different. I also use my techniques to place people in positions that are compatible with their managerial style, and I help them develop their ability to perform additional roles so that they can advance in the organization.

But to be able to accomplish this growth, a person must first know who and what he is.

Can Identify Excellence and Weaknesses in Others

Many managers fear excellence in others. They fear employing someone who might replace them, those who excel in areas where they are weak. That's maybe the source of the expression, "'A'-grade leaders hire 'A'-grade people. 'B'-grade people hire 'C'-grade people." They are like the racehorse owner who enrolls ponies in the races, expecting to win the Triple Crown. These managers are not leaders. A leader is not afraid to be replaced. He or she knows their value and that there will always be a position for them to fulfil. They work with faith, not with fear.

Can Accept and Appreciate Differences in Others

When we reach the stage at which we can recognize the qualities of others, the next step is to figure out how to collaborate with them. Can you see value in difference? Can you accept, respect, and nourish it?

Accepting also means understanding that you're never going to find the perfect person. So, can you work with someone who complements you and who excels in areas where you are weak? Can you experience that and not feel threatened?

The superior-subordinate-superior type of relationship is common in research and development (R&D) departments. An R&D manager may have "under" him PhDs who are geniuses in certain areas. These "subordinates" may be fantastic (E) types, whereas the R&D manager may be only an Administrator. Yet problem will arise if the Administrator wants to be both the best research director and the best researcher — if he wants to compete rather than support.

Knows how to Slow Down and Relax in Difficult Situations

As I mentioned above, if you look at a duck as it floats along in the water, on the surface it looks unperturbed and calm, but under the water its feet are working fast, very fast.

A good manager should, and a good leader *must*, be relaxed when conflict arises.

Being a good manager or leader means knowing how to disagree without being disagreeable. Some people actually *agree* disagreeably. We've probably all had the experience of finally reaching agreement with someone, after many hours of discussion, but the process was so painful that we never want to deal with that person again. Whether it's your marriage, your family, or your business, you often forget the content of a conflict — *What* were you fighting about? — but if you felt abused by the discussion you will never, ever forget *how* it was handled. The *how* is more important than the *what*.

On the other hand, you have probably also had the experience of having a conflict and a discussion with someone and at the end came to the conclusion that you did not agree. But you came away from this discourse feeling energized and wanting to relate more to this person because even though you disagreed, you never felt threatened or unheard. you learned something from this disagreement. As opposed to the previous case where you and a different person agreed, but the process made you feel so raw that you never wanted to see that person again.

What was the difference? Was the discourse handled with mutual trust and respect? What about the previous situation in which you agreed?

The same principle applies to international relations. How we handle our enemy is extremely important. Never disrespect your enemy because you will never find peace that way.

Creates a Learning Environment where Conflicts can be Resolved by Both Commanding and Granting Mutual Trust and Respect

Conflict is necessary and indispensable. Show me an organization without conflict, and I will show you a cemetery. Show me a marriage without conflict, and I will show you a marriage that has died, is dying, or will soon die. Show me a society where conflict is forbidden by law, such as a communist regime, and I will show you a stymied society.

A collaborative leader must have patience and be tolerant of the conflicts that inevitably arise among colleagues with different styles and strengths and different interests. He must be able to harness conflicts — accepting the pain that this process requires. For me, good management is not about how much financial theory you know, or how well you interpret financial statements, or how skilled you are at strategic planning. To me, good leadership is about how much pain you can take in working with others. The higher you go up the ladder, the greater the pain.

I often joke that one way to identify a good leader is by the depth of the scars on his tongue. Leaders have to bite their tongues. They must know what to say and how much to say, and they must be able to handle the frustration of *not* saying what's on their minds, when that is the appropriate response.

The Lifecycle Location

I have already said more than enough times that we need a complementary team. All team members should have (I) in their style. All should qualify to be leaders, but the question of who would lead still exists. Being a complementary team does not mean all are equal. Someone has to be the first among equals. Someone must have the final word in case there is a conflict of interests or even styles, and there is no emerging consensus. Who then is the leader of leaders?

This should be determined by the evolving mission of the organization and its changing location on the lifecycle.

All organizations, like all living organisms, have a lifecycle and undergo predictable and repetitive patterns of behavior as they grow and develop.[3] At each new stage in its development, an organization is faced with a unique set of challenges. How well or poorly management addresses these challenges and leads a healthy transition from one stage to the next has a significant impact on the success or failure of the organization.

3. Adizes, Managing Corporate Lifecycles .op cit

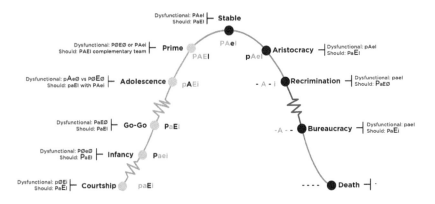

Leading an organization through lifecycle transitions is not easy. The methods of getting to Prime through balanced growth in the growing stages and through revitalization in the aging stages are not always obvious The same methods that produce success in one stage can create failure in the next. Fundamental changes in leadership and management all require an approach that delicately balances the amount of control, the (A) role, and flexibility, the (E) role, needed for each stage. Leaders who fail to understand what is needed (or not needed) can inhibit the development of their companies or plunge them into premature aging.

The style of leadership needed has to be a behavioral model of the next stage that the company should be in (next in growing, previous in aging). Thus, for the courtship, infancy, and go-go stages, the desired style is (PaEi) or better if one can find this person, the rare (PaEI). In adolescence, where the organization needs to turn inward and get organized to be "better" (rather than just seeking for "more,") leadership needs the (A) role but without losing the (E) role. In aging, depending on the stage, if there is still time to rejuvenate, a (PaE) is needed.

CHAPTER 17

Common Mission, Vision, and Values[1]

This chapter looks at the last of the four variables that cause mutual trust and respect.

Consider a marriage. A healthy marriage enables children to grow up healthy. The spouses complement each other's styles.[2] They have a process and a culture of mutual trust and respect so that their inevitable conflicts do not become destructive. But what happens if the two partners have different ideas of what a marriage is all about? One might want an open marriage, while the other wants a traditional, monogamous marriage. These two definitions of marriage are mutually exclusive. So, what now?

That's simple. It is not going to work.

---

1. Ichak Adizes, *How to Define an Organizational Mission* (Santa Barbara, CA: Top Leaf Video Series, the Adizes Institute, 2004), https://www.youtube.com/watch?v=DimbEdNfwWQ.
2. See Adizes with Madanes, *The Power of Opposites*.

For a team to work together as a team, there must be a shared vision and shared values. We should be different in style but united in vision and values and interests

Values are what we believe in. Vision is a statement of the desired in light of the expected: Where do we want to go, given where we are right now, and how far we can reasonably expect to get in the time available?

How do you design the vision and determine the values of a company?

At the Adizes Institute, we train people to do this. The detailed methodology is in our manuals, and the process takes about six days.[3]

Common vision and values provide (I)ntegration which is fundamental to any organization that wants to promote mutual trust and respect that wants to be healthy, *symbergetic*, synergetic and symbiotic.

As we discussed earlier, without (I)ntegrating, an organization can never become greater than the sum of its parts. Lacking a universal sense of shared values and a common goal, the organization will always be in danger of falling apart if its founder dies or leaves.

To remember the four factors, let us use the analogy of cooking a gourmet dish.

First, we need to decide what we want to cook. Is it an Italian or a Mexican dish? At what quality? To know this is to have a *common vision and values.*

Next, we need good, healthy, fresh ingredients. The ingredients represent the *people* in the organization Now we need a recipe for how and in what sequence to cook the ingredients. For us that is the systemic, *constructive decision-making process.* We also need appropriate

---

3. If you are interested in being trained and/or certified in the methodology, email academy@adizes.com or ltd@adizes.com.

hardware, cooking utensils. In our case, that is the diversified, complementary, *organizational structure.*

If we have made a decision on which dish we want to have, and we have the right ingredients, the recipe, and the hardware to cook, we will have a great dish to serve. That is, as long as the cook is a good cook — meaning a leader who commands and grants mutual respect and trust; one that animates the culture that he needs to develop and nourish — a culture of mutual trust and respect — for synergy and symbiosis, that nourishes and protects the health of the organization.

Summary

Change is here to stay. It is accelerating. With it, problems are accelerating, too. Change causes disintegration manifested by problems, which if not treated become a crisis.

A healthy organization can handle change better than a sick organization.

A healthy organization is symbergetic (growthful) and symbiotic (interdependent for a reason: all benefit from what is contributed).

To be synergetic, the organization needs to be composed of a complementary diversity of leadership styles that will make the system effective and efficient in the short and long run, fulfilling the PAEI roles. The diverse styles lead to a diversity of complementary functions in the company and can cross-pollinate each other's ideas and create better decisions.

A complementary team composed of diversified styles can have conflict. To avoid it becoming destructive, the team has to work with mutual respect.

Making the right decisions is not enough. They need to be implemented. For that, common interest is necessary so the diversified components of the system will cooperate and contribute.

Because of change, common interest is not stable. Conflict can emerge. To avoid this conflict, mutual trust is needed, faith that there is common interest in the long run.

To make conflict constructive, there must be a culture of mutual trust and respect.

To build and nourish a culture of MT&R, there must be common vision, mission, and values; a complementary organizational structure; a constructive decision-making process; and people staffing the organization that command and grant mutual trust and respect.

A collaborative leader is one who builds and leads such an organization. There is no ideal executive as an individual, which is the old paradigm that needs to change. What is required is a complementary team that will build and nourish a healthy organization with a culture of mutual trust and respect. It will handle change more successfully than one that is not healthy.

This book is a summary of several of my books, each of which take a component discussed in this book and explore the subject more deeply. I hope and pray this was clear enough to encourage you to learn more.

With respect,
Ichak K. Adizes
Santa Barbara, California

Appendix

CONTENT ANALYSIS

The following exercises are designed to help you practice content analysis and codification using PAEI. Content analysis, a research technique from the field of sociology, can be used to decipher PAEI orientations. This technique is useful for performing both qualitative and quantitative research.

The following are speeches from different leaders, which I have coded to demonstrate how content analysis may be used. Let's begin with President Obama's 2009 inaugural speech.

President Obama's Inaugural Address

My fellow citizens: I stand here today humbled by the task before us, grateful for the trust you have bestowed [I], mindful of the sacrifices borne by our ancestors.

I thank President Bush for his service to our nation [I], as well as the generosity and cooperation he has shown throughout this transition [I].

Forty-four Americans have now taken the presidential oath. The words have been spoken during rising tides of prosperity and the still waters of peace. Yet, every so often, the oath is taken amidst gathering clouds and raging storms. At these moments, America has carried on not simply because of the skill or vision of those in high office, but because we, the people, have remained faithful to the ideals [I] of our forebears and true to our founding documents [A].

So it has been; so it must be with this generation of Americans.

That we are in the midst of crisis is now well understood. Our nation is at war against a far-reaching network of violence and hatred. Our economy is badly weakened, a consequence of greed and irresponsibility on the part of some, but also our collective failure [I] to make hard choices [P] and prepare the nation for a new age [E]. Homes have been lost, jobs shed, businesses shuttered. Our health care is too costly, our schools fail too many — and each day brings further evidence that the ways we use energy strengthen our adversaries and threaten our planet.

These are the indicators of crisis, subject to data and statistics. Less measurable, but no less profound, is a sapping of confidence across our land [I]; a nagging fear that America's decline is inevitable, that the next generation must lower its sights.

Today I say to you that the challenges we face are real [P]. They are serious and they are many. They will not be met easily or in a short span of time [A]. But know this, America: They will be met [P].

On this day, we gather because we have chosen hope over fear [E], unity of purpose over conflict and discord [I]. On this day, we come to proclaim an end to the petty grievances and false promises, the recriminations and worn-out dogmas that for far too long have strangled our politics [I]. We remain a young nation, but in the words of Scripture, the time has come to set aside childish things. The time has come to reaffirm our enduring spirit [I]; to choose our better history

[E]; to carry forward that precious gift, that noble idea passed on from generation to generation [P]: the God-given promise that all are equal [A], all are free, and all deserve a chance to pursue their full measure of happiness [E].

In reaffirming the greatness of our nation, we understand that greatness is never a given. It must be earned [P]. Our journey has never been one of short-cuts or settling for less [P]. It has not been the path for the faint-hearted, for those that prefer leisure over work, or seek only the pleasures of riches and fame. Rather, it has been the risk-takers [E], the doers [P], the makers of things [P] — some celebrated, but more often men and women obscure in their labor [P] — who have carried us up the long rugged path toward prosperity and freedom [P].

For us, they packed up their few worldly possessions and traveled across oceans in search of a new life [E]. For us, they toiled in sweatshops, and settled the West, endured the lash of the whip, and plowed the hard earth [P]. For us, they fought and died, in places like Concord and Gettysburg, Normandy and Khe Sanh.

Time and again these men and women struggled and sacrificed and worked till their hands were raw so that we might live a better life [P]. They saw America as bigger than the sum of our individual ambitions [E], greater than all the differences of birth or wealth or faction [I].

This is the journey we continue today [P]. We remain the most prosperous, powerful nation on Earth. Our workers are no less productive than when this crisis began [P]. Our minds are no less inventive [E], our goods and services no less needed than they were last week, or last month, or last year [P]. Our capacity remains undiminished [A]. But our time of standing pat, of protecting narrow interests and putting off unpleasant decisions — that time has surely passed [E]. Starting today, we must pick ourselves up, dust ourselves off, and begin again the work [P] of remaking America [E].

For everywhere we look, there is work to be done [P]. The state of the economy calls for action, bold and swift. And we will act [P], not only to create new jobs [E], but to lay a new foundation for growth [E]. We will build the roads and bridges, the electric grids and digital lines that feed our commerce [P] and bind us together [I]. We will restore science to its rightful place and wield technology's wonders to raise health care's quality and lower its cost [E]. We will harness the sun and the winds and the soil to fuel our cars and run our factories [E]. And we will transform our schools and colleges and universities to meet the demands of a new age [E]. All this we can do [P]. All this we will do [P].

Now, there are some who question the scale of our ambitions, who suggest that our system cannot tolerate too many big plans. Their memories are short, for they have forgotten what this country has already done [P], what free men and women can achieve [P] when imagination [E] is joined to common purpose [I], and necessity to courage. What the cynics fail to understand is that the ground has shifted beneath them [E], that the stale political arguments that have consumed us for so long no longer apply [E].

The question we ask today is not whether our government is too big or too small, but whether it works [P] — whether it helps families find jobs at a decent wage [A], care they can afford [A], a retirement that is dignified [A]. Where the answer is yes, we intend to move forward [P]. Where the answer is no, programs will end [E]. Those of us who manage the public's dollars will be held to account [A], to spend wisely [A], reform bad habits [E], and do our business in the light of day [A], because only then can we restore the vital trust between a people and their government [I].

Nor is the question before us whether the market is a force for good or ill. Its power to generate wealth and expand freedom is unmatched. But this crisis has reminded us that without a watchful eye, the market can spin out of control [A]. The nation cannot prosper long when it favors only the prosperous [I]. The success of our economy has always depended not just on the size of our gross domestic product, but on the reach of our prosperity, on the ability to extend opportunity to every willing heart [I] — not out of charity, but because it is the surest route to our common good [I].

As for our common defense, we reject as false the choice between our safety and our ideals [I]. Our Founding Fathers — our Founding Fathers, faced with perils we can scarcely imagine, drafted a charter to assure the rule of law and the rights of man [A] — a charter expanded by the blood of generations. Those ideals still light the world [E], and we will not give them up for expedience sake [P].

And so, to all the other peoples and governments who are watching today, from the grandest capitals to the small village where my father was born, know that America is a friend of each nation, and every man, woman and child who seeks a future of peace and dignity [I]. And that we are ready to lead once more [E].

Recall that earlier generations faced down fascism and communism not just with missiles and tanks, but with sturdy alliances and enduring convictions [I]. They understood that our power alone cannot protect us, nor does it entitle us to do as we please. Instead, they knew that our power grows through its prudent use [A]; our security emanates from the justness of our cause [A], the force of our example [P], the tempering qualities of humility and restraint [I].

We are the keepers of this legacy [A]. Guided by these principles once more we can meet those new threats that demand even greater effort [P], even greater cooperation and understanding between nations [I]. We will begin [E] to responsibly [I] leave Iraq to its people [P] and forge a hard-earned peace in Afghanistan [P]. With old friends and former foes [I], we will work tirelessly [P] to lessen the nuclear threat and roll back the specter of a warming planet [E].

We will not apologize for our way of life, nor will we waver in its defense. And for those who seek to advance their aims by inducing terror and slaughtering innocents, we say to you now that our spirit is stronger and cannot be broken [P] — you cannot outlast us [P], and we will defeat you [P].

For we know that our patchwork heritage is a strength, not a weakness [I]. We are a nation of Christians and Muslims, Jews and Hindus, and nonbelievers [I]. We are shaped by every language and culture, drawn from every end of this Earth [I]; and because we have tasted the bitter swill of civil war and segregation, and emerged from that dark chapter stronger and more united [I], we cannot help but believe that the old hatreds shall someday pass [I]; that the lines of tribe shall soon dissolve [I]; that as the world grows smaller, our common humanity shall reveal itself [I]; and that America must play its role [P] in ushering in a new era of peace [E].

To the Muslim world, we seek a new way forward [E], based on mutual interest and mutual respect [I]. To those leaders around the globe who seek to sow conflict, or blame their society's ills on the West, know that your people will judge [A] you on what you can build, not what you destroy [P].

To those who cling to power through corruption and deceit and the silencing of dissent, know that you are on the wrong side of history, but that we will extend a hand if you are willing to unclench your fist [I].

To the people of poor nations, we pledge to work alongside you to make your farms flourish and let clean waters flow [P]; to nourish starved bodies and feed hungry minds [P]. And to those nations like ours that enjoy relative plenty, we say we can no longer afford indifference to the suffering outside our borders [I], nor can we consume the world's resources without regard to effect [A]. For the world has changed, and we must change with it [E].

As we consider the road that unfolds before us [E], we remember with humble gratitude those brave Americans [I] who at this very hour patrol far-off deserts and distant mountains [P]. They have something to tell us, just as the fallen heroes who lie in Arlington whisper through the ages.

We honor them [I] not only because they are guardians of our liberty [A], but because they embody the spirit of service [P] — a willingness to find meaning in something greater than themselves [E].

And yet at this moment, a moment that will define a generation, it is precisely this spirit that must inhabit us all [I]. For as much as government can do, and must do [P], it is ultimately the faith and determination of the American people upon which this nation relies [P]. It is the kindness to take in a stranger when the levees break [I], the selflessness of workers who would rather cut their hours than see a friend lose their job [I] which sees us through our darkest hours. It is the firefighter's courage to storm a stairway filled with smoke [P], but also a parent's willingness to nurture a child [I] that finally decides our fate.

Our challenges may be new [E]. The instruments with which we meet them may be new [E]. But those values upon which our success depends — honesty [A] and hard work [P], courage [E] and fair play [I], tolerance [I] and curiosity [E], loyalty [P] and patriotism [I] — these things are old. These things are true. They have been the quiet force of progress throughout our history.

What is demanded, then, is a return to these truths. What is required of us now is a new era of responsibility [A] — a recognition on the part of every American that we have duties to ourselves, our nation, and the world; duties [P] that we do not grudgingly accept, but rather seize gladly [P], firm in the knowledge that there is nothing so satisfying to the spirit, so defining of our character than giving our all to a difficult task [P].

This is the price and the promise of citizenship [A]. This is the source of our confidence — the knowledge that God calls on us to shape an uncertain destiny [E]. This is the meaning of our liberty and our creed, why men and women and children of every race and every faith can join in celebration across this magnificent mall; and why a man whose father less than sixty years ago might not have been served at a local restaurant can now stand before you to take a most sacred oath.

So let us mark this day with remembrance of who we are and how far we have traveled. In the year of America's birth, in the coldest of months, a small band of patriots huddled by dying campfires on the shores of an icy river. The capital was abandoned. The enemy was advancing. The snow was stained with blood. At a moment when the outcome of our revolution was most in doubt, the father of our nation ordered these words be read to the people:

"Let it be told to the future world . . . that in the depth of winter, when nothing but hope and virtue could survive . . . that the city and the country, alarmed at one common danger, came forth to meet (it)." [P]

America: In the face of our common dangers, in this winter of our hardship, let us remember these timeless words. With hope and virtue [E], let us brave once more the icy currents [P], and endure what storms may come [P]. Let it be said by our children's children that when we were tested, we refused to let this journey end [P], that we did not turn back nor did we falter [P]; and with eyes fixed on the horizon [E] and God's grace upon us [I], we carried forth [P] that great gift of freedom and delivered [P] it safely to future generations [E].

Thank you. God bless you. And God bless the United States of America.[1]

It emerges that President Obama's style is first (P) fifty five times then (I) forty-three times, then (E) thirty seven times and last (A) 21 times. The (P) content of his speech can be attributed to the situation the United States was in at that time. He had to refer to the crisis and what needed to be done. *Thus, his (P)-oriented speech was more of a situational imperative than a style.* I believe, his style is one of a (paEI).

1. https://obamawhitehouse.archives.gov/blog/2009/01/21/president-Barack
-obamas-inaugural-address.

The following write-ups are for the reader to classify. My classification, for your comparison, follows.

Jocko Willink, Retired U.S. Military Commander and Leadership Consultant

Principle number one: discipline equals freedom.

That's not a contradiction — it's an equation. Discipline might appear to be the opposite of freedom. But, in fact, discipline is the path to freedom.

Discipline is the driver of daily execution. Discipline defeats the infinite excuses that hold you back.

Some people think motivation is what will compel them to get things done. But motivation is just an emotion — a feeling, and like all feelings, it's fickle: it comes and goes. You can't count on motivation to be there when you need to get through truly challenging times.

But you can count on discipline. Discipline is something you dictate.

Motivation won't make you exercise every day; discipline will. Motivation won't stay up late and finish a project for you; discipline will. Motivation isn't going to get you out of bed in the morning; discipline will. Make discipline part of your daily life and your daily life will get better.

Principle number two: stay humble.

In life, you are going to have to do things that you don't want to do. Maybe things that you don't think you should have to do — things that offend your precious ego.

When I got done with Basic SEAL Training and reported on board SEAL Team One, you know what I was assigned to do? I was assigned to clean toilets. That's right — despite having just graduated some of the most difficult military training in the world, despite being assigned to an "elite" commando unit — my first mission at the actual SEAL Team was to clean toilets. Not exactly a glorious job.

But you know what? I did it. I did it to the best of my ability and took pride in doing it well. And that attitude got noticed: if I cared that much about how clean the toilets were, people knew I would do a good job with even more important assignments. After a short period of time, I got those more important assignments. But it was humility that opened the door for me.

Now, being humble does not mean that you shouldn't be confident. You certainly have to believe that you are a capable person. But don't let confidence turn into arrogance. So, keep your ego in check and stay humble.

The third and final principle: take ownership of everything. I call this "Extreme Ownership."

In the military, the best leaders and the best troops were the ones that took ownership of everything in their world — not just the things they were responsible for, but for every challenge and obstacle that impacted their mission.

When something went wrong, they cast no blame, they made no excuses. They took ownership of the problem and fixed it.

You can implement this attitude as well — not only in your job, but in your life. Let other people blame their parents, their boss, or the system. Let weaker people complain that the world isn't fair. You are the leader of your life: take ownership of everything in it.

So: be disciplined in all that you do. Don't subject yourself to the whims of motivation. Stay humble and be willing to do what needs to be done.

And: take extreme ownership of your life and everything in it.

Then: choose the hard path — the path of responsibility, hard work, and sacrifice. The path of discipline, humility, and ownership that ultimately leads to freedom.

If you follow these principles, then nothing in the world will stop you.[2]

Elon Musk, Founder and CEO of Tesla and Spacex

All right. I'd like to thank you for leaving "crazy person" out of the introduction.

So, I thought — I was trying to think what's the most useful thing that I — what I can say that can actually be helpful and useful to you in the future.

And I thought, perhaps tell the story of how I sort of came to be here. How did these things happen? And maybe there are lessons there. I often find myself wondering, how did this happen?

When I was young, I didn't really know what I was going to do when I got older. People kept asking me. But then eventually, I thought the idea of inventing things would be really cool.

And the reason I thought that was because I read a quote from Arthur C. Clarke, which said that "A sufficiently advanced technology is indistinguishable from magic." And that's really true.

If you go back say, three hundred years, the things we take for granted today, you'd be burned at the stake for. Being able to fly. That's crazy. Being able to see over long distances, being able to communicate, having effectively with the Internet as a group mind of sorts, and having access to all the world's information instantly from almost anywhere on the earth. This stuff that really would be magic — that would be considered magic in times past.

2. https://assets.ctfassets.net/qnesrjodfi80/4bwFAVZfObntTlfoX4EGrz/702f9358 b68d2ee6ed9dc1c4310ca1aa/Willink-Discipline-Freedom-Transcript.pdf.

In fact, I think it actually goes beyond that. There are many things that we take for granted today that weren't even imagined in times past, that weren't even in the realm of magic. So, it actually goes beyond that. So, I thought, well, if I can do some of those things — basically if I can advance technology — then that is like magic and that would be really cool.

I always had an existential crisis, because I was trying to figure out "what does it all mean?" Like what's the purpose of things? And I came to the conclusion that if we can advance the knowledge of the world, if we can do things that expand the scope and scale of consciousness, then we're better able to ask the right questions and become more enlightened. And that's the only way forward.

So, I studied physics and business, because I figured in order to do a lot of these things you need to know how the universe works, and you need to know how the economy works. And you also need to be able to bring a lot of people together to work with you to create something. Because it's very difficult to do something as individuals if it's a significant technology.

So, I originally came out to California to try to figure out how to improve the energy density of electric vehicles — basically to try to figure out if there was an advanced capacitor that could serve as an alternative to batteries. And that was in 1995.

That's also when the Internet started to happen. And I thought, well, I could either pursue this technology, where success may not be one of the possible outcomes, which is always tricky, or participate in the Internet and be part of it. So, I decided to drop out.

Fortunately, we're past graduation, so, I can't be accused of recommending that to you. And I did some Internet stuff, you know. I've done a few things here and there. One of which is PayPal.

Maybe it's helpful to say, one of the things that was important then in the creation of PayPal was how it started. Because initially — the initial thought with PayPal was to create a conglomeration of financial services, so if you have one place where all of your financial services needs could be seamlessly integrated and works smoothly.

And we had a little feature, which was through e-mail payments. Whenever we'd show the system off to someone, we'd show the hard part, which was the conglomeration of financial services, which is quite difficult to put together. Nobody was interested.

Then we showed people e-mail payments, which was quite easy, and everybody was interested. So, I think it's important to take feedback from your environment. You want to be as closed-loop as possible.

So, we focused on e-mail payments and tried to make that work. And that's what really got things to take off. But, if we hadn't responded to what people said, then we probably would not have been successful. So, it's important to look for things like that and focus on them when you seem them, and you correct your prior assumptions.

Going from PayPal, I thought well, what are some of the other problems that are likely to most affect the future of humanity? It really wasn't from the perspective of, "what's the best way to make money," which is okay, but it was really "what do I think is going to most affect the future of humanity."

So, the biggest terrestrial problem we've got is sustainable energy — but the production and consumption of energy in a sustainable manner. If we don't solve that in this century, we're in deep trouble.

And the other one being the extension of life beyond earth to make life multi-planetary. So that's the basis for — the latter is the basis for SpaceX and the former is the basis for Tesla and SolarCity.

When I started SpaceX, initially, I thought that well, there's no way one could start a rocket company. I wasn't that crazy. But then, I thought, well, what is a way to increase NASA's budget? That was actually my initial goal. I thought, well, if we could do a low-cost mission to Mars, Oasis, which would land with seeds in dehydrated nutrient gel, then hydrate them upon landing. And you'd have this great photo of green plants in a red background.

The public tends to respond to precedence and superlatives. And this would be the first life on Mars and the furthest life had ever traveled as far as we know.

And I thought, well, that would get people really excited and increase NASA's budget. So obviously the financial outcome from such a mission would probably be zero. So, anything better than that was on the upside.

So, I went to Russia three times to look at buying a refurbished ICBM . . . because that was the best deal. And I can tell you it was very weird going there in late 2001/2002, going to the Russian rocket forces and saying, "I'd like to buy two of your biggest rockets, but you can keep the nukes." That's a lot more. That was ten years ago, I guess.

They thought I was crazy, but I did have money. So, that was okay.

After making several trips to Russia, I came to the conclusion that my initial impression was wrong about — because my initial thought was, well, that there is not enough will to explore and expand beyond Earth and have a Mars base, that kind of thing. That was wrong.

In fact, there's plenty of will, particularly in the United States. Because the United States is a nation of explorers, so people who came here from other parts of the world. I think the United States is really a distillation of the spirit of human exploration. But if people think it's impossible, then well it's going to completely break the federal budget, then they're not going to do it.

So, after my third trip, I said, okay, what we really need to do here is try to solve the space transport problem and started SpaceX. And this was against the advice of pretty much everyone I talked to.

One friend made me watch a bunch of videos of rockets blowing up. Let me tell you he wasn't far wrong. It was tough going there in the beginning. Because I never built anything physical. I mean I built like a model rocket as a kid and that kind of thing. But I never had a company that built any physical. So, I had to figure out how to do all these things and bring together the right team of people.

And we did all that, and then, failed three times. It was tough, tough going.

Think about a rocket, the passing grade is 100 percent. And you don't get to actually test the rocket in the real environment that is going to be in. So, I think the best analogy for rocket engineers is, if you want to create a really complicated software, you can't run the software as an integrated whole, and you can't run it on the computer it's intended to run on, but the first time you run it on the computer, it must run with no bugs. That's basically the essence of it. So, we missed the mark there.

The first launch, I was picking up bits of rocket near the launch site. And we learned with each successive flight. And we were able to, eventually with the fourth flight in 2008, reach orbit. That was also with the last bit of money that we had. Thank goodness that happened. I think the saying is fourth time is the charm?

So, we got the *Falcon 1* to orbit. And then, began to scale it up to the *Falcon 9*, with an order of magnitude more thrust, it's around a million pounds of thrust. We managed to get that to orbit, and then developed the *Dragon* spacecraft, which recently docked to the Space Station and returned to earth from the Space Station.

That was a white-knuckle event. It was a huge relief. I still can't believe it actually happened.

But there's lot more that must happen beyond for humanity to become a space-ranked civilization and ultimately a multi-planet species. And that's something I think is vitally important. And I hope that some of you will participate in that either at SpaceX or other companies. Because it's just really one of the most important things for the preservation and extension of consciousness.

It's worth noting that Earth has been around for four billion years, but civilization, in terms of having writing, has been about ten thousand years, and that's being generous.

So, it's really somewhat of a tenuous existence that civilization and consciousness has been on Earth. And I'm actually fairly optimistic about the future of Earth. So, I don't want to, people sort of have the wrong impression like we're all about to die. I think things will most likely be okay for a long time on Earth. Not for sure, but most likely.

But even if it's 99-percent likely, a 1-percent chance is still worth spending a fair bit of effort to ensure that we have — back up the biosphere, and planetary redundancy if you will. And I think it's really quite important.

And in order to do that, there's breakthrough that needs to occur, which is to create a rapidly and completely reusable transport system to Mars, which is one of those things that's right on the borderline of impossible. But that's the sort of the thing that we're going to try to achieve with SpaceX.

And then, on the Tesla front, the goal with Tesla was really to try to show what electric cars can do. Because people had the wrong impression, and we had to change people's perceptions of the electric vehicle. Because they used to think of it as something that was slow and ugly, with low range, like a golf cart. So, that's why we created the Tesla Roadster, to show that it can be fast, attractive, and long range.

And it's amazing how even though you can show that something works on paper, and the calculations are very clear, until you actually have the physical object, and they can drive it, it doesn't really sink in for people. So, I think that is something worth nothing.

If you're going to create a company, the first thing you should try to do is create a working prototype. Everything looks great on Power-Point. You can make anything work on PowerPoint. If you have an actual demonstration article, even if it's in primitive form, that's much more effective in convincing people.

So, we made the Tesla Roadster, and now we're coming out soon with Model S, which is a four-door sedan. Because we made the Tesla Road-ster people said, "Sure we always knew you could make a car like that, it's an expensive car and it's low volume and small and all that but can you make a real car?" Okay, fine, we're going to make that, too. So, that's coming out soon.

And so that's where things are and hopefully, there are lessons to be drawn there.

I think the overreaching point I want to make is you guys are the ma-gicians of the twenty-first century, don't let anything hold you back. Imagination is the limit. Go out there and create some magic. Thank you.[3]

Jim Farley, CEO of Ford

The following was extracted from Farley's speech to his Ford employ-ees on his first day in the job:

"You have all heard the saying: 'Ford is at its best with our backs against the wall.' It's true. You all have stepped up many times in crisis. But I want to put my foot down here and say we can't settle for that. The best teams and best companies in the world don't think that way. The world today is too competitive. We must be our best every day. Let's start today."

---

3. https://singjupost.com/elon-musks-commencement-speech-at-caltech-full
-transcript/?singlepage=1.

"We must and will turn around our automotive operations and compete like a challenger. We have to improve product quality and make it a reason to choose Ford. We will benchmark against the best. Drive decisions through vehicle and customer data. We are going to reduce costs and address underperforming businesses. Customers will not pay for waste. Bottom line: Our goal is to improve revenue, margin, free cash flow, and our brand image every year."

"Complexity is a killer. We need to reduce or eliminate complexity and reduce bureaucracy by an order of magnitude — fewer platforms, fewer meetings, easier processes. We'll make Ford an effortless company to do business with. That's what customers expect."

"We sell one million F-Series a year and four hundred thousand Rangers, two hundred thousand Mustangs — that's scale that others just don't have. I want you to picture our F-Series customers out on the north slope of Alaska. They're working at 70 below. Whose truck do you think they're going to trust when they need it most? Electric is the smart thing to do. It's where so much of the value creation is in our sector today. And it's the right thing to do. It's time to be bolder."

"These past two months, I've met with many Ford employees around the world — designers, engineers, dealers, the people who punch in to build our cars and trucks every day. You told me what needs to change at our company. Your responses were formative in making the plan and operating model we shared today. I saw your determination. Now I'm asking you to drive the change you asked for."[4]

4. https://www.freep.com/story/money/cars/ford/2020/10/01/new-ford-ceo-jim -farley/5878815002/.

About the Author

For more than fifty years, Dr. Ichak Kalderon Adizes has developed, tested, and documented the proprietary methodology that bears his name. The Adizes Symbergetic Methodology is used to manage and lead change for exceptional results, effectively and efficiently, and without destructive conflict. *Leadership Excellence Magazine* named Dr. Adizes one of the "Top Thirty Thought Leaders on Leadership," and PRovoke Media (formerly The Holmes Report) named him one of the "Best Communicators Among World Leaders" in 2017 — alongside Pope Francis, Angela Merkel, and the Dalai Lama.

In 2019, in recognition of his contributions to management theory and practice, Dr. Adizes received a Lifetime Achievement Award from the International Academy of Management. He has also been awarded twenty-one honorary doctorates from universities in eleven countries.

Dr. Adizes is a former tenured faculty member at UCLA. He has taught as a visiting professor at Stanford University, Tel Aviv University, and Hebrew University, and as a lecturer with the Columbia University Executive Program. He has served as dean of the Adizes Graduate School for the Study of Organizational Therapy and Collaborative Leadership and was an academic advisor to the International School of Management for the Academy of National Economy of the Russian Federation.

He is the founder of the Adizes Institute, an international change-management company based in Santa Barbara, California, that delivers the Adizes Program for Symbergetic change management to clients in the public and private sectors. In addition to advising prime ministers and cabinet-level officers across the world, Dr. Adizes has delivered the Adizes program to a wide variety of companies ranging from start-ups to members of the Fortune 100.

Dr. Adizes lectures in four languages and has appeared before well over two hundred and fifty thousand senior-level executives in more than fifty-two countries, and several million over the Internet. His book *Managing Corporate Lifecycles* was named one of the "Ten Best Business Books" by *Library Journal.* He is an international bestseller and has published twenty-eight books, translated into a combined total of thirty-six languages.

Dr. Adizes is married with six grown children. Living in Santa Barbara, California, he loves to play the accordion, and practices yoga and Heartfulness meditation.

BOOKS BY THE AUTHOR

Publications.Adizes.com

1. Adizes, I. *The Power of Collaborative Leadership*. Forthcoming, 2023.

2. Adizes, I. *Systemic Coaching*. Forthcoming, 2023.

3. Adizes, I. *The Accordion Player: My Journey from Fear to Love*. Forthcoming, 2023.

4. Adizes, I. *What Matters in Life*. Forthcoming, 2023.

5. Adizes, I. *Insights On Socio-Political Issues: Volume III*. Santa Barbara, CA: Adizes Institute Publications, 2019.

6. Adizes, I. *Insights on Personal Growth: Volume III*. Santa Barbara, CA: Adizes Institute Publications, 2019.

7. Adizes, I. *Insights on Management: Volume III*. Santa Barbara, CA: Adizes Institute Publications, 2018.

8. Adizes, I., with Yechezkel and Ruth Madanes. *The Power of Opposites*. Santa Barbara, CA: Adizes Institute Publications, 2015.

9. Adizes, I. *Mastering Change*. Santa Barbara, CA: Adizes Institute Publications, 1992. Revised edition, Adizes Institute Publications, 2015.

10. Adizes, I. *Insights on Management: Volume II*. Santa Barbara, CA: Adizes Institute Publications, 2014.

11. Adizes, I. *Insights on Personal Growth: Volume II*. Santa Barbara, CA: Adizes Institute Publications, 2014.

12. Adizes, I. *Insights on Policy Issues: Volume II*. Santa Barbara, CA: Adizes Institute Publications, 2014.

13. Adizes, I. *Food for Thought: On What Counts in Life*. Santa Barbara, CA: Adizes Institute Publications, 2012.

14. Adizes, I. *Food for Thought: On Change and Leadership*. Santa Barbara, CA: Adizes Institute Publications, 2012.

15. Adizes, I. *Food for Thought: On Management.* Santa Barbara, CA: Adizes Institute Publications, 2012.

16. Adizes, I. *Insights on Management: Volume I.* Santa Barbara, CA: Adizes Institute Publications, 2011.

17. Adizes, I. *Insights on Personal Growth: Volume I.* Santa Barbara, CA: Adizes Institute Publications, 2011.

18. Adizes, I. *Insights on Policy: Volume I.* Santa Barbara, CA: Adizes Institute Publications, 2011.

19. Adizes, I. *How to Manage in Times of Crisis (And How to Avoid a Crisis in the First Place).* Santa Barbara, CA: Adizes Institute Publications, 2009.

20. Adizes, I. *Leading the Leaders: How to Enrich Your Style of Management and Handle People Whose Style Is Different from Yours.* Santa Barbara, CA: Adizes Institute Publications, 2004.

21. Adizes, I. *Management/Mismanagement Styles: How to Identify a Style and What to Do About It.* Santa Barbara, CA: Adizes Institute Publications, 2004.

22. Adizes I. *Corporate Lifecycles: How Organizations Grow, Age, and Die.* Initial publication by Prentice Hall, 1990. Reprint, Santa Barbara, CA: Adizes Institute Publications. New revised edition: *Managing Corporate Lifecycles: Complete Volume* or *Volume 1 and Volume 2,* Santa Barbara, CA: Adizes Institute Publications, 2004.

23. Adizes, I. *The Ideal Executive: Why You Cannot Be One and What to Do About It.* Santa Barbara, CA: Adizes Institute Publications, 2004.

24. Adizes, I. *Conversations with CEOs.* Santa Barbara, CA: Adizes Institute Publications, 2004.

25. Adizes, I. *The Pursuit of Prime.* Santa Monica, CA: Knowledge Exchange, 1996. Reprint, Santa Barbara, CA: Adizes Institute Publications.

26. Adizes, I. *How to Solve the Mismanagement Crisis.* Homewood, IL: Dow Jones/ Irwin, 1985. Reprint, Santa Barbara, CA: Adizes Institute Publications.

27. Adizes, I., and E. Mann Borgese, eds., *Self-Management: New Dimensions to Democracy.* Santa Barbara, CA: ABC-CLIO, 1975. Reprint, Santa Barbara, CA: Adizes Institute Publications.

28. Adizes, I. *Industrial Democracy: Yugoslav Style.* New York Free Press, 1971. Reprint, Santa Barbara, CA: Adizes Institute Publications.

VIDEOS BY THE AUTHOR

https://www.youtube.com/c/adizesofficial/
https://www.youtube.com/c/DrIchakAdizes-channel/

WEBSITES

https://www.ichakadizes.com/
https://adizes.com/

THE ADIZES® SYMBERGETIC™ METHODOLOGY FOR MANAGING CHANGE

This theory and its protocols on how to manage change with any system — an individual, a marriage, a for profit or nonprofit company, and society — has been tested successfully for over fifty years in over fifty countries. It is transferable and teachable, and as of 2022 there are over seventy Certified Associates worldwide who practice and teach this methodology through the Adizes institute in their country. For more info, see www.adizes.com.

THE ADIZES INSTITUTE

Through its ten offices, the institute serves companies worldwide to manage change. Its services encompass corporate transformation to reach Prime, online leadership training, digital support apps, executive search, C-level coaching, family coaching, training and certification of organizational symbergists (those that teach and practice the methodology), and the Adizes Graduate School, whose purpose is to train university faculty in the methodology and to support scientific research.